# STAGING GROWTH

A volume in the series

Culture, Politics, and the Cold War

Edited by Christian G. Appy

# STAGING GROWTH

## MODERNIZATION, DEVELOPMENT, AND THE GLOBAL COLD WAR

EDITED BY

DAVID C. ENGERMAN

NILS GILMAN

MARK H. HAEFELE

MICHAEL E. LATHAM

UNIVERSITY OF MASSACHUSETTS PRESS

AMHERST AND BOSTON

Printed in the United States of America

LC 2002013898

ISBN 1-55849-369-7 (library cloth); 370-0 (paper)

Designed by Milenda Nan Ok Lee
Set in Adobe Minion and Futura Bold
Printed and bound by Sheridan Books, Inc.

Library of Congress Cataloging-in-Publication Data

Staging growth : modernization, development, and the global Cold War / edited by David C. Engerman . . . [et al.].
p. cm. — (Culture, politics, and the cold war)
Includes bibliographical references and index.
ISBN 1-55849-369-7 (lib. bdg. : alk. paper) — ISBN 1-55849-370-0 (pbk. : alk. paper)
1. Globalization. 2. World politics. 3. Democracy. 4. Political culture. 5. Cultural policy. 6. Social change—Cross-cultural studies. 7. Developing countries—Economic conditions. I. Engerman, David C., 1966– II. Series.
D857 .S73 2003
338.9—dc21

2002013898

British Library Cataloguing in Publication data are available.

*To Our Teachers*

## CONTENTS

# ACKNOWLEDGMENTS

Many individuals and institutions helped us complete this volume. The history departments at Brandeis, Fordham, and Harvard all provided essential intellectual resources and support, as did Harvard's Charles Warren Center and the Johns Hopkins University–Nanjing University Center for Chinese and American Studies. A grant from the Mazer Fund at Brandeis University supported the publication of this collection. We are grateful to Chris Appy, the series editor, and Clark Dougan, our editor at the University of Massachusetts Press, for listening to our ideas, guiding us through the production process, and showing us ways to produce a better book. Akira Iriye helped bring this project to conclusion. Finally, and most important, we thank our contributors for their outstanding essays. Michael Adas, Laura Belmonte, Gregg Brazinsky, Christina Klein, Victor Koschmann, and Michael Mahoney all enriched our understanding of modernization theory, development, and the Cold War world. By joining a scholarly "Mod Squad" that coordinated its efforts from places as diverse as London, Oxford, Paris, Rome, Nerja, San Francisco, Ithaca, New Haven, Los Angeles, Stillwater, Boston, Cambridge, New York, New Brunswick, Washington, Tokyo, and Nanjing, they gave us some insight into the global forces that will shape the future as well.

David C. Engerman
Nils Gilman
Mark H. Haefele
Michael E. Latham

# FOREWORD

AKIRA IRIYE

For several years now, historians of international relations have been raising important new questions and proposing fresh ways of dealing with them. For too long, the scholarly literature in international history has been satisfied with chronicling foreign policies and strategies of states, in particular those that are called great powers. States as powers have been taken as the key units of analysis, and their interactions at the geopolitical level have provided the usual scheme of periodization. In the bulk of writings in the field, the most common chronology is still one that privileges interstate conflict and wars.

However, some of the most imaginative of the younger scholars—as well as a small minority among the older generation—have been dissatisfied, if not bored, with conventional chronologies and state-centric frameworks and have proposed new ways of examining the history of international relations. For some of them, a thematic, not a chronological, approach to history has seemed to provide the clue to reexamination, and for others a comparative global framework has appeared to be preferable to conventional emphases on one or two nations.

The contributors to this volume exemplify these new perspectives. Most of their essays do take the Cold War as the basic chronological framework, but they are far less interested in the origins and development of the Cold War than in using it in order to understand larger themes, the themes of modernization and development. The essays, therefore, are much less about the Cold War than about broader forces that shaped the world in the second half of the twentieth century. Actually, as some of the authors point out, modernization and development had emerged as key forces in world history much earlier, and they proved to be far more enduring than wars, hot or cold. Moreover, since modernization and development are transnational phenomena, it makes little sense to discuss them merely in a national framework. They are part of the phenomenon of globalization and, therefore, can be understood only in a global comparative framework. Most of the essays are self-consciously comparative, seeking to explore how different countries and cultures sought to grapple with the implications of modern development.

The individual essays in this volume deal with modernization and development in different contexts and look at their varied aspects. But all the authors raise some fundamental questions. Is modernization the same thing as Westernization? Is the idea of modernization universally valid? Does modernization bring about global integration? Do countries follow similar trajectories as they undertake development? If so, will all nations and societies ultimately come to look alike, to converge? Or, on the contrary, will different countries develop differently, owing to their indigenous cultural and "national character" traits?

Put this way, the questions are those that are being addressed today by commentators on the world scene. Writer after writer has been fascinated by the polarity between what Benjamin R. Barber has termed "McWorld" and "Jihad," that is, between what sociologists call "globality" and "locality." Modernization and development have been global forces, but this has not produced a homogenous world with interchangeable parts. Even more interesting, despite the transnational momentum created by forces of modernization and development, sovereign states as principal units of human action have been preserved. Indeed, if the twentieth century was a century of globalization, it also witnessed unprecedented scales of interstate slaughters and genocide.

Ultimately, therefore, we shall have to explore the relationship between transnational forces and international relations, between global trends and local loyalties, between the modern world and the modern state.

By examining the evolution of modernization and development, both in theory and in practice, and by situating their discussion in the context of the Cold War, the authors of these studies help us begin to come to grips with these questions. The process of modernization and development could, in theory, have integrated the world, although the Cold War, again in theory, could have divided it. In reality, as the essays collected in this volume demonstrate, in many ways the Cold War helped accelerate such a process, whereas the end of the Cold War, while undoubtedly producing a more globalized world, also disunited it by encouraging cultural self-consciousness and reaffirmation in all parts of the globe. All these are fascinating phenomena, and there is no better way to understand them than to turn to these superb essays.

STAGING GROWTH

We will lift Shanghai up and up, ever up, until it is just like Kansas City.

—Kenneth Wherry, 1940

# INTRODUCTION: MODERNIZATION, INTERNATIONAL HISTORY, AND THE COLD WAR WORLD

MICHAEL E. LATHAM

A conservative Nebraska Republican, relentless critic of New Deal liberalism, and sometime isolationist, Senator Kenneth Wherry was hardly the typical proponent of an American campaign to modernize the world in its own image. Yet on the eve of a global war in which civilization itself seemed to hang in the balance, even he embraced a hope that the foreign could be made familiar, that economic aid, military support, and political guidance would defeat the imperial Japanese, radically alter China's future, and drive that nation toward the liberal, capitalist, democratic endpoint most clearly represented by the United States. Since the early twentieth century Americans had imagined the world's most populous country as a "feudal society poised at the brink of modernity" and reveled in the "thrilling vision of a China purged of its traditionalism."[1] Social change, in such expressions, was identified with progress, inevitability, and convergence, not difference or contingency. It was a matter of technical expertise and operational planning, not searing conflict or structural crisis. By 1949, however, Mao Zedong made it clear that the "purging" would produce some unanticipated results. China's culture, history, and politics mattered in ways that a modernizing ideology, grounded in linear, universalist assumptions, failed to recognize or understand. The Yangtze, it turned out in the end, had little in common with the Missouri, and China's Communist revolution created a society that left Wherry and his Cold War colleagues perplexed, anxious, and fearful. Even at the start of the twenty-first century, despite claims that the solvents of free trade and internet-age communications would swiftly liberalize and democratize the "Middle Kingdom," China remains dominated by a state that tightly controls the media, seeks to restrict political discourse, and, above all, aims to promote change on its own terms and in the directions of its own choosing. Perhaps unsurprisingly, China does not march in lockstep toward the American heartland.[2]

As the essays in this volume reveal, American modernizers confronted a Cold War world that frequently defied their expectations. Grounded in Enlightenment thinking, nineteenth-century conceptions of national identity, and a sense of America's overwhelming postwar affluence and apparent historical success, modernization theory promised both a framework for objective social analysis and a powerful vehicle for social engineering. American theorists and policymakers alike believed that the Cold War marked a period of crisis, an era in which an ideological contest of uncertain duration would define the future course of the world. How, they asked, could the United States defeat communism and create a global environment in which America's liberal, capitalist, pluralist values would be most likely to survive and prosper? Modernization's claim to accelerate the passage of decolonizing societies through a dangerous and destabilizing transition provided an appealing answer. Scientifically derived, modernization theory promised to be eminently useful: it would define the conditions for "take-off" to begin, find the relevant lessons embedded in the American past, identify the essential levers of progress, and help policymakers manipulate them. For those who promoted and refined it, modernization itself became an ideology, a firmly held set of mutually reinforcing ideas about the "passing" of traditional society, the integration of social, economic, and political change, and the opportunity for the United States to channel a "revolution of rising expectations."[3]

For those aspiring to "development," however, modernization became the subject of intense debate, negotiation, and division, a discourse in which meanings, goals, and values were redefined in a wide variety of specific historical experiences and political contexts.[4] Although Americans frequently understood modernization as a matter of empirical truth and claimed the authority to define its parameters, elites in the "developing areas" interrogated its categories and selectively appropriated its ideals to suit their own diverse needs and purposes. Recognizing that fact opens up a history that transcends the oft-told narratives of U.S.-Soviet competition. As one prominent scholar has argued, "reconceptualizing the Cold War as part of contemporary international history" instead of a narrower "political conflict between two power blocs" requires that historians devote new attention to the global relationships among "ideology, technology, and the Third World."[5] The essays in this volume, analyzing modernization theory's creation, deployment, and interpretation across cultural boundaries, take an important step in that direction.

## MODERNIZATION AND ITS SOURCES

As a vision of social change and progress, modernization certainly predates the Cold War, and seems to have survived it as well. Enlightenment thinkers, Michael Adas explains in his essay, commonly used measures of scientific and technological accomplishment to mark the scope of progress, draw lines between "civilization" and "savagery," and justify plans for Western colonial dominance. Although the trenches of World War I may have tempered European enthusiasm by demonstrating that machines might lead to unprecedented carnage instead of utopian harmony, the idea of imposing a scientifically defined order continued to hold great appeal on the other side of the Atlantic. Technology, advocates of American expansion believed, could inspire changes in behavior and thought—it could instill a new sense of rationality, efficiency, and respect for empiricism in contrast to native passivity. From the Great Plains to the Philippine Islands, the engineer became part of the advance guard of "civilization," and Manifest Destiny, most commonly understood as the mission of a chosen people to expand across the continent, came to reflect a twentieth-century sense of prophetic universality, a conviction that the wider world would be transformed, improved, and set on a new and better historical course by the dissemination of American ideals and values.[6]

Yet if its roots ran deeper than the Cold War, modernization theory was most fully articulated at the height of that era. In the context of American concern about the appeal of communism in the decolonizing and developing world, modernizers sought to counter Lenin's argument with their own model of historical convergence. As Nils Gilman demonstrates in this volume, Walt Rostow's "Non-Communist Manifesto" plotted stages of growth leading toward an "Age of High Mass Consumption," not the abolition of private property in a worker's paradise. Where Lenin insisted that a dictatorship of the proletariat might direct the forces of class struggle toward the Communist secular utopia, American modernizers emphasized consensual democracy and liberal capitalism as the engines of progress. Where the Communists talked of a perfection yet to be realized, American modernizers claimed that they had already reached the promised land. Their full employment economy, tools of fiscal management, steadily increasing economic growth, and elite-led democratic government led them to identify an "end of ideology" in which the great social questions of equality, freedom, race, and class were reduced to mere technical matters. Led by the experts, Americans would pursue the liberal vision that continued to guide history's "first new nation." They would also define their own past as a blueprint for others to follow.

Striking as they are, the parallels between the visions of Enlightenment intellectuals and the claims of twentieth-century American social scientists also raise challenging questions about the relationship between previous imperial discourses and newer claims about the mission of modernization. Where older European approaches typically insisted on inherent differences between peoples based on immutable biology, starting in the 1930s scholars like Franz Boas, Margaret Mead, and Ruth Benedict described a more malleable world differentiated by the concept of culture. "In this view," Akira Iriye points out, "race was of far less importance than history; it was now possible to think that nations interacted with each other through their respective ways of life."[7] The very idea of culture, and the assumption that liberal, progressive values would flow across political borders, allowed American modernizers to speak in different terms than their predecessors.

The fixed, immutable barrier between "savagery" and "civilization" now became a spectrum along which the "traditional" might move toward the "modern," a great transition through which nations might not only advance up to their limited potential but actually "develop" and asymptotically approach the full modernity that characterized the countries they followed down a common historical path. The imperial and modernizing projects, Adas observes in this volume, were fundamentally different in these terms. Where modernizers spoke of "privileged social mobility, expanding political participation, and the democratization of political institutions as measures of the degree of modernity attained by different postcolonial societies," nineteenth-century imperialists never considered the matter in that light. "The political context in which the improvers worked," they believed, "was a given: limited reforms might be suggested, but the colonial administration was normally considered beyond the purview of their civilizing efforts. Thus . . . modernization as it was understood in the earlier decades of the Cold War was inconceivable in the colonial context."

At the same time, however, Adas and other contributors to this volume suggest a strong resonance between modernization and older imperial discourses invoked to promote not merely formal territorial acquisition but also projects of cultural manipulation and external control. Although the final ends of colonial administration efforts and modernization programs were defined differently, modernizers echoed their predecessors by speaking a similar language stressing the parallel concepts of deficiency, tutelage, reform, and rationalization. Michael Mahoney's essay on the case of Mozambique, for example, deliberately blurs the lines between imperialism and modernization by analyzing the way that the Portuguese government shifted toward universalist, development-centered claims as a justification for maintaining colonial control. Newly independent African nations, Portuguese ministers like Franco Nogueira insisted, were completely unprepared for the demands they faced and would simply collapse into poverty and long-term dependence on either the Western or the Communist sides of the Cold War divide. Mozambique's people, he claimed, would enjoy a distinct advantage. Enjoying full rights as Portuguese citizens, they would benefit from sweeping development efforts in education, social services, and industrialization. For Portugal, modernization and its claims of order, rationality, efficiency, and, above all, economic growth became ways to explain the need for prolonged African tutelage. Like their American colleagues at work in Vietnam, Portuguese officials also reached toward modernization as a means to win the "hearts and minds" of a people that increasingly demanded nothing short of full independence on their own terms. Though the Portuguese explicitly rejected the comparison, their "villagization" programs, involving the relocation and concentration of Mozambique's peasantry into settlements under the surveillance of military force, shared stunning similarities with the U.S. government's attempt to shore up its South Vietnamese client state through a Strategic Hamlet Program. In both cases, fences and watchtowers separated inhabitants from anticolonial guerrillas while the government claimed that development programs in health care, education, agriculture, and public administration would earn the loyalty of a population caught up in the great transition from tradition to modernity. The specific tactic, moreover, also replicated a classic colonial method of counterinsurgency deployed by the Spanish in Cuba, the United States in the Philippines, and the British in South Africa and Malaya. Despite protestations to the contrary, development and violence often went hand in hand.[8]

In cases like these, modernization came to reflect one of the Cold War's most profound ironies. Modernization, its American advocates believed, would provide the means to deal with a decolonizing world of nationalist aspirations. It would accelerate the historical trajectory of "traditional" societies through a destabilizing yet necessary transition. It would also show indigenous elites the correct route to the promised land of liberal, capitalist growth and, to borrow Graham Greene's formulation, promote the rise of an effective, independent "third force" standing between imperial control and Marxist revolution.[9] As Walt Rostow insisted, modernization would replace colonialism. It would foster "a new post-colonial relationship between the northern and southern halves of the Free World. . . . As the colonial ties are liquidated, new and most constructive relationships can be built . . . a new partnership among free men—rich and poor alike."[10] Yet despite the language of enlightened progress, modernizers frequently attempted to set the terms of debate, tried to define when and how development would be pursued, and relied on imperial practice to derail anticolonial revolution.

Further research into the sources of modernization theory and their relationship to previous visions of progress and control might also consider the way that Americans perceived "traditionals" within their own borders. As scholars like Donald Pease have argued, American views of the foreign abroad have been strongly influenced by the way that they attempted to define the status of the "others" at home.[11] From the late nineteenth through the twentieth centuries, Native Americans, immigrants from Southern Europe, African Americans, and Mexican Americans were frequently identified as peoples afflicted with a sense of fatalism, a debility of mind as much as material condition. Those categories, derived from domestic impressions and experience, were often deployed abroad, and liberal attempts to address what social scientists like Oscar Lewis called the "culture of poverty" within the United States resonated strongly with modernization programs overseas.[12] Kennedy administration planners expected that the Alliance for Progress could inspire Latin Americans to create a New Deal of their own. Lyndon Johnson hoped to build a Tennessee Valley Authority on the Mekong, a project that would bring the embattled peasantry into a new, productive world of aspiration and hope. The Peace Corps trained volunteers on Native American reservations and in New York slums. It deployed community development strategies in Andean villages and Iranian towns even as the War on Poverty promoted them in the black inner-city neighborhoods of Los Angeles and Chicago. In each setting, liberals envisioned modernization as a means to solve problems rooted in culture as much as structural inequity. Acknowledging those parallels sheds some light on the nature of modernization as a framework that blended paternalism and idealism. Liberal experts, implicitly praising their own modern expertise, rationality, and analytical toughness, identified deficiencies in the populations they studied and claimed superior knowledge of how they might be remedied. At the same time, however, they understood their work as part of an altruistic obligation, a project through which they would share their domestic accomplishments with a world that desperately wanted to emulate them.[13]

## COLD WAR CULTURE AND MODERNIZATION'S MIRROR IMAGE

"The sickness of the world," publisher Henry Luce told the readers of *Life* magazine in 1941, "is also our sickness." Either the United States would recognize its responsibility to promote "Democracy and Freedom and Justice" in a seamless, fluid world of competing ideologies, or "the words themselves and what they mean die with us—in our beds. . . . America is responsible to herself as well as to history, for the world-environment in which she lives."[14] After the triumph of World War II, that internationalist vision gained immense popularity and, as historian John Fousek argues, American nationalism played a decisive role in framing the "broad public consensus that supported Cold War foreign policy." When dreams of "one world" were replaced by a sense of sharp international polarization, "U.S. government and opinion leaders asserted the notion of U.S. global responsibility more forcefully than ever. The world might be divided, but the United States was still responsible for the peace and well-being of the whole. Rather than receding before an international system that was not so easily unified, pacified, or reconstructed, the discourse of American nationalist globalism grew ever more pronounced."[15] American responsibility, moreover, demanded a sustained projection of American identity. As Harry Truman insisted in 1950, the "powerful Communist campaign aimed at swaying peoples around the world" required that Americans "make ourselves known as we really are—not as Communist propaganda pictures us. We must pool our efforts with those of other free peoples in a sustained, intensified program to promote the cause of freedom against the propaganda of slavery. We must make ourselves heard round the world in a great campaign of truth."[16]

Shaped by those demands, modernization theory was more than a model and instrument of global change. It also became a framework through which Americans defined their purposes as well as themselves. Laura Belmonte's analysis of U.S. propaganda programs, for example, reveals that American plans to "sell capitalism" involved the construction of a sharp contrast between the culture of thriving "free enterprise" and the Soviet world of forced labor, sinecures, and oppression. While capitalist modernity allowed Ford Motor Corporation employees to enjoy a home stocked with appliances, a new car, and the satisfaction of sending four kids to college, Soviet workers toiled in abysmal conditions, lacked consumer goods, and lived lives of gray drudgery. In their attempt to counter the "myth of the Communist paradise," American planners spoke of creativity and productivity, not alienated "organization men." They spoke of collective bargaining, growing classlessness, and women happily fulfilled at home, not racism, inequality of income, or pervasive gender discrimination. As Christina Klein convincingly demonstrates, moreover, those appealing images were not restricted to the Voice of America or the U.S. Information Agency. They also suffused American popular culture. Musicals like *The King and I* presented modernization as a sentimental act. Not merely a strictly scientific, masculine process, it also became a maternal task, an act of love that expanded the world's enlightened community as it caressed away the reserves of tradition to create "new men and women." In contrast to Soviet violence, which demanded vigilant containment, modernizers pursued an integrative, anticolonial approach, and their nation's history became the source of lessons for others to follow. Through the immensely popular musical spectacle, America's nineteenth-century abolitionism was invoked to challenge the timeless culture of Siamese tradition, repel British imperialism, and, for contemporary viewers, to counter the dangers of Soviet "slavery." As Anna told the King's children what they should become, she also told American audiences who they were and what their preeminently modern society should stand for. In a clear, unmistakable contrast to Russia's brutal repression of the "captive nations," Americans would pursue a more benevolent, nurturing mission. Patiently instructing the childlike, they would draw on their own historical experience to lead the "undeveloped" to a fully mature freedom.

Even in the midst of the Cold War, however, those polar oppositions proved difficult to sustain. Rather than a clear-cut distinction between the Soviet system and their own society, an expression of unambiguous Cold War truth, American modernizers often defined the process of social change through a framework that tended to wash away the contrast between themselves and their ideological enemies. Modernization theory, as Nils Gilman suggests, might even be thought of as a kind of "capitalist mirror image" of Leninism. Though American visions of the true and only heaven certainly differed from Soviet visions of the "end of history," both models stressed the ability of enlightened elites to accelerate an inevitable, universal movement through historical stages and posited that technological diffusion would engender a new consciousness as well as a new society.

Most important, American theorists frequently defined modernity in terms that made the educated, industrialized "first" and "second" worlds appear to have far more in common with each other than either did with the static, passive, and unenlightened "tradition" of the "third world." Modernizers, one scholar argues, dealt with a "pair of abstract and hardly precise binary distinctions." Paired, dichotomous terms like "traditional and modern" or "Communist and free" seemed to "derive their meanings from their mutual opposition more than from any inherent relationship to the things described." As a result, the problem of placing the Soviet system into the realm of "modernity" led American theorists to rely on the ideal of the "natural." It led them toward an analysis of what a "mature" or "fully developed" modern society would look like in the absence of "artificial" or "forced" control. The Communist world, many of them concluded, was indeed "modern, technologically sophisticated, [and] rational to a degree," but also "authoritarian (or totalitarian) and repressive, and ultimately inefficient and impoverished by contamination with ideological preconceptions and burdened with an ideologically motivated socialist elite." The "first world," however, was more "purely modern, a haven of science and utilitarian decision-making, technological, efficient, democratic, free—in short, a natural society unfettered by religion or ideology."[17]

That appeal to the natural may have allowed modernization theorists to claim the kind of objectivity usually reserved for their physical science colleagues, but in the long run it proved incapable of conveying the kind of distinction that Harry Truman and succeeding American Cold Warriors insisted on. When the economist Walt Rostow reflected on the "essentially biological field of economic growth," he described societies as natural, organic wholes, but he could not persuade more critical foreign nationalists to accept his view of a world in which every country faced a stark choice between the two global alternatives of liberal freedom and totalitarian oppression.[18] Jawaharlal Nehru, David Engerman explains, wanted India to join a "West" of industrialized modernity, literacy, and diminished poverty. Impressed with the rapid growth rates generated by the Soviet Union, he turned toward five-year plans, production quotas, price regulation, and massive public investment because he sought to emulate Russian economic accomplishments. Yet Rostow and his MIT associates, fearing the worst, failed to recognize that Nehru's admiration for Soviet planning did not extend to Soviet politics. For the American team from the Center for International Studies, the course to "true" modernity could not be reconciled with Soviet arms deliveries, Russian economic aid, and Russian-inspired industrialization at the expense of agriculture. Indians committed to nonalignment and an independent course to development rejected American protest, and when reports of Central Intelligence Agency funding appeared, they rejected the MIT presence altogether. Although Rostow and his colleagues defined modernity in two distinct, mutually exclusive variants, they found that those aspiring to progress often framed their choices in frustratingly original ways.[19]

The ambivalence of modernization theorists on the question of democracy, moreover, paralleled the ambivalence of American policymakers on the subject. It also made it particularly difficult to stake a firm moral claim in the Cold War struggle. Theorists like Edward Shils and Daniel Bell, Nils Gilman observes, wrote with a distrust of mass politics and a strong aversion to the passion and irrationality they saw in populism.[20] Like their government, they preferred the stability that might be promoted by technocratic elites, leaders more inclined toward progressive, staged reform instead of sweeping, structural revision guided by popular demands. At the height of the Cold War, the Protestant theologian and State Department adviser Reinhold Niebuhr tried to present a clear, unequivocal argument about the difference between the "free world" and the Communist one. The Communists, he argued, committed staggering atrocities while claiming "unqualified sanctity." Marxist visions of modernity heralded the "appearance of a kingdom of perfect righteousness in history," yet Communists used that "moral façade" to "pose as the liberators of every class or nation which they intended to enslave."[21] As the United States itself continued to support dictators like Ngo Dinh Diem, Anastasio Somoza, and Mohammed Reza Pahlavi as defenders of liberty, such indignant declarations increasingly fell flat. A close analysis of the theory and practice of modernization suggests that, while hardly equivalent, the Cold War's two "modernities" invoked the logic of history in surprisingly similar ways. It also shows that a world of immense complexity and fluidity existed outside both of them.

## DEPOLITICIZATION, SELECTION, AND CONTESTATION

Created in the Cold War context, modernization theory was part of a mutually reinforcing system of knowledge and power. Its history, in the anthropologist James Ferguson's terms, reflects the "set of complex, shifting relations that exists between the academic social sciences and the various kinds of knowledge and theory that circulate within the world of development." As theory moved from the scholarly world into the realm of government institutions and multilateral agencies, it became a means of Cold War control as much as a way to engineer "progress." Cold War visions of American national security needs, moreover, frequently shaped the very questions that scholars asked and the set of assumptions that guided their research. Rather than addressing the questions that emerged from within their disciplinary practices, they increasingly accepted the external boundaries imposed by the needs of their sponsors and sought to provide answers tailored to the set of instruments that policymakers had at their disposal.[22] As Mark Haefele points out in this volume, MIT's Center for International Studies intended to "undertake no research that does not . . . grow out of the necessity to know something in order to be able to do something." Though not all American social scientists worked with such a policy-driven focus, the networks of government and foundation funding, shared assumptions about the goals of "development," and a powerful sense that the United States could engineer a better world all drove universities into a tighter relationship with the American state and its political objectives. Along with the new "area studies" fields and a dramatic expansion in psychological and behavioral research, proponents of modernization benefited directly from government desires to use the insights and lessons of economics, political science, and sociology to analyze Soviet strengths and weaknesses, guide decolonization, and defeat revolution.[23] Walt Rostow, Haefele explains, wrote a "manifesto" against communism, not a dispassionate evaluation. He also told policymakers that foreign aid could rapidly catalyze "take-offs" in the impoverished world, insisted that development would quickly defeat the Communist "disease of the transition," and, like several of his colleagues, moved easily between Cambridge classrooms and State Department offices.

Yet modernization theory, with its claims to universality and assumptions about the malleability of the "traditionals," often failed to fit the world it promised to order. In particular, questions of culture and history tended to disappear from arguments that were often far more instrumental than analytical. Defining a common trajectory away from the timeless, "traditional" world of fatalism and passivity and charting the relative advance of nations up the rungs of the developmental ladder folded a world of diversity and complexity into a common, simple schema. Countries as diverse as Ecuador and Iran, the Congo and Burma, could be studied through the same basic framework, and with the same basic set of assumptions. Problems of politics were reduced to matters of mere administration as modernizers evaluated the world with categories drawn from their own sense of national success.[24] In Vietnam that way of thinking bolstered American confidence that a "war of national liberation" might be defeated through a combination of military counterinsurgency and comprehensive development. Yet, as Haefele argues, repeated efforts to drive South Vietnam through a "take-off" into modernity that would win the "hearts and minds" of its citizens failed miserably. No matter how much development aid the United States poured into the country, American officials could not turn Ngo Dinh Diem's dictatorial regime into a progressive, enlightened government. Nor could they convince the Vietnamese to discard their deeply held commitment to national unification and social revolution in favor of an ideology imposed by an external force. In the eyes of many Vietnamese, the American approach was every bit as imperial as that of their previous French and Japanese adversaries. In the end, Vietnamese culture and history mattered immensely, and the "traditionals" turned out not to be so malleable after all.[25]

Understanding cases like that of Vietnam requires that one pay close attention to the different ways that those on the "receiving" end of modernization responded to it. In varied conditions, cultures, and political situations, aspirations for social change and progress led to a widely varied range of results. "One cannot accept the power of the development idea," Frederick Cooper and Randall Packard have recently argued, "without realizing that the possibility that modern life and improved living standards could be open to all, regardless of race or history of colonial subjugation, was in the 1950s a liberating possibility, eagerly seized by many people in the colonies." That insight points historians toward questions about the way that leaders in the decolonizing and developing worlds responded to the promise of modernization by selecting and appropriating some of its components while rejecting others.[26] In such situations, the discourse of modernization could be enlisted for profoundly anti-imperial, even revolutionary purposes. As Michael Mahoney's treatment of FRELIMO demonstrates, the results were often surprising. Where the revolutionaries had once based their struggle for Mozambican independence on ideals of African cultural nationalism, by 1971 they embraced a vision of development grounded in Marxism's claim to scientific analysis and universal validity. Instead of embracing "tradition" in opposition to Portugal's modernizing claims, FRELIMO attempted to frame an alternative "modernity" that promised to sweep away both the backward past and the colonial present. Accepting the terms of a debate with Portugal over the direction of "development," FRELIMO, as Mahoney notes, sought to become "more modern than thou." That vision of modernity, however, was expressed in ways that fit neither Rostow's expectations nor Lenin's. Development would indeed be pursued through a single party and centralized state planning, but revolutionaries like Samora Machel also expected that it would depend more on the insight, judgment, and practical skill of illiterate peasants than on the formal knowledge of a "privileged class" of technocratic elites. FRELIMO's dreams of development, shaped by a specific set of historical circumstances and conditions, clearly defied Cold War categories.

That process of selection and adaptation also took place outside situations of formal colonialism. Victor Koschmann's analysis of the way that Japanese intellectuals disputed the arguments of American social scientists and officials provides a compelling example of the fact that, even within the so-called free world, understandings of modernity were never stable or hegemonic. The American theorists at the Hakone Conference considered modernization an empirically validated scientific fact, an objective truth revealed by literacy rates, evidence of social mobility, industrialization, mass media, and urbanization. Though they accepted the possibility that different national cultures might find different paths to modernity, they spoke as if the American Occupation, postwar economic resurgence, and constitutional reforms made Japan a clear model for other Asian states to follow, a point on the road to progress that would demonstrate what a liberal, capitalist country could achieve. U.S. Ambassador Edwin Reischauer, Koschmann explains, argued the case even more forcefully. Gradual expansion of democracy and a well-maintained equilibrium between government leadership and private initiative, he insisted, made Japan a clear success story. Japanese "opposition intellectuals," however, found that praise unjustified and even dangerous. Where American theorists hewed closely to the "objective" realm of statistics and indices, they raised the more controversial problem of ideology and values to argue that Japanese democracy was an imperfect and incomplete project, not an achieved condition. Declarations that Japan had arrived at a full modernity qualifying it for Asian leadership, they concluded, ominously echoed the rationale used to justify imperial expansion during the Pacific War. Rather than celebrating a fulfillment of modernization's promise at the "end of history," Japanese critics instead attacked a conservative, nationalist complacency by focusing on the significance of their country's past. They fused the insights of Marx and Weber to express their concerns with persistently low working-class wages and structural inequality as well as continued paternalism and "semifeudal" influences on socioeconomic life. As Koschmann argues, Japanese "opposition intellectuals" still embraced a vision of an integrated modernity, a functional system in which forces in the economic, political, and social realms influenced one another. But rather than discarding history in favor of universalism, they emphasized the impact of their country's specific experience and defined their own professional responsibility as one of engaged criticism, not "objective" validation.

Gregg Brazinsky's analysis of the Korean response to modernization theory presents an equally compelling case. Troubled by South Korea's corrupt, repressive government, rising student protest, economic stagnation, and signs of interest in reunification with the North, U.S. policymakers worried about their ally's vulnerability to Communist appeals. By promoting theories of modernization in Korean universities, American officials hoped to contain dissent and inspire activists to seek progress along liberal, capitalist lines. Through university appointments, television programs, book translations, and cultural exchange programs, they recruited philanthropic foundations for a comprehensive campaign to channel Korean aspirations and demonstrate appropriate steps toward a destined progress. Korean intellectuals, however, transformed modernization theory to suit their own questions and goals. Rather than an indivisible set of prescriptions imposed from outside, for Koreans modernization became a body of thought from which they might choose particular ideas and discard others. Critically interrogating modernization theory in light of their own national history and experience, they also revised some of the model's core assumptions. As Brazinsky explains, Koreans challenged claims that modernization required Westernization and criticized the very idea of a temporal dichotomy between tradition and modernity. Although the West had indeed modernized first, Korean culture had long revered the "modern" value of human liberation. Korea's Confucian reverence for knowledge and scholarship, along with a Buddhist concern for the quality of human life, they maintained, might also promote a distinctly Korean future, a destiny free from some of the worst excesses of Western materialism. Where Talcott Parsons and other American modernizers celebrated Max Weber's conclusion that Protestant asceticism had generated a uniquely Western modernity, Koreans appealed to their own religious inheritance to define an alternative that emphasized progress but rejected the language of cultural subordination.[27] Where Americans defined modernization in terms of separate, sequential stages, universality, and convergence, Koreans declared that tradition could actually facilitate modernization and insisted that their own past would lead them in distinct, but equally modern directions.

A framework that ordered the world and defined its trajectory, modernization theory reflected a profound sense of achievement, a belief that all nations would ultimately follow in the American wake and a sense that American power could shape a more liberal, progressive world. The essays in this volume, however, demonstrate that definitions of modernity itself became the subject of intense debate. Rather than engineering a rapid global convergence on a common endpoint, American modernizers encountered a world of political and cultural difference. When visions of development and progress crossed national and cultural borders, they often took on new, unanticipated forms.

## SURVEYING THE RUINS

As the Cold War finally drew to a close, the historian Christopher Lasch described modernization theory as a decayed, yet curiously resilient structure, a decrepit old ruin that just wouldn't collapse. A generation of criticism, he acknowledged, had "again and again exposed the inadequacies of the modernization model, even for an understanding of the West." Yet "it still stands . . . a deserted mansion, its paint peeling, its windows broken, its chimneys falling down, its sills rotting; a house fit only for spectral habitation but also occupied, from time to time, by squatters, transients, and fugitives."[28] Since the late 1960s modernization theory has indeed taken a beating from all sides. Conservatives like Samuel Huntington and Robert Nisbet, Nils Gilman explains, attacked the framework as a failed liberal dream. Its authors, they insisted, had constructed abstract, ideal types, yet claimed they represented historical conditions. They had failed to produce a rigorous account of the causes of change, and relied instead on an argument that merely placed static, frozen "snapshots" in order and described them as evolutionary evidence toward progress. On the Left, dependency theorists like Andre Gunder Frank and world systems theorists like Immanuel Wallerstein drew on Marxist analyses to invert modernization's overall conclusions. In the context of the Vietnam War and a growing rejection of liberal optimism, they held that stagnation and poverty were accelerated by the historical force of capitalism, not alleviated by contact with it. What passed for development resulted in exploitation, not benign modernity. By the early 1990s, finally, poststructural thinkers like Ashis Nandy, Wolfgang Sachs, and Arturo Escobar declared war on modernization as well as on its theoretical challengers.[29] The Enlightenment and its heirs, whether they stood on the Right or Left, were equally guilty of constructing binary systems of classification, making false claims to scientific objectivity, and imposing regimes of brutal violence, relentless surveillance, and repressive control on the human lives of their subjects. If conservatives like Huntington and radicals like Frank tried to take apart the frame of modernization in order to create a better design for social analysis, poststructural critics insisted that the building was simply beyond repair. Far better, they suggested, to dispense with grand theory altogether—to burn the mansion to the ground and spread the ashes to the winds.

Yet, as Lasch recognized, the old building still stands. While modernization may have lost credibility as a grand theory, many of its aspirations and ideals are still with us. In the World Bank, the United Nations, and nongovernmental organizations like CARE and World Vision, social change may no longer be cast in Rostovian universals. But hopes that development can fight disease, promote education, raise living standards, and give the world's poor greater life chances endure.[30]

The contributors to this volume help us understand that ongoing dialogue by placing it in historical perspective. Rather than advocating reconstruction or demolition, they go within the mansion's walls to investigate its architecture and learn why so many once found it such an appealing place to live. Their questions are important because in the rush to disavow modernization theory's arrogance, ethnocentricity, and imperial assumptions, scholars have often left vital questions about its context, intellectual assumptions, and political role unexplored. In a Cold War defined by competing ideologies and visions of civilizational progress, modernization became a powerful framework for analysis and prescription, a most influential way of understanding the world and charting its future.

In the post–Cold War era, modernization theory's sense of destiny has certainly faded and scholars have increasingly turned away from its rigidities to describe transnational phenomena. Rather than considering America's ability to channel and direct the world's future, social theorists have hastened to investigate cultural and economic changes that are mutual and reciprocal, not binary or unidirectional. Rather than a simple "passing of the traditional," analysts have turned to describe globalization, an internationalization of human migration, finance, communications, markets, and culture that has produced a host of overlapping group, religious, and ethnic identities.[31] Yet, as this volume reveals, the fundamental questions about development and progress that modernizers raised in the Cold War world will continue to shape our own.

## NOTES

This essay was written at the Johns Hopkins University–Nanjing University Center for Chinese and American Studies, Nanjing, People's Republic of China.

1. Frank Ninkovich, "The Rockefeller Foundation, China, and Cultural Change," *Journal of American History* 70 (March 1984): 801–2.

2. Wherry quoted in Eric F. Goldman, *The Crucial Decade: America, 1945–1955* (Westport, Conn.: Greenwood Press, 1956), 116–17. Maurice Meisner, *Mao's China and After: A History of the People's Republic*, 3d edition (New York: Free Press, 1999), provides a strong synthesis of China's revolutionary past.

3. For an overview of this argument, see Michael E. Latham, *Modernization as Ideology: American Social Science and "Nation Building" in the Kennedy Era* (Chapel Hill: University of North Carolina Press, 2000), 1–19.

4. As Nick Cullather observes, in historical analyses of development the term "ideology" tends to suggest "the durability of fixed ideas," while "discourse" alludes to "a fluid exchange of signifiers and meanings," a vocabulary open to contestation and challenge. See Cullather, "Development? It's History," *Diplomatic History* 24 (fall 2000): 649.

5. Odd Arne Westad, "The New International History of the Cold War: Three (Possible) Paradigms," *Diplomatic History* 24 (fall 2000): 551.

6. On this theme, see Anders Stephanson, *Manifest Destiny: American Expansion and the Empire of Right* (New York: Hill and Wang, 1995). Walter L. Williams, "United States Indian Policy and the Debate over Philippine Annexation: Implications for the Origins of Imperialism," *Journal of American History* 66 (March 1980): 810–31, stresses the continuity in American thought from continental expansion to the creation of an overseas empire.

7. Akira Iriye, *Cultural Internationalism and World Order* (Baltimore: Johns Hopkins University Press, 1997), 7.

8. On modernization and American attempts to defeat "wars of national liberation," see D. Michael Shafer, *Deadly Paradigms: The Failure of U.S. Counterinsurgency Policy* (Princeton: Princeton University Press, 1988), and Latham, *Modernization as Ideology*, 151–207. Stuart Creighton Miller, *"Benevolent Assimilation": The American Conquest of the Philippines, 1899–1903* (New Haven: Yale University Press, 1982), and James Scott, *Seeing Like a State: How Certain Schemes to Improve the Human Condition Have Failed* (New Haven: Yale University Press, 1998), provide sharp analyses of additional cases.

9. See his famous novel, set in Saigon during the Viet Minh struggle against French imperialism, *The Quiet American* (London: William Heinemann, 1955).

10. Memorandum, Rostow to Theodore Sorensen, 16 March 1961, National Security Files, box 325, "Rostow, Foreign Aid, 3/16/61–3/18/61," John F. Kennedy Library, Boston.

11. See Donald Pease, "Imperial Discourse," *Diplomatic History* 22 (fall 1998): 605–15.

12. Scholars often made the comparison between the foreign and the domestic explicit. See, for example, Oscar Lewis, *La Vida: A Puerto Rican Family in the Culture of Poverty—San Juan and New York* (New York: Random House, 1966).

13. On the concept of the "culture of poverty," see Michael B. Katz, *In the Shadow of the Poorhouse: A Social History of Welfare in America* (New York: Basic Books, 1986), and idem, *The Undeserving Poor: From the War on Poverty to the War on Welfare* (New York: Pantheon, 1989). Kennedy adviser Lincoln Gordon insisted on the relevance of American experience in *A New Deal for Latin America: The Alliance for Progress* (Cambridge: Harvard University Press, 1963). Lloyd Gardner analyzes Johnson's liberal vision in *Pay Any Price: Lyndon Johnson and the Wars for Vietnam* (Chicago: Ivan R. Dee, 1995). On the Peace Corps and liberal idealism, see Elizabeth Cobbs Hoffman, *All You Need Is Love: The Peace Corps and the Spirit of the 1960s* (Cambridge: Harvard University Press, 1998). Fritz Fischer, *Making Them Like Us: Peace Corps Volunteers in the 1960s* (Washington: Smithsonian Institution Press, 1998), takes up the problem of paternalism.

14. Henry Luce, "The American Century," as reprinted in *Diplomatic History* 23 (spring 1999): 160, 165–66.

15. John Fousek, *To Lead the Free World: American Nationalism and the Cultural Roots of the Cold War* (Chapel Hill: University of North Carolina Press, 2000), 2, 124.

16. Truman as cited in Allan A. Needell, " 'Truth Is Our Weapon': Project TROY, Political Warfare, and Government-Academic Relations in the National Security State," *Diplomatic History* 17 (summer 1993): 404.

17. Carl E. Pletsch, "The Three Worlds, or the Division of Social Scientific Labor, circa 1950–1975," *Comparative Studies in Society and History* 23 (October 1981): 573–74.

18. See Rostow, *The Stages of Economic Growth: A Non-Communist Manifesto* (Cambridge: Cambridge University Press, 1960), 36. For another formulation of modernization as a natural process, see Talcott Parsons, *Societies: Evolutionary and Comparative Perspectives* (Englewood Cliffs, N.J.: Prentice-Hall, 1966). As critics pointed out, those appeals to nature shared striking similarities with older formulations of cultural and racial difference. See, for example, Ali A. Mazrui, "From Social Darwinism to Current Theories of Modernization: A Tradition in Analysis," *World Politics* 21 (October 1968): 69–83.

19. Interestingly enough, as David Engerman points out, American intellectuals had long wrestled with the problem of defining modernity in opposition to communism. During the Great Depression's moment of capitalist crisis, moreover, many of them also softened their analysis of Soviet industrialization in ways that blamed massive famine on the "passivity" of a "traditional" peasantry instead of

the Stalinist state. See Engerman, "Modernization from the Other Shore: American Observers and the Costs of Soviet Economic Development," *American Historical Review* 105 (April 2000): 383–416.

20. Note, for example, Bell's argument against McCarthyism on the grounds of its irrationality and populist excess, instead of its violation of civil liberties, in *The Radical Right* (Garden City, N.Y.: Doubleday, 1963).

21. Reinhold Niebuhr, "The Hard Utopians: Communism," in Harry R. Davis and Robert C. Good, eds., *Reinhold Niebuhr on Politics* (New York: Charles Scribner's Sons, 1960), 27, 30.

22. James Ferguson, "Anthropology and Its Evil Twin: 'Development' in the Constitution of a Discipline," in Frederick Cooper and Randall Packard, eds., *International Development and the Social Sciences* (Berkeley: University of California Press, 1997), 150.

23. On the relationship between the Cold War and American social research, see Sigmund Diamond, *Compromised Campus: The Collaboration of Universities with the Intelligence Community, 1945–1955* (New York: Oxford University Press, 1992); Ellen Herman, *The Romance of American Psychology: Political Culture in the Age of Experts* (Berkeley: University of California Press, 1995); Ron Robin, *The Making of the Cold War Enemy: Culture and Politics in the Military-Industrial Complex* (Princeton: Princeton University Press, 2001); André Schiffrin, ed., *The Cold War and the University: Toward an Intellectual History of the Postwar Years* (New York: New Press, 1997); and Christopher Simpson, ed., *Universities and Empire: Money and Politics in the Social Sciences during the Cold War* (New York: Free Press, 1998).

24. James Ferguson, *The Anti-politics Machine: "Development," Depoliticization, and Bureaucratic Power in Lesotho* (Cambridge: Cambridge University Press, 1990), provides a particularly strong analysis of this problem.

25. On the revolution's sources and ideals, see Mark Philip Bradley, *Imagining Vietnam and America: The Making of Postcolonial Vietnam* (Chapel Hill: University of North Carolina Press, 2000); James P. Harrison, The *Endless War: Vietnam's Struggle for Independence* (New York: Columbia University Press, 1989); Jeffrey Race, *War Comes to Long An: Revolutionary Conflict in a Vietnamese Province* (Berkeley: University of California Press, 1972); and Marilyn Young, *The Vietnam Wars, 1945–1990* (New York: HarperCollins, 1991). Latham, *Modernization as Ideology,* 151–207, analyzes the failure of Kennedy's modernization efforts.

26. Cooper and Packard, "Introduction," in *International Development and the Social Sciences,* 9. On the theme of selection, see Catharine Hall, "Histories, Empires and the Post-Colonial Moment," in Iain Chambers and Lidia Curti, eds., *The Post-Colonial Question: Common Skies, Divided Horizons* (London: Routledge, 1996), 65–77.

27. For Weber's original argument, see *The Protestant Ethic and the Spirit of Capitalism* (London: Routledge, 1992). For its incorporation into modernization

theory, see S. N. Eisenstadt, ed., *The Protestant Ethic and Modernization: A Comparative View* (New York: Basic Books, 1968).

28. Christopher Lasch, *The True and Only Heaven: Progress and Its Critics* (New York: Norton, 1991), 162.

29. See Ashis Nandy, ed., *Science, Hegemony, and Violence: A Requiem for Modernity* (Delhi: Oxford University Press, 1988); Wolfgang Sachs, ed., *The Development Dictionary: A Guide to Knowledge as Power* (London: Zed Books, 1992); and Arturo Escobar, *Encountering Development: The Making and Unmaking of the Third World* (Princeton: Princeton University Press, 1995). Among poststructural scholars writing about modernization and development, the work of Michel Foucault has proven most influential. See, for example, *Discipline and Punish: The Birth of the Prison* (New York: Vintage, 1979).

30. See, for example, the ideals expressed in Amartya Sen, *Development as Freedom* (New York: Random House, 1999).

31. See Arjun Appadurai, *Modernity at Large: Cultural Dimensions of Globalization* (Minneapolis: University of Minnesota Press, 1996).

# PART I

# DEVELOPING MODERNIZATION

# MODERNIZATION THEORY AND THE AMERICAN REVIVAL OF THE SCIENTIFIC AND TECHNOLOGICAL STANDARDS OF SOCIAL ACHIEVEMENT AND HUMAN WORTH

MICHAEL ADAS

In the years after World War I, bitter debates between leading European intellectuals over the perils of mechanization and Americanization, as well as the future of industrial societies more generally, called into question the scientific and technological measures that had been deployed for centuries to demonstrate European intellectual, organizational, and moral superiority. Over the nineteenth and early twentieth centuries these gauges of material achievement and potential for progressive social development had come to be essential elements of the civilizing mission rhetoric that was pervasively deployed to justify Western colonial dominance over much of the rest of humanity. Anguished European responses to the longer-term effects of the war contrasted dramatically with the upsurge of enthusiasm across the Atlantic for inventors and innovation, for the mass consumer products of industrial technology, and for the same visions of progress and unlimited improvement that the war had led many European leaders and social commentators to dismiss as cruel delusions. While the British and French in particular struggled to shore up empires under siege and find ways to rebuild their shattered societies, the Americans grew increasingly assertive in the exercise of their newly won political and economic influence. Just as the decline of Europe's global hegemony opened the way for the emergence of the United States as the premier world power, European doubts concerning the very foundations of their civilizing mission strengthened the Americans' growing conviction that *they* knew best how to reform "backward" societies that were racked by poverty, natural calamities, and social unrest.

Although the term "modernization" was rarely used until after World War II, in the 1920s and 1930s American educators, missionaries, and engineers promoted political, economic, and cultural transformations in China, the Philippines, and Latin America that were as fundamental and wide-ranging as those proposed by development specialists in the 1950s and 1960s. In the interwar period—as in the decades when modernization was in vogue—industrial, democratic America was seen to be the ideal that less fortunate societies ought to emulate. America's path to political stability and prosperity through the rational management of its resources, through the application of science and technology to mass production, and through efforts to adapt the principles of scientific investigation to the study of human behavior was increasingly held up as the route that "underdeveloped" and unstable societies were destined to travel as they "entered the modern age." Though the ideology of modernization would not begin to be fully articulated until the 1950s, when its ascendancy was buoyed by Cold War imperatives and it was recast in the development jargon of the post–World War II era, its basic tenets had begun to be formulated long before. Through it the scientific and technological measures of social achievement and cultural adaptiveness that European ideologues had increasingly privileged in the nineteenth century were revived and reworked. In modernization theory they found their broadest application and their most elaborate expression. But the presuppositions that undergirded modernization theory were deeply rooted in both America's own historical experience and broader currents of Western thought that extended in some cases back into the early decades of European overseas expansion in the fifteenth and sixteenth centuries.

Religion, specifically the profession of Christianity, was the most critical marker by which Europeans distinguished themselves from the people they encountered overseas through most of the early modern era, from roughly 1450 to the early 1700s. But for many European travelers, merchants, and missionaries, social practices (such as marriage patterns and the position of women) and especially the material culture exhibited by the different peoples contacted were viewed from the outset as critical gauges of the level of savage degradation or civilized advancement these societies exhibited. An early emphasis on the sophistication of the indigenes' architecture, transport systems, tools, and perceptions of time and space gave way in the eighteenth century to more generalized assessments of the capacity of different groups—which were increasingly identified as races—for scientific reasoning and experimentation.

In the following century, as the industrial revolution steadily widened the gap in material productivity and mastery of the natural world between Western Europeans and the rest of humanity, machines became the chief measures of societal achievement and human worth and potential. Estimates of the capacity of different human groups to unlock the secrets of nature and in turn harness their discoveries to industrial production, or to invent ever more lethal weaponry and more rapid communications systems, became critical determinants of the ranking they received in the hierarchies of racial types the Europeans were so fond of devising in the nineteenth century. A whole range of attributes came to be associated with different human groups on the basis of European perceptions of their scientific and technological achievements. European writers and colonizers represented themselves as rational, energetic, in control, progressive-minded, disciplined, punctual, and efficient. Varying combinations of contrasting qualities were attributed to different colonized peoples, who were essentialized as superstitious, indolent, fatalistic, reactionary, disorganized, oblivious to time, and hopelessly wasteful.

Advocates of colonial expansion regularly deployed these contrasts between Europeans and non-Europeans to justify European overseas dominance, formulate colonial policy, and make sense of the responses of the colonized. They were also invoked by Americans involved in colonizing efforts from the 1890s to World War I, and—often in rather different ways—by proponents of modernization theory in the 1920s and 1930s and especially in the era of the Cold War. Though European precedents had a major impact on American thinking about these issues, scientific and technological measures of human worth can be traced to the first years of settlement in North America. And they became a prominent feature of the ideologies associated with the continental and overseas expansion that proved critical to the transformation of scattered colonial enclaves in the late seventeenth century into a powerful American nation with aspirations to global hegemony by the beginning of the twentieth.

From the time of the earliest European contacts in North America, chroniclers, missionaries, and settlers made much of the technological gap between the peoples of the "Old World" and those of the "New." As was the case in Africa, the European perception that the Amerindians lacked religion and followed strange customs had more to do with the relegation of the New World "natives" to the status of savages than what they lacked in material culture. But the myth that the Indians were hunters rather than agriculturists, which persisted despite considerable evidence of their aptitude for farming, and the vision of America as a land of abundant resources that the indigenous peoples had not begun to tap, chiefly because their technology was too primitive, buttressed the arguments of those who sought to justify the Indians' subjugation and displacement. The settlers' association of civility with human domination over nature and their view of the new continent as a sparsely populated wilderness led thinkers on both sides of the Atlantic to the conclusion that its Indian inhabitants were savages, much in need of assistance from the "industrious men" and "engins" that only Europe could provide.[1]

Although Thomas Jefferson's "agrarian idealism" predominated in the decades when America was transformed from a patchwork of settlement colonies into an expanding nation, technological advance was increasingly seen as essential to the growth and well-being of the fledgling republic. As John Kasson has argued, Jefferson, himself an inventor of considerable ingenuity, came to see the controlled introduction into the United States of the industrial technology being developed in Great Britain as "a welcome ally in the republican enterprise."[2] Many of Jefferson's contemporaries assigned technology an even more essential role. Merchants and politicians, ministers and educators, hailed the machine as the answer to the new nation's shortage of labor, as a means by which the unity of the rapidly expanding republic would be preserved, and as a vital source of prosperity and progress. Inventors were compared to magicians and men to "republican machines." Machines were lauded "not simply as functional objects but as signs and symbols of the future of America."[3] Technological development was increasingly equated with the rise from barbarism to civilization, and machines were viewed as key agents for the spread of the American version of civilization in the New World wilderness. Throughout the nineteenth century, prominent politicians, writers, and artists caricatured the Indians as slothful, technologically impoverished, and unprogressive vestiges of backward societies that must either adopt the white man's way or perish. The shortcomings of the Indians were set against the virtues of the expansive European pioneers whose hard work, discipline, thrift, foresight, and technological ingenuity were transforming the underdeveloped wilderness into a land of unprecedented prosperity.[4] At century's end, all of these ideas were brought together in Frederick Jackson Turner's seminal essays on the impact of the moving frontier on Indian societies and the course of American history more broadly.[5]

As the United States industrialized, the "special affinity between the machine and the New Republic" was increasingly emphasized.[6] A number of prominent and often-quoted American thinkers, including Nathaniel Hawthorne, Henry Thoreau, and Henry Adams, shared their European counterparts' ambivalence toward, if not pronounced hostility to, the industrial order as dehumanizing and environmentally degrading. And a few anti-industrialists followed Ruskin and Morris in attempting to resurrect artisan production.[7] But the great majority of Americans exulted in the power and productivity of the new technology: "they grasped and panted and cried for it."[8] As in Europe and the colonial world, the railway became the premier symbol of the advance of industrialism in the United States. John Stilgoe has shown how extensively railroads had transformed the American landscape by the last decades of the nineteenth century, pervading virtually all aspects of American life from commerce and advertising to education and recreation.[9] In this same period, industry increasingly eclipsed agriculture as the dominant sector in the U.S. economy and the main influence on American social life. By the late 1880s the combination of science and technology found in American industry was matched only by that of Germany, and the United States was outstripping its

European competitors in the production of iron and steel. Many Americans had come to regard machines as objects of aesthetic pleasure; others proclaimed them divinely ordained instruments for building the nation and strengthening its moral resolve.[10]

If it had been predictable that the Europeans, who had excelled all other peoples in the mastery of the natural world in the early industrial era, would come to regard scientific and technological accomplishments as key measures of human worth, it was perhaps inevitable that Americans would do so. Though they might concede European superiority in the fine arts, philosophy, and the other pursuits of "high culture," Americans came to regard invention and technological innovation as endeavors in which they could surpass all other peoples, including the British who had played vital roles in the industrialization of the United States.[11] In the middle decades of the nineteenth century, American thinkers exercised significant influence in promoting scientific and technological standards for judging human worth, from the contributions of Samuel Morton and Josiah Nott toward "scientific" racism to the emphasis placed by ethnologists such as Lewis Henry Morgan on the role of technology in the evolution of society.[12] At the turn of the century, when the United States became increasingly involved overseas, assumptions of its material and technical superiority became a central element in the American version of the civilizing mission. In response to the perceived backwardness, poverty and social turmoil they encountered in Hawaii and China and over much of the Caribbean, American diplomats, merchants, and missionaries envisioned sweeping reforms and promoted projects for improvement modeled on those undertaken in the preceding decades in the United States itself.[13]

The fullest elaboration of America's civilizing mission ideology was prompted by the conquest of the Philippines at the turn of the century. The decision to retain the islands as a colonial possession forced politicians and colonial officials to develop policies and programs that would justify the violent subjugation of the recalcitrant Filipinos. Anticipating an emphasis later found in the writings of the modernization theorists, American colonizers stressed the political dimensions of reform and reconstruction in the new colony. But their vision of good government extended far beyond the "peace, order, and justice" formula that was the focus of British and French advocates of imperial expansion. From the outset, the U.S. role was defined as one of tutelage rather than paternalistic domination. American officials explicitly argued that economic reforms and education were undertaken to create a prosperous Filipino middle class from which moderate political leaders, committed to representative democracy and continuing economic ties to the United States, could be drawn. Though the timetable was vague, the Americans' well-publicized intent was to prepare the Filipinos for self-rule.[14]

The preparation of the Filipinos for independence was never seen in purely political terms. It was clear to most American policymakers that legislatures and elections would have little meaning until the backward and impoverished society that they saw as the legacy of centuries of Spanish rule was thoroughly reconstructed. Perhaps more than in any other colony, the role of the engineer as civilizer was touted by politicians in Washington and officials in the islands themselves. No American personified this ideal more than the energetic W. Cameron Forbes, an impatient businessman turned colonial administrator. Forbes, whose main purpose as governor general was to direct the rebuilding and expansion of the road and railway networks of the islands, was "very much a man of the age of steel and machine . . . who believed unquestioningly that things modern were things progressive" and whose journals were full of "celebrations of the new, the speedy, the mechanical, and, perhaps above all else, the efficient." As he saw it, the Filipinos could not get enough of the new technology that colonization had made available to them. Whenever he met them, Forbes remarked, the Filipinos asked immediately for railroads: "They are crying for them, and from all sides I am pressed with questions as to their probability, how soon can they have them, etc."[15]

The centrality of the technological and scientific components of America's colonial mission in the Philippines was summed up concisely by J. Ralston Hayden in the mid-1920s in an early retrospective assessment of American rule: "The old Spanish legal codes were largely rewritten and modernized, a modern government was organized and successfully operated, a great system of popular education was created, a census taken, a modern currency system was established, a program of public works including the construction of roads, bridges, port improvements, irrigation works, artesian wells, school houses, markets and other public buildings laid down and carried out, an admirable public health service was inaugurated."[16] In this same period American military and civilian engineers oversaw similar projects in the Caribbean.[17] Although the political dimensions of these contemporary development efforts were considerably circumscribed, and their scale and the extent of the opportunities for full collaboration with local peoples was substantially reduced compared to those in the Philippines, they were all premised on the assumption that the American path to modernity could serve as a model for the rest of the world.

Involvement in World War I further enhanced the already high esteem in which Americans held inventors and machines. Despite some misgivings about the war's indecisive outcome, the conflict strengthened their conviction that they were a people destined by virtue of their scientific and technological prowess to shape the future of less fortunate societies. There were, of course, individuals such as Ernest Hemingway and Ezra Pound who fled from the growth and the consumer-crazed society that the United States had become by the early 1920s. But the great majority of Americans reveled in the spectacles and creature comforts of "the machine age." Their experience of the Great War had been very different from that of the European adversaries. In the two and half years before the United States entered the war, American production, profits, and employment had soared in response to the insatiable demand for food and war matériel of its future allies. American merchants competed with Japanese traders for the overseas markets that hard-pressed European combatants had been forced to abandon.[18]

America's late entry into combat meant that its soldiers were spared the long years of futile slaughter in the trenches. By the time substantial numbers of doughboys were actually fighting in the spring of 1918, German offensives had broken the trench stalemate and restored a war of motion and maneuver. In the counteroffensive that forced the Germans to sue for peace in November, the Allies made extensive use of the new military technology, particularly tanks and airplanes, which had been developed during the war years. The lessons of the final offensives were not lost in the interwar years on George Patton, George Marshall, and other future army commanders, or on Billy Mitchell and like-minded advocates of massed air power. In their view, American industry had done much to keep the Allies in the war; European and American scientific research and inventiveness had devised the weapons that had carried them to victory.[19]

As a result of their late entry into combat and the end of the trench stalemate, the numbers of American servicemen killed were far lower than those of the other major combatants: just over 50,000 dead in battle compared to the millions lost by the British, French, or Germans. These totals suggest that, in contrast to the European combatants, America's "lost generation" was literary rather than literal. Hemingway and John Dos Passos notwithstanding, postwar disillusionment in the United States was largely a consequence of the failure of the peace process rather than the disenchantment with modern mechanized warfare that was so pervasive among European survivors and intellectuals. Thorstein Veblen's scathing 1922 critique of the folly of intervention best summed up American frustration over involvement in a conflict that had ended so indecisively as to make future wars appear inevitable. One of Veblen's main concerns was the great boost the war had given to Billy Sunday's brand of religion and the threat that the postwar religious revival posed for the "material sciences," whose methodology Veblen considered the "most characteristic and most constructive factor engaged in modern civilization."[20]

In the decades after World War I, applied science and technology pervaded American life to a degree that greatly exceeded that experienced by any other society throughout history. Between 1917 and 1940, the number of American households that were electrified increased from less than 25 to over 90 percent. The automobile, produced on Henry Ford's moving assembly line in Dearborn for the first time in 1913, became an item of mass consumption. The family car and commercial airlines gave Americans unprecedented mobility; the radio, the great expansion of telephone networks, motion pictures, and mass advertising radically transformed American communications. A great proliferation of new appliances from vacuum cleaners and electric stoves to toasters and washing machines brought the American home irretrievably into the machine age. The impact of machine design was evident in American architecture and the fine arts. Streamlining and Art Deco graced the most fashionable homes and offices, and automakers vied to perfect the new styles. Henry Ford was widely regarded as the prophet of a new age of "heroic optimism," in which science and invention were hailed as the keys to American prosperity and the best antidotes to social ills. Politicians and intellectuals celebrated factories as the modern equivalents of medieval cathedrals and praised industry for its simplicity and truth. Alfred North Whitehead judged successful those organisms that "modified their environments." Charles Beard proclaimed science and "power-driven machinery" the hallmarks of Western civilization.[21]

Even when the Great Depression brought major challenges to the capitalist foundations of the American industrial order, few questioned the primacy of the machine in the United States or any progressive society. The 1930s were dominated by massive construction projects—dams, highways, tunnels, and bridges—designed to generate energy for and to extend the range of the technology Americans continued to view as the key to their rise to global power and as essential means of eradicating poverty both at home and overseas.[22] In the era between the two world wars, the long-standing assumption that technological innovation was essential to progressive social development came to be viewed in terms of a necessary association of mechanization with modernity. As Richard Wilson has argued, in American thinking the "machine in all of its manifestations—as an object, a process, and ultimately a symbol—became the fundamental fact of modernism."[23] Modernization theory represented an extension of this association—which was grounded in the American and Western European historical experience—to the peoples and cultures of the non-Western world. Though the lexicon of American educators and policymakers in overseas areas remained rudimentary and their conceptualizations crude by the social science standards of the 1960s, many of the presuppositions that later informed paradigms of tradition and modernity were evident in their curricula and proposals for reform.

L. G. Morgan, for example, viewed the teaching of "modern science" as indispensable to China's efforts to bring its antiquated society into the "modern world." Morgan, who taught Chinese students for many years, believed that beyond advances in practical knowledge and technique, training in the Western sciences would instill a much-needed sense of discipline and precision in the youth of China. He averred that it would enhance their critical faculties, render them more "cool and logical," and enable them to overcome the passivity that he identified as a major impediment to Chinese innovation and growth.

Morgan suggested that a modern mind-set, if propagated in China by the study of Western scientific learning, would enable the Chinese people to root out the sources of their backwardness and poverty, from bad roads to corrupt government. He was confident that at least some Chinese were capable of mastering even the most advanced scientific theories of the West. He urged the Chinese to emulate the Japanese, who had build a strong and prosperous nation within a generation because they had adopted the scientific approach transmitted through Western-style education.[24]

Morgan's fellow educator George Twiss provided a more detailed analysis of the obstacles in "old" China that would have to be surmounted if the living standards of the Chinese people were to be improved and the country's resources "developed." His discussion of these impediments singled out many of the "barriers to development" stressed by later modernization theorists: ancient customs and beliefs, poor communications, and a low level of control over the natural environment. His solutions were standard fare among modernizers of the post–World War II era: Western education, "modern" science, and industrialization.[25]

After World War II, the modernization paradigm supplanted the beleaguered civilizing mission as the preeminent ideology of Western dominance. American social scientists were the main exponents of the new ideology, which was much more systematically and coherently articulated than its predecessor. Competing theories of the dynamics and stages of the transition from "tradition" to "modernity" were debated by academics and, as the essays that follow illustrate in a variety of ways, their jargon-laden discourse played a major role in policy formation with respect to the "underdeveloped," "developing," or "emerging" nations of the "third world." New hierarchies of the levels of social development—the first, second, third, and (somewhat later) fourth worlds; postmodern, modern, traditional, primitive; mature, developing, underdeveloped—replaced the civilized/barbarian/savage scale that had long served as the standard. Like the minority of nineteenth-century European and American colonizers who stressed their roles as "improvers," modernization theorists rejected the long-standing conviction that racial or innate deficiencies were responsible for the lowly position that non-Western peoples usually occupied in these hierarchies. The postwar convergence of revulsion against Nazi atrocities perpetrated in the name of racial purification, and African and Asian nationalist challenges to the claims of racial superiority by the colonial overlords had much to do with the decidedly antiracist premises of the new ideology. Like the earlier improvers, the modernizers assumed that all peoples not only could but would "develop" along the scientific-industrial lines pioneered by the West. As Ali Mazrui has argued, a social evolutionist teleology informed this assumption.[26] But the modernizers drastically reduced the time frame in which the process of social advance was to occur. In contrast to the centuries envisioned by even the most sanguine colonial improvers, the transition to modernity was plotted in decades. In the more advanced of the "emerging" nations, it could conceivably occur within one person's lifetime.

The nonracist assumptions of the modernization theorists were linked to a second major premise that distinguished their models of development from those of the colonial era. Though the modernizers regarded American and European capital and technical assistance as vital to development in the postcolonial world, they envisioned Africans and Asians—not Westerners—as the main agents of the transformation of backward societies. The very nature of the colonial relationship had dictated that the European colonizers consider their ongoing control essential for the task of civilizing savage and barbaric societies. But the process of decolonization, which coincided with the decades when modernization theory peaked in influence, rendered this vision of Western paternalism obsolescent. Concerns about the composition and methods of the new elites who were to oversee the transition from tradition to modernity, as well as anxiety about communism's appeal in the generally impoverished former colonies, explain the much greater emphasis in much of the literature on modernization on political aspects of societal transformation in contrast to the colonial rhetoric of improvement. Some of the more influential proponents of modernization theory privileged social mobility, expanding political participation, and the democratization of political institutions as measures of the degree of modernity attained by different postcolonial societies.[27] Even the most radical of the nineteenth-century colonial reformers had given little attention to these issues. The political context in which the improvers worked was a given: limited reforms might be suggested, but the colonial administration was normally considered beyond the purview of their civilizing efforts. Thus contrary to Walt W. Rostow's assessment of the impact of imperialism,[28] modernization as it was understood in the early decades of the Cold War was inconceivable in the colonial context.

The ultimate outcome of the transformation of traditional into modern societies was also unthinkable in the colonial era. Even in its most benevolent manifestations, the underlying aim of the civilizing mission was to reshape colonial economies in ways that would make them more compatible with the metropolitan economies of each imperial system. Modernization paradigms have almost invariably been based on the assumption that industrialization is essential for full development, for genuine modernity—even though their creators have rarely thought through the implications of this outcome for the economies of the developed nations. Their ideal is a world of industrially competitive nations interacting in a capitalist, free-trade, global framework. But the reality for much of the postcolonial world has been the continuing economic dependence of the great majority of the primary product-oriented former colonies on the industrialized West (and, in the last decades of the Cold War, Japan and neighboring nations on the Pacific Rim).

Although modernization theory differs in important ways from its European colonial civilizing-mission predecessors, in most of its more influential formulations it shared an emphasis on the scientific and technological measures of human worth and achievement that have long been vital components of ideologies of Western dominance. Marion Levy, for example, began his elaborate mid-1960s disquisition on the social effects of the transition from tradition to modernity with the assumption that the degree to which a society had been modernized could be measured by the extent to which it had made use of inanimate power and employed tools "to multiply the effect of effort."[29] Wilbert Moore treated modernization and industrialization as if they were synonymous, while C. E. Black regarded the "revolution in science" in early modern Europe and the later application of scientific discoveries to "the practical affairs of man in the form of technology" as essential preconditions for the "ascent" to modernity.[30] Rostow also stressed as necessary conditions for modernity the importance of the rise of scientific thinking and the growing capacity of humans to manipulate their natural environment. The "take-off" and "drive to maturity," which Rostow argued must follow if meaningful modernization were to occur, were measured in purely economic and technological terms: in the ability of societies to save for investment in industrial growth a designated portion of what they produced.[31]

Given the varying emphases of different advocates of the modernization paradigm and their predilection for scientific-sounding stage sequences, corollaries, and axioms, the centrality of scientific-technological gauges has often been obscured. But the continuing importance of those standards has been underscored by the very characteristics that have been used to distinguish the traditional from the modern. Modernity is associated with rationality, empiricism, efficiency, and progressive change; tradition connotes fatalism, veneration for custom and the sacred, indiscipline, and stagnation. Joseph Kahl, who provided one of the more detailed listings of these attributes, averred that traditional *men* are passive and fatalistic largely because they lack the sophisticated technology required to "shape the world to their own desires." Modern *men*, he argues, make use of ever more advanced technology to remake their environment and change their social systems in ways intended to promote both their own careers and the development of their societies as a whole.[32] Two of the key criteria by which Alex Inkeles distinguished "Modern Men" in six "developing" countries in the mid-1960s were their belief in the efficacy of science and medicine (and a corresponding rejection of fatalism and passivity) and their insistence that people be "on time" and "plan their affairs in advance." In an earlier essay, Inkeles also stressed the "modern man's" ability to "dominate his environment in order to advance his own purposes and goals," and the high level of technology normally associated with modern cultures.[33]

The emphasis on men in the thinking of influential modernization theorists such as Kahl and Inkeles exemplified a persistence in academic discourse and actual policy formulation of the masculine orientation that had predominated in the civilizing projects of European colonizers for centuries as well as among late nineteenth-century American proconsuls in Hawaii, the Philippines, and the Caribbean. Like their Western European counterparts, American officials assumed that the unprecedented achievements in experiment and invention, which they invoked to demonstrate Western superiority, were the products of male ingenuity and male artifice. Colonial proposals to train physicians and railway engineers were drawn up with male students in mind, just as colonial development schemes and postindependence modernization initiatives (both capitalist- and socialist-inspired) have been for the most part male-oriented.[34] As Catherine Scott has recently shown, in the writings and policy formulations of leading advocates of modernization paradigms for postcolonial societies the attributes of modernity are invariably gendered male, those of tradition, female.[35]

Modernization theory also shared the assumption of its civilizing mission predecessor that there was a single viable path to development. In part, of course, this constricted and rather unimaginative vision of what was in effect the future of humanity was a response to the alternatives provided by the West's Communist rivals in the Cold War. But it also represented a pronounced enthnocentrism and a none too subtle form of cultural imperialism. Modernization paradigms were premised on "an imperialism of values which superimpose[d] American or, more broadly, Western cultural choices on other societies, as in the tendency to subordinate all other considerations (save political stability perhaps) to the technical requirements of economic development."[36]

Ironically, despite the great emphasis in the literature on the Cold War on tensions and rivalries between the capitalist West and the Soviet bloc, the peoples of postcolonial societies that made up the third world were faced with a similar sort of cultural imperialism in the various Communist routes to development from Stalinism to Maoism. Rivals on both sides of the Cold War divide privileged fossil-fueled, large-scale, top-down drives for industrialization as the essence of modernity. Proponents of the two approaches might clash over the role of the state and the market in the development process, but they shared the conviction that traditional or "feudal" beliefs, customs, and institutions were little more than impediments to the inevitable transformation of backward non-Western economies and societies into fully modern ones. Both placed a premium on unbridled scientific investigation and technological innovation; neither evinced much concern, at least until the 1970s, for the environmental consequences of the globalization of the industrialization process. Even more than in the West, the Soviets and later the Maoists stressed the importance of heavy industry and the application of science to everything from production to social organization.[37] And the main architects of both major Communist alternatives were largely oblivious to ecological concerns. Consequently, the outcomes of their five-year plans often proved devastating to the environment of the regions where these initiatives were concentrated.[38]

Postcolonial leaders in the third world might deplore the draconian means by which Communist regimes pursued development, but they (and often American intelligence operatives) were impressed by both Soviet and Maoist successes in achieving rapid industrial growth, raising living standards, and building formidable military establishments which could stand up to those of the West. Faced with the ethnocentrism of the assumption by developmentalists on both sides of the Cold War divide that only the scientific-industrial path to development could enable postcolonial societies to achieve modernity, those engaged in the struggle against injustice and poverty in the emerging nations faced a dilemma in the truest sense of the term—a choice between undesirable alternatives. If they refused technical assistance and scientific borrowing from the industrialized West and the Soviet bloc in order to resist neocolonial domination or cultural imperialism, their societies would be denied essential tools, skills, and knowledge for their development programs. This assistance was all the more critical because the newly independent states confronted much greater demographic and economic obstacles than those faced by nations that had industrialized earlier. But the full industrial transformation of postcolonial societies along either Western or Communist lines might well prove calamitous, given the limited and diminishing resources available and the new burdens these changes would impose on an already severely stressed global environment.

Escape from this global predicament was impeded by the fact that potential alternatives to the capitalist or Communist routes to development—such as the Gandhian approach that favored community-oriented projects, grassroots initiatives, and labor-intensive technologies—were scorned in the decades of the Cold War by both American and Soviet theorists and field specialists. These "alternative technology" approaches were also marginalized by most postcolonial regimes.[39] And a final irony of the end of the Cold War rivalries between the liberal capitalist and Communist blocs was a further diminution of the appeal of "appropriate technologies" and grassroots development initiatives. The presumed triumph of globalization based on the liberal capitalist model has sparked a revival of modernization theory and the resurgence of a development teleology grounded in the Enlightenment project and visions of an industrialized world order.

## NOTES

This essay appeared in an earlier form as the epilogue to Michael Adas, *Machines as the Measure of Men: Science, Technology, and Ideologies of Western Dominance*. 

1. James Rosier as quoted by Karen Kupperman in *Settling with the Indians: The Meeting of English and Indian Cultures in America, 1580–1640* (Totowa, N.J.: Rowman & Littlefield, 1980), 80 (quoted portions), 81–90. Kupperman points out (86, 104–6) that a number of observers thought the Indians' technology admirably suited to the American environment.

2. John Kasson, *Civilizing the Machine: Technology and Republican Values in America, 1776–1900* (New York: Grossman, 1982), 22–25 (quoted portion, 25).

3. Ibid., 29–30, 32 (quoted phrase), 35, 38, 41 (quoted portion), 46–47.

4. For samples of these judgments regarding the Indians to the end of the nineteenth century, see Roy Harvey Pearce, *The Savages of America* (Baltimore: Johns Hopkins University Press, 1953), esp. 66–71, 82–91, 165–66, and Robert E. Berkhofer, Jr., *The White Man's Indian* (New York: Knopf, 1978), 91–96.

5. Frederick Jackson Turner, *The Frontier in American History* (New York: Holt, Rinehart, & Winston, 1920).

6. Leo Marx, *The Machine in the Garden* (London, 1964), 203.

7. Ibid., chap. 5, contains superb discussions of early intellectual hostility to the coming of the machine age. For late nineteenth- and early twentieth-century variations on these responses, see Jackson Lears, *No Place of Grace: Antimodernism and the Transformation of American Culture, 1880–1920* (New York: Pantheon, 1981), especially chap. 2, which includes a fine analysis of the origins and weaknesses of the crafts movement in the United States.

8. Perry Miller, quoted in Marx, *Machine in the Garden*, 208.

9. John Stilgoe, *Metropolitan Corridor: Railroads and the American Scene* (New Haven: Yale University Press, 1983).

10. Perhaps no work captures these sentiments as exuberantly as Andrew Carnegie's *Triumphant Democracy* (New York: Scribner, 1886). See also: Kasson, *Civilizing the Machine*, chap. 4; Marx, *Machine in the Garden*, 190–226; and Robert Rydell, *All the World's a Fair* (Chicago: University of Chicago Press, 1984). For

the integration of scientific research into American industry, see David Noble, *America by Design: Science, Technology, and the Rise of Corporate Capitalism* (Oxford: Oxford University Press, 1977).

11. Marx, *Machine in the Garden*, 205. See also Andrew Carnegie's extensive comparisons in *Triumphant Democracy*.

12. Samuel Morton, *Crania Americana* (Philadelphia: J. Dobson, 1839); Josiah Nott (and George Gliddon), *Types of Mankind* (London: J. B. Lippincott, 1854); and Lewis Henry Morgan, *Ancient Society* (1877; Cambridge: Harvard University Press, 1964).

13. See, for examples, Peter Buck, *American Science and Modern China, 1876–1936* (Cambridge: Cambridge University Press, 1980); K. R. Howe, *Where the Waves Fall* (Honolulu: University of Hawaii Press, 1984); and Howard Gillette Jr., "The Military Occupation of Cuba, 1899–1902: Workshop for American Progressivism," *American Quarterly* 25, no. 4 (1973): 410–25.

14. Of the substantial literature on political initiatives in the Philippines in the early decades of American rule, the best studies include: Peter Stanley, *A Nation in the Making: The Philippines and the United States, 1899–1921* (Cambridge: Harvard University Press, 1974); Glenn A. May, *Social Engineering in the Philippines* (Westport, Conn.: Greenwood Press, 1980); Bonifacio S. Salamanca, *The Filipino Response to American Rule, 1901–1913* (n.p.: Shoe String Press, 1968); and Oscar M. Alfonso, *Theodore Roosevelt and the Philippines, 1897–1909* (Quezon City: University of the Philippines Press, 1970).

15. Stanley, *Nation in the Making,* 96–106 (quoted portions, 99, 104).

16. Quoted in Michael Onorato, *A Brief Review of American Interest in Philippine Development and Other Essays* (Manila: MCS Enterprises, 1972), 3.

17. Hans Schmidt, *The United States Occupation of Haiti, 1915–1934* (New Brunswick: Rutgers University Press, 1995), and Bruce Calder, *The Impact of Intervention: The Dominican Republic during the United States Occupation of 1916–1924* (Austin: University of Texas Press, 1984).

18. On the economic impact of the war on the United States, see David M. Kennedy, *Over Here: The First World War and American Society* (Oxford: Oxford University Press, 1980); Frederic L. Paxson, *American Democracy and the World War* (New York: Cooper Square, 1966); and the classic contemporary reckonings by Grosvenor Clarkson and Robert F. Wilson.

19. For the most detailed survey of American military preparations for the war, see Edward M. Coffman, *The War to End All Wars* (Madison: University of Wisconsin Press, 1968). On the role of technology in the Allied victory and America's military future, see George C. Marshall, *Memoirs of My Services in the World War, 1917–1918* (Boston: Houghton Mifflin, 1976), especially chaps. 10 and 11; M. Blumensen, ed., *The Patton Papers, 1885–1940* (Boston: Houghton Mifflin, 1972), 446–59; William B. Mitchell, *Memoirs of World War I* (New York: Random House, 1960) and *Winged Defense* (New York: Putnam, 1925); and Michael Sherry, *The*

*Rise of American Air Power* (New Haven: Yale University Press, 1987), esp. chaps. 2 and 3.

20. Veblen's essay "Dementia Praecox" originally appeared in *Freeman* 5 (1922). I have used the reprint in Leon Ardzooni, ed., *Essays on Our Changing Order* (New York: Viking Press, 1934), 423–36 (quoted portion, 430–31). Even Hemingway's disillusionment had more to do with the bungling Italian commanders and the Italian general staff than with mass mechanized killing per se. See, for example, the analysis of his wartime experiences in Michael S. Reynolds, *Hemingway's First War: The Making of "A Farewell to Arms"* (Princeton: Princeton University Press, 1976), especially chaps. 4 and 5.

21. The comparisons to cathedrals and exemplifications of truth are quoted in Richard D. Wilson et al.., *The Machine Age in America, 1918–1941* (New York: Harry N. Abrams, 1986), 24, 30. See also Alfred North Whitehead, *Science and the Modern World* (New York: Macmillan, 1925), 295–96, and Charles Beard, *Whither Mankind?* (New York: Longmans, Green, 1929), 14–15. This summary of the ascendancy of technology in the 1920s draws heavily on the essays in the Wilson catalog; William Leuchtenburg's useful survey, *The Perils of Prosperity, 1914–32* (Chicago: University of Chicago Press, 1958); Walter Polakov, *The Power Age* (New York: Covici, Friede, 1933); and Siegfried Giedion's *Mechanization Takes Command* (New York: Oxford University Press, 1969).

22. Frank Ninkovich, "The Rockefeller Foundation, China, and Cultural Change," *Journal of American History* 70, no. 4 (1984): 799–820; David Lilienthal, *TVA: Democracy on the March* (New York: Harper & Bros., 1944); Merle Curti and Kendall Birr, *Prelude to Point IV: American Technical Missions Overseas, 1838–1938* (Madison: University of Wisconsin Press, 1954); and Randall E. Stross, *The Stubborn Earth: American Agriculturalists on Chinese Soil, 1898–1937* (Berkeley: University of California Press, 1986).

23. Wilson, *Machine Age*, 23.

24. L. G. Morgan, *The Teaching of Science to the Chinese* (Hong Kong: Kelly & Walsh, 1933), esp. pp. xii–xiii, 51–52, 55–62, 69.

25. Twiss, *Science and Education in China* (Shanghai: Commercial Press, 1925), pp. 12, 39–41, 48–60.

26. Ali Mazrui, "From Darwin to Current Theories of Modernization," *World Politics* 21, no. 1 (1968): 69–83.

27. This is clearly evident in many of the classics of the modernization genre: e.g., David E. Apter, *The Politics of Modernization* (Princeton: Princeton University Press, 1965); Gabriel A. Almond and James S. Coleman, *The Politics of Developing Areas* (Princeton: Princeton University Press, 1960); and Samuel P. Huntington, *Political Order in Changing Societies* (New Haven: Yale University Press, 1968).

28. W. W. Rostow, *The Stages of Economic Growth: A Non–Communist Manifesto* (Cambridge: Cambridge University Press, 1964), 27.

29. Marion Levy, *Modernization and the Structure of Societies* (Princeton: Princeton University Press, 1966), 11–12.

30. Wilbert Moore, *Social Change* (Englewood Cliffs, N.J.: Prentice-Hall, 1963), chap. 5; and C. E. Black, *The Dynamics of Modernization* (New York: Harper & Row, 1967), 7, 10–11.

31. Rostow, *Stages of Economic Growth,* chaps. 2–5.

32. Joseph Kahl, *The Measurement of Modernism* (Austin: University of Texas Press, 1968), esp. 4–6, 18–20. For an earlier expression of these criteria, see Bert F. Hoselitz, "Non-Economic Barriers to Economic Development," *Economic Development and Cultural Change* 1, no. 1 (1952–53): 14–15.

33. Alex Inkeles, "Making Men Modern: On the Causes and Consequences of Individual Change in Six Developing Countries," *American Journal of Sociology* 75, no. 2 (1969), esp. 210–11; and "The Modernization of Man," in Myron Weiner, ed., *Modernization: The Dynamics of Growth* (New York: Basic Books, 1966), 141–44.

34. In what has become a very large literature on these issues, two works remain seminal: Ester Boserup, *Women's Role in Economic Development* (London: Allen & Unwin, 1970), and Barbara Rogers, *The Domestication of Women: Discrimination in Developing Societies* (London: St. Martin's Press, 1980).

35. Catherine V. Scott, *Gender and Development: Rethinking Modernization and Dependency Theory* (Boulder, Colo.: Rienner, 1995), esp. chap. 2.

36. Dean Tipps, "Modernization Theory and the Comparative Study of Societies: A Critical Perspective," *Comparative Studies in Society and History* 15, no. 2 (1973): 210.

37. Kermit E. McKenzie, *The Comintern and World Revolution, 1928–1943* (London: Columbia University Press, 1964), esp. chap. 5; Robert Lewis, *Science and Industrialization in the USSR* (New York: Holmes & Meier, 1979); Maurice Meisner, *Mao's China: A History of the People's Republic* (New York: Free Press, 1977), chaps. 9, 13, and 16; and Jonathan Spence, *The Search for Modern China* (New York: Norton, 1990), chaps. 20, 22, and 23.

38. On the Soviet Union, see Murray Feshbach and Alfred Friendly, Jr., *Ecocide in the U.S.S.R.* (New York: HarperCollins, 1992); for China, see Vaclav Smil, *The Bad Earth: Environmental Degradation in China* (Armonk, N.Y.: M. E. Sharpe, 1984) and *China's Environmental Crisis* (Armonk: M. E. Sharpe, 1993).

39. See, for examples, Francine R. Frankel, *India's Political Economy, 1947–1977* (Princeton: Princeton University Press, 1978), and James C. Scott, *Seeing Like a State* (New Haven: Yale University Press, 1998), especially chaps. 7 and 8.

## FURTHER READING

Adas, Michael. *Machines as the Measure of Men: Science, Technology, and Ideologies of Western Dominance.* Ithaca: Cornell University Press, 1989.

Jordan, John M. *Machine Age Ideology: Social Engineering and American Liberalism, 1911–1939*. Chapel Hill: University of North Carolina Press, 1994.

Kasson, John. *Civilizing the Machine: Technology and Republican Values in America, 1776–1900*. New York: Grossman, 1976.

Marx, Leo. *The Machine in the Garden*. London: Oxford University Press, 1964.

Mazrui, Ali. "From Darwin to Current Theories of Modernization," *World Politics* 21, no. 1 (1968): 69–83.

Schmidt, Hans. *The United States Occupation of Haiti, 1915–1934*. New Brunswick: Rutgers University Press, 1971.

Stanley, Peter W. *A Nation in the Making: The Philippines and the United States, 1899–1921*. Cambridge: Harvard University Press, 1974.

Tipps, Dean. "Modernization Theory and the Comparative Study of Societies: A Critical Perspective," *Comparative Studies in Society and History* 15, no. 2 (1973): 199–226.

Modernity is a style of life.
The ensemble of behaviors
that compose the modern style
is given its coherence by a
frame of mind—toward the
here and the hereafter, toward
permanence and change,
toward oneself and one's
fellow men.

—Max Millikan and
Donald Blackmer,
*The Emerging Nations* (1961)

# MODERNIZATION THEORY, THE HIGHEST STAGE OF AMERICAN INTELLECTUAL HISTORY

NILS GILMAN

Let me start my analysis of modernization theory's place in postwar American intellectual history with a few words about this essay's title. The phrase "highest stage" is of course meant to invoke Lenin's classic *Imperialism, the Highest Stage of Capitalism* (1917). In this text Lenin argued that the World War I era imperialism of the great powers in Africa and Asia, far from representing a throwback to feudal forms of economic organization, was the natural culmination of capitalism—the penultimate stage before capitalism would reach its final world-historical crisis. Lenin implied that the colonies stood in the same relation to the metropole as the proletariat did to the bourgeoisie. Just as the proletariat was bound to supersede the bourgeoisie through revolution, so too was the backward colonial world (rather than the industrialized center, as Marx had claimed) the place where the revolution would begin. Leninism repositioned the political and economic weaknesses of postcolonial countries as a historico-philosophical strength: instead of being doomed to continued backwardness and long-haul attempts to "catch up," as suggested by even nonracist colonial dogma, Leninist philosophy suggested that the formerly enthralled would be the true leaders of the historical process.

By linking the struggle for socialism to the struggle for independence from colonial overlords, Lenin forged an attractive philosophy for Western-educated leaders of colonial resistance movements. These leaders were drawn to his idea that their own inclination to national liberation also represented the apex of historical consciousness generally. Moreover, that Lenin's Soviet Union had in the span of a generation gone from being a backward and vanquished nation to one of the world's great powers lent credence to Lenin's worldview in the eyes of many postcolonial leaders. The apparent success of the Soviet Union in achieving rapid and sustainable industrialization caused grave concern among American policymakers and social scientists—not least because of the dangerous example it set for the postcolonial nations. What could have presented a more appealing prospect to a leader of a poor nation still smarting from the past and continued humiliations of (post)colonialism? This, at least, was the great worry of American social scientists and policymakers in the early postwar years, a fear only exacerbated by the neutralism propounded by many prominent postcolonial leaders, like Indonesia's Sukarno, Egypt's Gamal Abdal Nasser, and India's Jawaharlal Nehru. The success of a militant "developmentalist" communism in China, that quintessentially "backward" land, represented the nightmare worst-case scenario.

It was in this febrile ideological moment that modernization theory would emerge, formulated in part to counter the appeal of Leninism in the postcolonial countries. Fears that the USSR was providing a superior example of development animated thinking among American social scientists and those in charge of policy toward the postcolonial world. At the Massachusetts Institute of Technology's Center for International Studies (CENIS), the think tank that housed many of the most prominent modernization theorists, the Soviet threat was the essential starting point for thinking about development. Its director, Max Millikan, argued: "A much extended program of American participation in the economic development of the so-called underdeveloped states can and should be one of the most important elements in a program of expanding the dynamism and stability of the Free World and increasing its resistance to the appeals of Communism. The best counter to Communist appeals is a demonstration that these same [development] problems are capable of solution by other means than those the Communists propose."[1] One CENIS scholar, Lucian Pye, put it even more bluntly: "Any discussion of American policy toward the underdeveloped areas of the world which seeks to be realistic must treat explicitly the problem of communism in the context of the Cold War."[2] The idea of modernization provided a theoretical basis for that policy by explaining why and when communism could interrupt the capitalist formula of development, and by providing an alternative to the Communist model. As the geography of the Cold War shifted from Europe to Asia with the Korean War, it became ever more important to connect anticommunism with development.

Modernization theorists proposed technocratic reform to undermine the appeal of more radical redistributions of political power and resources that Communists claimed they favored. In creating this alternative to Leninist proposals about development, however, these scholars would replicate many of the historico-philosophical features of Lenin's own philosophy. Nowhere is this more evident than in the writings of the man most associated with modernization theory, the CENIS economist Walt Whitman Rostow. Lenin and Rostow shared a belief in an immanent historical process that proceeded through inexorable "stages" to a secular utopia. Both believed that the relevant unit of economic and political analysis was the individual nation-state. And both also believed that this process was "revolutionary," irreversible, and most important, salutary. What separated Rostow from Lenin (and Marx) was his appreciation of capitalist modernity as fulfilling rather than alienating. In other words, according to Rostow's "Non-Communist Manifesto," *The Stages of Economic Growth,* it was not communism but "the Age of High Mass Consumption" that represented the happy outcome of history. In fact, Rostow even referred to this stage of economic growth as the "highest" one.

## CONVERGENCE ON THE HIGHEST STAGE

Another way in which the modernization theorists replicated Leninist thought was with the idea that modernization was an inexorable process, but one which could be accelerated by the right kinds of leaders. To be sure, modernization theorists rejected Lenin's argument that this process was best facilitated by an anticapitalist revolutionary vanguard party, instead proposing that it should be led by a procapitalist vanguard of technocratic social planners. Yet if Lenin and the modernization theorists differed on political terms, they nonetheless shared the quintessential Enlightenment dogma that there exists a universal historical process, paradoxically both immanent and guided, in which a single modernity would eventually emerge. All the world's diversity would in due course "converge" on a single structural unity. Even if they differed sharply in the political details of that vision, modernization theory and Leninism both believed that technology and industrial civilization had features that transcended their political contexts; both Lenin and the modernization theorists deemed Frederick Taylor's *Principles of Scientific Management* (1911) a key text. Assembly lines and factories were the world's destiny, both sides agreed. In these ways modernization theory became a kind of capitalist mirror image of Leninism, a Leninism shorn of class struggle as its central historical motor. Instead of projecting the Soviet Union (or some shortly-to-be-achieved version of that state) as the final culmination of history, the modernization theorists, in usually tacit ways, imagined the United States as the apex of development.

While debates flourished about its normative and positive features, its necessary and sufficient conditions, or how to achieve it, most postwar American social scientists agreed that "development" meant achieving a unique goal: modernity. Whether it was Talcott Parsons arguing that specific, universalistic, achievement-oriented values were the hallmark of modernity, or Daniel Lerner claiming that modernity resulted from exposure to mass media and communications technologies, or David McClelland declaring that a population with high *n* Ach (the psychological "need for achievement") would create modernity, or Alex Inkeles claiming that the factory experience created "modern" notions about family, life, and politics, modernization theorists agreed that modernization was a totalizing, monolithic phenomenon which again and again, regardless of time and place, worked the same basic results for the same basic reasons.[3] The world was homogenizing: all countries, insofar as they were "modern," would eventually look more or less alike, and modern people would all think, act, feel, and behave more or less alike. The notion that the world was converging from a congeries of traditional lifeways onto a unique modernity was the central leitmotif of modernization theory.

Two factors accounted for the convergent tendencies of contemporary global civilization. First was the role of elites. All modernizing societies were led by "modernizing elites," who by definition possessed "modern" psychocultural traits. These elites would bend (possibly recalcitrant) populations to their modernizing will. The tautological nature of this argument did not seem to jar its proponents, such as David Apter or Edward Shils. The second reason for convergence lay in technological diffusion. Having denied class struggle a causal role in history, Walt Rostow suggested, "In Britain and the well-endowed parts of the world populated substantially from Britain the proximate stimulus for take-off was mainly, but not wholly, technological."[4] Even someone as averse to technological determinism as Parsons agreed that factories, the media, and bureaucracies were destined to crowd out older ways of producing, communicating, and organizing. Parsons's student Marion J. Levy used a linear scale based on the use of inanimate power sources and tools to measure the "degree" of modernization.[5] Complex machinery, McClelland claimed, "represents symbolically the new age, introduces a new kind of social mobility and ultimately should spread attitudes typical of the modern era."[6] According to the modernization theorists there was only one form of technological modernity (albeit an ever-evolving one).[7]

These arguments are best observed in the industrial theorist Clark Kerr, whose participation in the modernization paradigm has rarely been noted. Although he used Saint-Simon's term "industrialism," Kerr employed this term to mean the same thing his contemporaries would mean when they used the term "modernization": industrialization, Kerr explained (tautologically), was the "transition from the traditional society toward industrialism." Developing an argument first expressed at a 1954 conference, "Human Resources and Labor Relations in Underdeveloped Countries," Kerr's *Industrialism and Industrial Man* provided both a description of labor relations at the terminus of the industrialization process (something that Kerr believed had already been more or less achieved in the United States) and an analysis of how industrialism could be achieved in postcolonial countries. In Kerr's view, modernization was a convergent process in which the lifeways of rich countries inexorably displaced *anciens régimes* in postcolonial settings. "Industrialization came into a most varied world," Kerr explained:

> a world with many cultures, at many stages of development from the primitiveness of quasi-animal life to high levels of civilization, under the rules of many different elites and beliefs. . . . Into the midst of this disparity of systems there intruded a new and vastly superior technique of production; a technique which by its very nature always pushed for identity since the modern was always the more superior. This technique knew no geographical limits; recognized no elites or ideologies. Once unleashed upon the world, the new technique kept spreading and kept advancing.

The result of this convergence would be a homogenized world in which "the differences will be between and among individuals and groups rather than between and among the major geographical areas of the world." Kerr's breathtaking historical vision pictured an immense technological force, driven by its own internal and irresistible logic, sweeping away all hitherto existing societies. He believed that a "new culture based on mass tastes and mass consumption . . . gradually overwhelms the many and varied preexisting cultures. It is the great transformation—successful, all-embracing, irreversible." The essential unifying force was technology: "The same technology calls for the same occupational structure around the world. . . . Social arrangements will be most uniform from one society to another when they are most closely tied to technology." As in the case of development economics, any traditional cultural differences that might slow the process of industrialization were dismissed as mere "obstacles," destined for the dustbin of history.[8] Like other modernization theorists, Kerr expressed not a hint of romantic nostalgia about the loss of these counterworlds.

Kerr considered world history a story of the asymptotic approach of nations toward an ideal-typical baseline called modernity. In the beginning, there was "tradition." From time immemorial, traditional people had been mired in varied and discrete practices, the description and cataloging of which had been the primary responsibility of anthropologists and archaeologists. And yet, according to modernization theory, beneath that apparent diversity there existed a fundamental unity. All these times and places were inward-looking, passive toward nature, fearful of change, superstitious, unhealthy, and economically simple, to mention only a few commonalities. In this sense "tradition," for all the diversity encompassed by that term, was itself a unity. The first transition away from tradition had taken place in Europe and North America, and this process had then been exported to the rest of the world. Shils stated this point emphatically: "Historically, the modern type of society has originated only once, in the Western world, and hence its transformative effect on the rest of human society and culture must be understood from that base line, a fact which is at least implicit in the extremely wide contemporary concern with the problems of 'modernization.' "[9] Modernization theorists agreed that this "transformative effect" resulted in great turbulence for the countries concerned, making them particularly susceptible to "the Communist disease."[10] This turbulence also made it crucial for the postcolonial countries to think about the lessons that might be learned from the history of the "first movers."

A second crucial assumption of modernization theory was that the United States and Europe—including the Soviet Union—had already all but achieved modernity. As possessors of both unimpeachably modern elites and the highest technology available, "the West" was all but synonymous with modernity. In effect that meant that the present of the United States and Europe represented the future of poor and postcolonial lands. As CENIS stated in 1961, "Implicit . . . in the use of such words as 'transitional' and 'modernizing' are some basic assumptions which we have asserted rather than proved—that is, that these societies are indeed going through a process which will produce in them social and economic changes parallel to those which have occurred in modern Western states."[11] Even unpleasant aspects of modernization were merely way stations en route to the same beneficent modernity according to Kerr: "The urban slums are a symptom of a society in transition toward industrialism, as any tourist in Bombay, Osaka, Kirkuk, or Brazzaville can report."[12] Scholars studying postcolonial politics made the same assumption of convergence; as the political scientist Robert Ward put it, "The concept of 'political modernization' rests upon the hope that it validly and objectively defines the essential features of the political developments which have occurred in all so-called advanced societies and that it also represents the pattern toward which politically underdeveloped societies are now evolving."[13] Likewise, the historian Cyril Black observed that his fellow modernization theorists tended "to assume that the Western pattern will be reproduced all over the world in all its aspects. Indeed, modernization is frequently thought of as a process by which non-Western societies are transformed along Western lines."[14]

One debate that flourished among those studying modernization concerned the process by which convergence would take place. On one side of the debate, Rostow argued that convergence was inevitable because there existed a predetermined set of stages through which all countries would move during the process of economic development: as set out in *The Stages of Economic Growth,* "traditional society" begat the "preconditions for take-off" begat "take-off" begat "the drive for maturity" begat "the age of high mass consumption." In Rostow's schema, all societies in the world could be ranked along this single "developmental" axis. On the other hand, many modernization theorists believed that there were a variety of paths to modernity. Kerr, for example, argued that where "Marx had seen a unilinear course to history; we see a multilinear one. There are several roads, *each of which leads to industrialism.*"[15] Although Kerr suggested that the force of technology would lead to a globalization of "pluralist industrialism," some room did remain for human agency to advance or impede this outcome. Invoking Max Weber, Kerr claimed that any one of several groups of "industrializing elites"—including political leaders, industrial organization builders, top military officers, associated intellectuals, and sometimes leaders of labor organizations—could take charge of the development process, each with their own "style and emphasis." At the end of the day, however, a monolithic modernity would be the outcome.

In the present day, to be sure, there were two main variants of that singular modernity (the Soviet and the American), but even these were bound to converge, modernization theorists argued, since there was really only one form of modernity. Belying their historical image as strict anti-Communists, modernization theorists tended to see the Soviet Union as increasingly similar to the United States, in that both were manifestations of modernity.[16] As Parsons put it, "underneath the ideological conflicts [between capitalism and communism] that have been so prominent, there has been emerging an important element of wide consensus at the level of values, centering in the complex we often refer to as 'modernization.' "[17] This is not to say that the modernization theorists were political relativists; on the contrary, there existed good and evil paths to the inexorable convergence. Although the material transformation was everywhere quite similar, there were sharply divergent political paths to modernity. Even Rostow, who insisted on the unilinearity of the economic development process, was quick to point out that from a political perspective the transition was hardly unilinear. In his view, there were two political paths to modernity, the democratic-capitalist method of the free world and the "totalitarian" method employed by communism. Although communism represented a morbid path, both the Soviet Union and the United States were encompassed within history's highest stage, modernity. Regardless of the political-cultural trajectory employed, all countries were destined to wend their way toward a uniform industrial modernity.

## A SYNTHESIS OF POSTWAR AMERICAN SOCIAL THOUGHT

A third way this essay's title helps us to understand modernization theory is by suggesting that the theory embodied the highest flowering of American intellectual life. Although sardonic, this usage is illuminating in the following sense: the term "modernization" colligated many of the postwar period's dominant ideas about society, politics, and economics into an overarching whole that not only offered a supposedly scientific interpretation of what was happening in the postcolonial world, but also placed contemporaneous liberal ideas about American society within a wider metahistorical narrative.[18] As a grand unified theory of historical development with liberalism as its "primary ideology,"[19] modernization theory provided a vehicle for bringing together ideas otherwise aligned only by a general ideological eurhythmy. While the 1950s witnessed movements at odds with the postwar period's prevailing "conservative liberalism"[20]—such as the crypto-fascism of the John Birch Society, the realism of Hans Morgenthau's international relations theory, or the Marxism of the *Monthly Review*—for the most part, the first two postwar decades were strikingly ideologically monolithic. This section proposes that modernization theory's popularity can be fully understood only with reference to its central place in this profound if diffuse ideological moment.

If modernization theory suggested that the Soviet Union represented a pathological or diseased form of modernity, then the normal or healthy version represented an idealized portrait of the United States, as conceived in the liberal imagination. As the historian Georges Canguilhem observed in 1966, "Every conception of pathology must be based on prior knowledge of the corresponding normal state, [and] conversely, the scientific study of pathological cases becomes an indispensable phase in the overall search for the laws of the normal state."[21] For modernization theory there were two forms of developmental pathology: degenerative backwardness, on the one hand, and cancerous communism, on the other. In contrast to both these, modernization theory defined healthy modernity as a fully realized New Deal America: a god-fearing but secular society in which race and gender were of little import; a privately run, full-employment economy of well-paid workers, all of whom owned a house and a car; a formal democratic system in which widespread agreement existed about societal goals, the details of which would be worked out by technically trained public service elites. Modernization theory was thus the foreign policy analogue to "social modernism" at home, namely the idea that a meliorist, rationalizing, benevolent, technocratic state was capable of solving all social and especially economic ills.[22] Although the theorists knew that the United States had not reached ideal modernity (the segregated South was a particular problem), they believed that sooner or later their vision of modernity was bound to succeed in imposing itself. The template of modernity had been identified, and technocrats would soon realize it, both at home and abroad. The developmental state was thus the postcolonial analogue to the welfare state in the developed world.

As Fritz Fischer has suggested, the liberal intellectuals of the 1950s "intended to build other nations by letting the people of those nations follow the mythic American example." The modernization theorists sincerely believed that the United States represented the most enlightened form of civilization yet known, and felt as if they were doing the world a favor by aiding "them" to become more like "us."[23] Modernization theory positioned the 1950s United States as the endpoint of a progressive teleology for the world: the whole world was destined to converge with the model of modernity traced out by the contemporary United States. Modernization theory, in this sense, was a universalist faith. But its universalism did not mean the ecumenical reconciliation of all the various cultural, political, and economic traditions of the world in a higher order of circulation and exchange. Rather, it meant the imposition of "modern" (i.e., contemporary American) values on "backward societies," and the economic integration of all economies into the world capitalist system as junior members. Difference both at home and abroad would be annihilated through the delicious if lubricious salve of consumerism. Modernization theory was thus not just a discourse about what was *happening* in the third world, but was also a discourse about what the United States was *already* like.

Theorists of modernization drew their ideas about the contemporary United States (and hence modernity) from disparate elements of 1950s social science that otherwise rarely have been seen as forming a unity, including (1) the end of ideology debate, (2) the elite theory of democracy, and (3) consensus history. They unified these discourses by providing an overall cognitive framework for understanding the differences between the United States and the postcolonial world. (The theory in this sense offers a textbook example of Edward Said's proposition regarding how the West has constructed its identity in contrast to non-Western—or in this case "traditional"—others.) This synthesis was possible because all these discourses were themselves products of the reflection upon the difference between traditional and modern societies. By bringing these discourses together, modernization theory provided American intellectuals with an overarching, interlocking, global conception of historical change. What made modernization theory seem so compelling to scholars in a wide variety of disciplines was its ability to house so many of the live ideas of its era under one theoretical roof. The sociologists, political scientists, and historians all read one another and seemed to be agreeing on basic issues. Instead of causing suspicions, these tacit agreements made scholars believe that, by God, they were onto something. Because it synthesized all these critical discourses of the 1950s, moreover, modernization provides us with a key for unlocking the "mental climate" of American intellectuals during this period.

The phrase "the end of ideology" first appeared in the United States in a 1954 article by Edward Shils recounting what had happened at that year's meeting in Milan of the Congress for Cultural Freedom (CCF). The CCF was an anticommunist organization that had been formed in the early postwar period to rally intellectuals worldwide against the Soviet Union's postwar ideological offensive.[24] Borrowing the phrase "the end of ideology" from the French philosopher Raymond Aron, Shils remarked that this meeting of the CCF had witnessed a great deal *less* ideological disagreement than previous occasions. As far as Shils was concerned, this indicated that the ideological battle against the Soviet Union had effectively been won; a consensus had emerged that some version of social democracy represented the only decent way to organize a society. Shils speculated that perhaps this consensus had a wider import; perhaps it meant that we had reached a postideological era.[25]

Although Shils was the first to introduce the phrase to American audiences, it was his fellow sociologist Daniel Bell who made it famous. Bell asserted that since World War II the West had experienced an "exhaustion of political ideas." In contrast to the 1930s, American (and European) intellectuals in the 1950s arrayed themselves along a much narrower spectrum of ideological positions, defined by a basic political liberalism and social democratic ethos. Bell lamented that this ideological narrowing meant that intellectual life was a bit boring today, but overall it was good news, since it reflected the fact that the social problems of American life had essentially been solved. What social problems remained in the West had been clearly identified, and technocrats would soon find efficient solutions to them.[26] This narrowing of ideological dispute at home connected to claims of Clark Kerr and Talcott Parsons that the Soviet and American forms of modernity were converging. As Aron concluded, "by various paths, spontaneously or with the help of the police, the two great societies [the United States and the Soviet Union] have suppressed the conditions of ideological debate, integrated the workers, and imposed consensus."[27]

It is important to note the role of the postcolonial countries in the logical structure of the end of ideology argument. Shils and Bell were both at pains to make clear that their arguments did not apply to postcolonial intellectuals. Indeed, Shils punctuated the title of his essay

"The End of Ideology?" with a question mark precisely because of these intellectuals, who had continued to make noisy ideological protests at the Milan conference. Likewise, Bell noted that ideological fervor was still the norm rather than the exception among postcolonial intellectuals. Thus Bell did not title his essay "The End of Ideology" *tout court,* but rather "The End of Ideology *in the West.*" Bell's friend Seymour Martin Lipset would make sense of this ideological disjuncture between the West and the non-West by invoking the convergence hypothesis. In the long run, he asserted, industrial development would lead to a postideological democratization the world over. In the meanwhile, ideology remained appropriate for many postcolonial countries. "Ideology and passion may no longer be necessary . . . within stable and affluent democracies," Lipset argued, "but they are clearly needed in the international effort to develop free political and economic institutions in the rest of the world. It is only the ideological class struggle in the West which is ending."[28]

The second of the discourses to be synthesized by modernization theory was what has come to be known as "the elite theory of democracy," as proposed by political scientists including David Easton and Robert Dahl. This theory argued that democracies worked best if led by coherent, self-confident elites who agreed among themselves about basic societal goals. Effective pluralistic politics, as Shils put it, "requires a sense of affinity among the elites and a common attachment to the institutions and apparatus through which political life is carried on."[29] Ideally, these elites would present the masses with a limited range of options, which would then be parsed through formal democratic practices. Associated with "extremist" politics of both the Right and Left, populism was the great enemy. The elite theory of democracy also helped explain why convergence would take place: these scholars believed that elites everywhere had the same kinds of interests, namely, economic growth in the context of social stability and political order. Rational modern elites would focus their attention on solving the technical problems associated with creating sustainable economic growth. Applying technology would solve social problems; this meant promoting technological change if you were a first world elite, and importing appropriate technology if you were a third world elite. The elite theorists of democracy agreed with Bell that the masses were best off if they left social decision-making to trained experts who would solve the last few niggling details that stood in the way of the final completion of modernity.

These discourses from sociology and political science also resonated with the dominant historiographic trend of the era. The intellectual historian John Higham coined the term "consensus history" in 1959 to refer what he saw as a recent historiographical tendency to argue that American history was characterized by relative agreement on political matters, and that American society was relatively conflict-free.[30] The scholars Higham identified with consensus history were Louis Hartz, Clinton Rossiter, Daniel Boorstin, Edmund Morgan, and David Potter, among others. What the proponents of the end of ideology hypothesis claimed was true of the American present, the consensus historians claimed was true of all of American history. These historians claimed that Americans had always agreed about basic values and goals; the only disagreements were about the means of achieving those ends. As Hartz famously suggested in his classic work *The Liberal Tradition in America,* the United States had been "born free," albeit dominated by the liberal ideas of John Locke.[31] Boorstin likewise stated that American intellectual and political life had been characterized by consensus. Instead of its being dominated by one great idea, however, Boorstin suggested that the genius of American political life was that it was bereft of any political ideas whatsoever. Both these ideas were fundamentally related to the end of ideology hypothesis.[32] Boorstin suggested that America was a society with no ideology at all, while Hartz argued that America was characterized by ideological consensus about the virtues of Lockean liberalism. Although some of the consensus historians, like Hartz, were rather critical of the complacency that this historical consensus implied, other disciplines would echo the consensus hypothesis as a way of celebrating American economic achievement; to quote Kerr: "Consensus develops wherever industrialization is successful."[33] Thus we can see how the convergence hypothesis, the end of ideology, the elite theory of democracy, and consensus history locked together to form a logically tight picture of the contemporary world.

Modernization theory's brilliant synthesis of all these interrelated ideas and theories provided them with an additional measure of legitimacy; at the same time, they provided the theory with theoretical aid and comfort, lending it a patina of plausibility it might not have enjoyed in the absence of these surrounding discourses. From the end of ideology debate modernization theory adopted the notion that the ideological rumblings in traditional societies were but manifestations of their backward political cultures, and that development was therefore the policy solution to postcolonial political radicalism. Most notably in Walt Rostow's stages-of-growth model, but also in the psychosociological models of Alex Inkeles, David McClelland, and Everett Hagen, modernization theory drew on the convergence hypothesis to help buttress the claim that development meant acceding to a universal, uniform, technocratic industrial society. Finally, modernization theory used ideas about the United States from consensus history to construct the "modernity" half of the "modernity-tradition" couplet. Rostow would quote Hartz as saying that America was "born free," by which he meant that it was "a society that did not have to struggle against the weight of attitudes, values, and institutions that go with a traditional society."[34] The category of modernity was for modernization theory a kind of idealized portrait of the United States as painted by the consensus historians: a progressive, conflict-free society, run by benign technocratic elites, worthy of emulation by other countries.

Modernization theory, like these other discourses, suggested that other societies emulated us not only because we were rich, but also because we were a society characterized by political and social happiness. We find the single best unification of all these ideas in the words of Rostow, who in 1957 wrote:

> The United States is now within sight of solutions to the range of issues which have dominated its political life since 1865. Our central problem has been to reconcile the fact of industrialization with the abiding principles of democracy. The farm problem, the status of big business in a democratic society, the status and responsibilities of organized labor, the avoidance of extreme cyclical unemployment, social equity for the Negro, the provision of equal educational opportunity, the equitable distribution of income—none of all these great issues is fully resolved; but a national consensus on them exists within which we are clearly moving forward as a nation. If we continue to devote our attention in the same

> proportion to domestic issues as in the past, we run the risk of becoming a bore to ourselves and the world. We shall be quarrelling over increasingly smaller margins, increasingly narrow issues.[35]

Like Bell, Kerr, and Hartz, Rostow was principally worried about the insipid nature of contemporary America. For Rostow as for Lipset, the solution was to take the modernist mission of social reform out into the beleaguered postcolonial world. Modernization theory's errand into the world thus provided the solution to the last problem facing an almost perfected American society. As Robert Bellah would observe in 1970, the fundamental assumption of modernization theory was that "modern Western society, especially American society, in spite of all its problems, is *relatively* less problematic than the developing societies with their enormous difficulties in economic growth and political stability."[36] A year later, the political scientist Samuel Huntington would conclude that all these verdicts resulted from "an optimism of retroactive progress": satisfaction with the United States made social scientists optimistic about the American past and its relevance to other societies.[37]

## A CRISIS OF MODERNITY

To understand the third way in which the phrase "highest stage" helps illuminate modernization theory we should recall that Lenin's own use of this term was rather ironic. Imperialism was indeed the highest stage—but only of capitalism. In bringing capitalism to its apex, it also brought out all its contradictions, setting the stage for its collapse and supersession by communism. By applying the phrase "highest stage" to modernization theory, I therefore mean to suggest that by bringing together all the elements of American intellectual life in the early postwar years and crystallizing them into a totalizing configuration, the theory also engendered the forces under which it would disintegrate. Generally speaking, the critiques of modernization theory can be classified into three groups: conservative, left-wing, and what I will call postmodern. I will conclude that this multifold assault on the theory was in fact only a subplot in a much wider revolt against modernity itself.

Primary credit for the conservative critique of modernization theory no doubt belongs to Samuel Huntington.[38] In a seminal article of 1970, "The Change to Change: Modernization, Development, and Politics," Huntington provided a fundamental epistemological and ideological critique of modernization theory. He argued that the dichotomy of "traditional and modern" was fundamentally "asymmetrical," in that modernization theorists had defined "modernity" abstractly, and then created the category of "tradition" out of the historical leftovers. He wondered whether the historical phases described by modernization theory were actual stages in historical evolution or abstract Weberian ideal-types. This criticism mirrored the arguments of his fellow conservative Robert Nisbet, who a year earlier had published *Social Change and History,* a book which culminated in a polemic against the functionalism of Talcott Parsons, Marion J. Levy, Neil Smelser, and their followers. For Nisbet, the methodological weakness of functionalism was that it made all historical change a result of immanent social dynamics, thereby obscuring such "external" phenomena as imperialism and colonialism. Modernization theorists, Nisbet claimed, had attempted "to make concepts regarding change seem analytically useful within finite, concrete, and historical circumstances when these concepts are the products of developmental ways of thinking that were meticulously defined by their principal makers and users as non-finite, non-concrete, and above all, non-historical."[39] Likewise, Huntington claimed that modernization theory had never provided a rigorous account of the causes of political change, or proved the existence of supposed systemic connections between various aspects of modernization, or provided accurate or exclusive definitions of the putative stages of modernization. The principal function of modernization concepts, Huntington concluded, was "neither to aggregate nor to distinguish, but rather to legitimate."[40] Although he did not specify what he thought modernization theory was legitimating, the rest of his criticism made it clear.

Huntington proposed that the term "modernization" be replaced with the more neutral word "change." This terminological shift related to Huntington's rejection of two key tenets of the liberal view of modernization. First, he rejected liberalism's universalist belief that there existed a unique (liberal) cultural model toward which all societies were converging. Huntington radically separated the cultural characteristics of the West from the techno-scientifically driven process of human domination over nature. Late developers could adopt the technical advances first generated in the West without emulating the cultural particularities of the West. "Modernization and economic development," he concluded, "neither require nor produce cultural westernization."[41] In Huntington's opinion there was no reason to assume that material convergence would lead to or even encourage cultural convergence. Second, because economic convergence did not necessarily lead to cultural convergence, Huntington rejected the notion that modernization was either inevitable or a good thing. Whereas someone like Rostow or Kerr claimed that modernization, by providing "the right kind of revolution," was the solution to the threat of communism, Huntington argued that modernization to the contrary ought to be discouraged, since, as even Rostow admitted, it increased the risk of political disorder and hence the possibility of Communist takeover. Rejecting the notion that the United States had a moral obligation to help poor countries modernize, and instead proposing that "stability" was the main thing the United States ought to promote, Huntington argued that the United States ought to be trying to *prevent* development in the third world.

Huntington's critique of modernization theory stemmed from his conservative view of contemporary American institutions. Surveying the chaos of American political life in the late 1960s, Huntington did not conclude that the United States was an illiberal place (or that liberalism was itself a sham), but rather that it was an excessively liberal place, in which the government had lost the capacity to impose its will on the populace. Huntington believed that a (re)imposition of authority was needed both at home and abroad. (In the mid-1970s, he would coauthor an influential study whose major conclusion was that America's travails stemmed from its "excess" of democracy.)[42] Describing himself as a "Leninist Burkean,"[43] Huntington claimed that "the most important political distinction among countries concerns not their form of government but their degree of government."[44] He proposed that the higher the degree of government—the greater its ability to impose its will on the population—the more developed the government. The basic problem with most postcolonial countries was that they had a low degree of government. Even though he rejected the convergence hypothesis, Huntington agreed with the modernization theorists that the United States and the Soviet Union had more in common with each other than either did with developing countries. If anything, the Soviet Union was *more* developed than the United States, since it did a better job suppressing dissent and ensuring the obedience of its population.

The point of departure for the left-wing critique of modernization theory came from a group of Latin American neo-Marxists, including Rodolfo Stavenhagen of Chile and Fernando Henrique Cardoso (now the neoliberal president of Brazil), who emerged in the 1960s from the structuralist school of development economics started by Raúl Prebisch and the Economic Commission for Latin America (ECLA) in the 1950s. The fundamental premise of these scholars was that development could not be understood solely in the context of a uniform national experience of tradition or modernity, and instead had to be seen in an international context that involved a fundamental analysis of capitalism and exploitation, terms that had been systematically occluded in modernization theory. Known as dependency theorists, these critics charged modernization theory with having ignored the way in which structural factors could inhibit economic improvement for certain lands.[45] The sociologist Andre Gunder Frank would drive the reception and development of these ideas in the United States, but this reception cannot be fully understood without considering it within the wider context of the New Left, and specifically the protests against entrenched authority and the Vietnam War.

In his seminal essay "The Development of Underdevelopment," Frank argued that underdevelopment did not result from a lack of capitalism, as modernization theory claimed, but rather was the historical precipitate of capitalist development in the first world.[46] In other words, development in the first world was predicated on exploitation of the third world, the historical result of which was underdevelopment. Underdevelopment did not result from historical stagnation, but rather was the result of colonial policies such as the British deindustrialization of India, the destructive effects of the slave trade on Africa, and the razing of the Aztec and Inca civilizations. To Frank, the incursion of capitalism, far from improving the economic situation of indigenous peoples, had degraded their internal economic capacities. Frank also argued that other now-modern countries such as Switzerland and Japan had in no way replicated the protean English experience of development. This understanding of the economics of colonialism marked a return to Lenin's and Rosa Luxemburg's original conception of imperialism. Finally, citing a string of recent coups in Latin America, Frank not only denied Seymour Martin Lipset's claim that there existed a direct and positive relationship between economic development and democratization, but went one step further and argued that there was a negative relationship.

Having thus disposed of mainstream development economics and political modernization theory, Frank turned his attention to the sociological theory of modernization in "The Sociology of Underdevelopment and the Underdevelopment of Sociology."[47] In this article, he argued as Huntington and Nisbet had that Parsons's structural functionalism did nothing to distinguish rich countries from poor ones empirically. For example, cultural traits like particularism and ascribed status, which Parsons had indicated were signs of backwardness, clearly persisted in the United States. Frank wondered whether the fact that brothers Walt and Eugene Rostow both had important posts in the Johnson administration was the result of the "achievement orientation" of American society. By pointing out the status of the Rostows, exemplars of the technocracy and the first name in modernization theory, Frank connected his attack on modernization theory to a more general assault on the complacent American national identity grounding the modernization paradigm. He suggested that modernization theory, by ignoring the destructive effects of development on the former colonies, was little more than a self-serving mythology. As one observer commented, "Even before the naïve optimism of much early modernization theory had been exposed by the end of the post-war boom and the deepening U.S. involvement in Vietnam and other anticommunist ventures, Frank's polemical assaults, coinciding with the student revolt of the 1960s, had effectively demolished its pretensions to scientificity."[48] Modernization theory embodied in social scientific form everything that the New Left scorned about American society: its complacent and static view of itself, its combination of meritocratic ideology with old boy reality, and its combination of liberal self-congratulation with conservative practices.

The influence of the Vietnam War on the left-wing reaction against modernization theory must also be mentioned. To begin with, modernization theory's foremost public face, Walt Rostow, was widely seen as one of the architects of the war, in particular its strategy of terror-bombing the peasant populations in the North. In addition, as Michael Latham has pointed out, the "strategic hamlet" program in Vietnam was in various ways a direct outgrowth of modernization theory.[49] More subtle but perhaps most important of all, there was a general feeling on the part of the Left that a shared sense of cognitive arrogance—the sense that its proponents possessed the sole legitimate ("scientific") means for understanding the phenomena they sought to understand—explained both the apodictic enunciations of modernization theory and the way in which the Vietnam War was being prosecuted. Though he was never a modernization theorist per se, Defense Secretary Robert McNamara's faith in scientific knowledge as a solution to all political and military ills resonated all too readily with the theory of modernization.[50] Finally, the bitterness and outrage on the part of the Left about the Vietnam War help explain the polemical ire that Frank and others directed at the theory.

In the end, however, Frank's influence was more significant as an angry pamphleteer and passionate advocate of the poor than as a deep critic of modernization theory. His scheme of Western pauperization of the colonial world did nothing to explain the poverty of peoples like the Tibetans and the Yanamamo, who were virtually untouched by either colonialism or capitalism. It would be left to the sociologist Immanuel Wallerstein to develop a more sophisticated and theoretically sound version of dependency theory, which he would call world-systems theory. Like Frank's, Wallerstein's project was to extricate contemporary sociology from what he termed "the cul-de-sac known as modernization theory." Wallerstein scoffed that "We do not live in a modernizing world, but in a capitalist world." He continued: "What makes this world tick is not the need for achievement but the need for profit. The problem for oppressed strata is not how to communicate within this world but how to overthrow it. Neither Great Britain nor the United States nor the Soviet Union is a model for anyone's future. They are state-structures of the present, partial (not total) institutions operating within a singular world-system, which however is and always has been an evolving one."[51] For Wallerstein, the globe since the fifteenth century had been enmeshed in one single economic system that had to be analyzed as such. Under this "modern world-system," the world was divided into three essential geographic categories. First was the core, which consisted of the primary sites of capital accumulations, characterized by urbanization, rapid technological advance, skilled and relatively highly paid labor forces, and most important, political power. Second was the periphery, politically enfeebled places whose role in the world economy was to provide primary goods and foodstuffs at a cheap price to the core. On the periphery, technological growth tended to be slow, urbanization minimal, capital accumulation close to nil, and remuneration much lower than in the core. The linchpin of Wallerstein's analysis was the third category, the semiperiphery, defined as those liminal nations and regions on the rise (or sometimes fall) from the periphery to the core. Semiperipheries were crucial not only because their mobility deflected anger and revolutionary activity in the periphery by providing hope that peripheral areas could escape their position within the world economy, but also because they "served as good places for capitalist investment when well-organized labor forces in core economies cause wages to rise too fast."[52] This structural vision permitted Wallerstein to concoct a full-blown alternative metanarrative to counter modernization theory, which appeared in a multivolume work.[53]

In addition to these Right and Left critiques of modernization theory, there also emerged in the 1970s a number of others that are harder to classify on the traditional political spectrum. Many feminists and advocates of racial consciousness attacked the theory for color- and gender-blindness, which were features linked to its form of liberal universalism. These criticisms sometimes validated the local over the universal, seeing beauty in the differences of particular communities. Often this led to a revaluation of tradition, the category that had been the shorthand for everything that modernization theorists hoped to undo in bringing modernity to backward peoples. Yet another strand of the 1970s attack on the theory was an environmentalist critique. A belief in the possibilities of endless growth was being called into serious question in a variety of forums. The Club of Rome's manifesto *The Limits of Growth* (1972) claimed that the aim of societies should not be endless growth, which was unsustainable (which the Club attempted to "prove" using a then-sophisticated computer model), but rather a more symbiotic relationship between humankind and earth. In a similar vein, *Daedalus* dedicated its fall 1973 issue to the subject of the "No Growth Society."[54] As Mancur Olson noted in his introduction to the issue, the very traditional values that modernization theorists had decried as "obstacles to growth" might be appropriate and even necessary in a no-growth society. A rapid change in Americans' perception of reality and values, Olson intimated, had resulted in a profound change of consciousness and aesthetics. If TVA director and development enthusiast David Lilienthal spoke in the modernist voice of the 1950s and 1960s when he celebrated "the fruits of bigness,"[55] E. F. Schumacher captured the new spirit of the 1970s by arguing that "Small is Beautiful."[56]

While critics from these feminist, racialist, and environmentalist perspectives often allied themselves with leftist critics of modernization theory, their critiques were part of a wider attack on modernity that differed from leftist critiques. If we follow Jürgen Habermas in considering modernity the continuation of "the Enlightenment Project," then I would propose the most accurate expression under which to collect these various movements is *postmodernism*. This makes sense when we recall that modernization theory styled itself as the ultimate realization of the Enlightenment. Walt Rostow, for example, argued, "At home and abroad, the image of the United States as a national community dedicated to strive toward the values of the Enlightenment has not lost its relevance,"[57] in particular in "Asia [where] human beings seek the elevation of their human, social, political, and economic status, and they want this elevation to come about rapidly. They are moved by exactly the same set of ideas—the ideas of the Enlightenment—that yielded the American and French revolutions more than a century and a half ago."[58] Modernization theory shared with the Enlightenment a militant rationalism; a belief in the benign reconciliation of elitist direction with populist aspiration; a rational and scientific approach to religious, social, political, and economic issues; an essential secularism; a simultaneous sympathy for and fear of cultural nationalism; an abiding desire to construct an overriding metanarrative that would explain world history and guide secular action; and the belief that that conscious control of the historical process was possible. Considering these similarities, it becomes evident how the revolt against modernization theory had much in common with the anti-Enlightenment sensibilities of postmodernism.

The collapse of modernization theory under the force of these various critiques is emblematic of the "malaise" afflicting American society during the Nixon, Ford, and Carter administrations. The attacks on it were but an episode in a wider attack on conventional ways of doing things, hierarchical orderings of society, professorial privilege, wars in the postcolonial world, alienation in the workplace, sexual restraint, stable singular identities—in short, an attack on all of the hallmarks of the modernist ideal. Since modernization theorists' faith in the American social order underpinned their promotion of convergence on American-style modernity, the general social crisis of American social modernism in the 1960s and 1970s proved devastating to the theory. By 1981, David Riesman, a fellow traveler (albeit a skeptical one) of the modernization theorists in the 1950s, would be publicly "reconsidering" the American Dream, which he specifically stated was a dream of the possibility of "universal modernization."[59] By 1980, modernization theory, and the dream that underlay it, seemed dead.

## THE END OF A PARADIGM?

Nevertheless, modernization theory continued to live on in truncated form, and in recent years it even has experienced an explicit revival. Thus the final sense in which my title's Lenin reference suggests an important truth is that, in the case of both capitalism and modernization theory, the subject lives on despite the many fatal prognoses both have received over the years. Just as Lenin's predictions of capitalism's death turned out to be premature, so too have the predictions of modernization theory's demise turned out to have been rather hasty.

Many of the scholars associated with modernization theory were still in the prime of their careers when the compound crisis described in the last section erupted. What then succeeded modernization theory? Among economists, who had never been impressed with modernization theory anyway, monetarism began in the 1970s to replace the Keynesian focus on demand-drive GDP growth as the underlying engine of economic development. (The monetarist turn was part of a wider intellectual movement dissociated from the particular problems of poor nations.) For development practitioners like World Bank President Robert McNamara, a "Basic Needs" approach supplanted previous interests in large infrastructure projects. Though some modernization theorists continued to write about large patterns of political development, many others retreated into area studies programs, tacitly acknowledging the need to give greater attention to local particularisms. However, many of the modernization theorists who continued to have big theoretical ambitions moved into two other important intellectual movements, namely neoconservatism and communitarianism.

Neoconservatism would appeal to those who remained committed to the values of modernity as these were defined in the 1950s and early 1960s, but who were willing to pull back from the earlier temptation to impose these values on societies outside the United States. The neoconservatives registered their disappointment with the failure of the utopian promises of modernization, which had hoped for a "technologically based, prosperous future that would obviate ideological conflicts."[60] Despite their commitment to many of the values of modernity—such as rationality, linearity, scientific authority, and order—these intellectuals suspected that the *process* of modernization might be part of the problem, rather than the solution. As the belief in a postideological age crumbled, these intellectuals—including the likes of Seymour Martin Lipset, Lucian Pye, and Daniel Bell—revised their earlier optimistic views of the modernization process and instead hoped that, at a minimum, social and political order might be maintained. Instead of believing in a happy if boring modernity, these scholars now tended to agree with Bell in his 1975 assessment that capitalism contained certain fundamental "cultural contradictions"—in other words, that modernism's culture of rebellion undermined the work ethic and social stability necessary for society to run smoothly.[61] If these scholars were now being labeled conservatives rather than liberals, this had more to do with the shifting political sentiments of the country than with any ideological change of heart on their part. A similar interest in order would also animate the other major successor movement to modernization theory, communitarianism.

It is no coincidence that many of the most influential works of communitarianism, from Robert Bellah's *Habits of the Heart* (1984) to Robert Putnam's *Bowling Alone* (1999), were written by former modernization theorists.[62] While communitarianism asked the same questions as modernization theory about how to sustain social stability and increase welfare, it acknowledged that some of the certainties of modernization theory—notably the notion that "rationality" was the decisive cognitive element of modernity—had missed the mark. Communitarians still believed in modernity, but argued that a successful modernity had to be grounded in the right kinds of values—values that they agreed must have premodern roots. Modernity's "overemphasis on individual liberation" had led to a destruction of the common moral tenets and an "ethical vacuum." Exemplifying the transition from modernization theory to communitarianism was Amitai Etzioni, who wrote in *The New Golden Rule* (1996):

> On the highest level of generalization the issue with which this volume grapples is the synthesis of some elements of traditionalism with some elements of modernity, recasting both in the process. . . . Modern thinking . . . is best seen as a grand corrective to the social formations of the middle ages . . . and the paradigms that legitimated them. This volume argues that after the forces of modernity rolled back the forces of traditionalism, these forces did not come to a halt; instead in the last generation (roughly, from 1960 on), they pushed ahead relentlessly, eroding the much weakened foundations of social virtue and order while seeking to expand liberty ever more.[63]

Like other former modernization theorists, Etzioni believed that "order" ought to be given a new weight, reflecting his own changed views of American modernity, now characterized as licentious and disorderly instead of the acme of freedom. "Communal values" had to be reemphasized. The notion of a community grounded in essential value-consensus revealed Etzioni's continued reliance on a Parsonian framing of the "problem of modernity." Rather than advocate outright authoritarianism, like Samuel Huntington or Lucian Pye, Etzioni argued for a middle course between oppression and what he considered to be the virtual anarchy of modernity in full cry.

Except for Marxism, whose advocates had railed against modernization theory from the beginning, no master narrative emerged to replace modernization theory. During the 1980s, as postmodern sensibilities waxed, it became unfashionable even to attempt such narratives, with Marxians virtually the only ones even trying to tell big stories. However, since many scholars refused to accept the Marxian counternarrative, but remained uncomfortable living in a world without a big picture, modernization theory survived as the unstated, undefended, but nevertheless omnipresent liberal vision of historical change. Suited to triumphalist moments in American intellectual life, the theory was perhaps destined to experience a rehabilitation when American self-confidence returned after the hiatus of the 1970s. Just as it arose during America's period of greatest global hegemony, in the immediate wake of World War II, so it would be revived at the beginning of the post–Cold War period, when the apparent triumph of the Gulf War was still unquestioned and Asian economic implosion heralded the return of American hegemony. The Japanese-American Hegelian philosopher Francis Fukuyama spearheaded this rehabilitation.

In his celebrated essay "The End of History,"[64] Fukuyama claimed that, though unacknowledged, modernization theory continued to define the developmental horizon for most American social scientists. He began this essay with the extravagant claim that the United States was standing in 1989 at "the end of history," a fact which permitted American intellectuals (i.e., himself) to apprehend the meaning of the historical process, namely that liberalism in the classical sense was mankind's true calling. Grounding the convergence hypothesis in a Hegelian discourse about universal history, Fukuyama averred that technology "guarantees an increasing homogenization of all human societies," and asserted that "all countries undergoing economic modernization must increasingly resemble one another."[65] He claimed that the evidence supported Lipset's arguments about the correlation between democratic stability and rising per capita incomes, with the collapse of the Soviet Union providing the most dramatic vindication of this thesis.[66] Although Fukuyama admitted that there still existed ideological dissenters from neoliberalism, he dismissed these people as resentful losers who had to realize that the historical game was up and that the way of "the West" was the only way in the long run. Even if Fukuyama claimed that rehabilitating modernization theory would not mean a return to the "simple-minded and overly deterministic formulation . . . that posited that all societies would, in effect, end up like suburban America in the 1950s,"[67] he nevertheless judged everything from the position he believed History has itself identified as the endpoint of history, namely the United States in the 1990s. By providing modernization theory with a firm grounding in Hegelian philosophy, Fukuyama became, in effect, the Georg Lukács of modernization theory.

It is instructive to compare Fukuyama's rehabilitation of modernization theory with the recent work of Samuel Huntington, who as we saw was one of modernization theory's most forceful critics in the 1970s.[68] Though they never engaged each other directly, both made widely read big claims about the state of geopolitics in the 1990s, and the divisions between the two can be traced to their differing takes on modernization theory. Following modernization theory, Fukuyama argued that economic pressures tended to push societies, insofar as they want to be economically successful, toward a convergence on a high-trust model of modern social organization in which the state was best left out. By contrast, Huntington argued that contemporary history was leading toward a clash of incommensurable and irreconcilable "civilizations," the latter term being defined in a Toynbeean fashion.[69] There was no basis, Huntington claimed, for saying that any one of these civilizations was universal in the sense either of moral superiority or of having history on its side. Huntington instead seemed content to argue that simply because one of these civilizations was ours, we ought to fight like hell for it. Instead of assuming the cognitively arrogant position of Fukuyama, Huntington defended an amoral, self-interested, militarist Realpolitik. Whereas Fukuyama adopted the neoliberal orthodoxy about getting the state out of social and economic affairs, Huntington continued to defend the activist state as necessary in order to keep society in top fighting shape, as it were. Both Fukuyama and Huntington, it should be noted, rejected multiculturalism and postmodernism, Fukuyama from a cosmopolitan-universalist perspective, Huntington from an authoritarian-centralizing perspective.

In the 1990s modernization theory provided a vision of globalization as the realization of the economic, social, and political agenda of the Enlightenment. As Raymond Lee pointed out, the disintegration of communism had left "the First World as the only model of modernity to be emulated."[70] Modernization theory transformed itself in the 1990s from an anti-Communist creed to an argument for globalization. Even as postmodern skeptics decried development as a power-knowledge regime for extending the scope of capitalism, institutions like the World Bank and the United Nations continued to strive for the realization of the modernist dream of development. And with good reason, for the postcolonial regions themselves were still calling on rich nations to help them fulfill this dream. United Nations Secretary General Kofi Annan in a speech on 12 February 2000, called for a

"Global New Deal" to spread goods, jobs, and capital among all countries. Annan asked, "Can we not attempt on a global level what any successful industrialized country does to help its most disadvantaged or underdeveloped regions catch up?"[71] The promise of universal prosperity and modernity may have lost its charm for neoconservative or postmodern Americans (especially if it means giving up any of their own privileges), but it remains the fervent dream of the destitute everywhere. Perhaps some inkling of this fact helps explain the remarkable return of the discourse of modernity among the American foreign policy cognoscenti in the late fall of 2001.

## NOTES

1. Max Millikan, "Economic Policy as an Instrument of Political and Psychological Policy" [n.d.], 12, Millikan Papers, MIT Archives, box 10, folder 317.

2. Lucian W. Pye, "The Policy Implications of Social Change in Non-Western Societies," 1957, CENIS, working paper no. C/57–18, p. 73.

3. Alex Inkeles, "Making Men Modern: On the Causes and Consequences of Individual Change in Six Developing Countries," *American Journal of Sociology* 75, no. 2 (1969); Alex Inkeles and David Horton Smith, *Becoming Modern: Individual Change in Six Developing Countries* (Cambridge: Harvard University Press, 1974); Daniel, Lerner, *The Passing of Traditional Society: Modernizing the Middle East* (New York: Free Press, 1958); David McClelland, *The Achieving Society* (Princeton: D. Van Nostrand, 1961); Talcott Parsons and Edward A. Shils, eds., *Toward a General Theory of Action* (Cambridge: Harvard University Press, 1951).

4. W. W. Rostow, "The Making of Modern America, 1776–1940: An Essay on Three Themes," CENIS working paper no. C/60–6, pp. 3/4–3/5.

5. Marion J. Levy, Jr., *Modernization and the Structure of Society: A Setting for International Affairs* (Princeton: Princeton University Press, 1966), 9–15, 35–38.

6. McClelland, *The Achieving Society*, 403.

7. For an account which takes a long view of the Western obsession with technology as the defining feature of its alleged superiority over other lands, see Michael Adas, *Machines as the Measure of Men: Science, Technology, and Ideologies of Western Dominance* (Ithaca: Cornell University Press, 1989). Adas quotes Richard Wilson as saying that the "machine in all of its manifestations—as an object, a process, and ultimately a symbol—became the fundamental fact of modernism" (410).

8. Clark Kerr et al., *Industrialism and Industrial Man: The Problem of Labor and Management in Economic Growth* (Cambridge: Harvard University Press, 1960), 1n, 278–79, 296, 267, 284, 285.

9. Edward Shils, Manuscript to "Social Evolution and the Problem of Comparability," 1971, 1–2, Harvard University Archives, HUG (FP) 42.45.4.

10. W. W. Rostow, *The View from the Seventh Floor* (New York: Harper and Row, 1964). See also the essay that was probably Rostow's unacknowledged inspiration for this phrase, Robert Langbaum, "Totalitarianism: A Disease of Modernism?" *Commentary* 19, no. 5 (1955).

11. Max Millikan and Donald Blackmer, eds., *The Emerging Nations: Their Growth and United States Policy* (Boston: Little, Brown, 1961), 143.

12. Kerr et al., *Industrialism and Industrial Man,* 170.

13. Robert E. Ward, "Political Modernization and Political Culture in Japan," *World Politics* 15, no. 4 (1963): 571.

14. C. E. Black, ed., *The Transformation of Russian Society* (Cambridge: Harvard University Press, 1961), 8.

15. Kerr et al., *Industrialism and Industrial Man,* 12.

16. Arnold S. Feldman, "The Nature of Industrial Societies," *World Politics* 12, no. 4 (1960).

17. Quoted in Jeffery Alexander, *Fin de Siècle Social Theory* (New York: Verso, 1995), 8.

18. See ibid.

19. Robert Bellah, "Meaning and Modernization" (1965), in *Beyond Belief: Essays on Religion in a Post-Traditional World* (New York: Harper and Row, 1970), 69.

20. Richard Pells, *The Liberal Mind in a Conservative Age: American Intellectuals in the 1940s and 1950s* (New York: Harper and Row, 1985).

21. Georges Canguilhem, *The Normal and the Pathological* (New York: Zone Books, 1991), 51.

22. Anthony Woodiwiss, *Postmodernity USA: The Crisis of Social Modernism in the United States* (London: Sage, 1993).

23. Fritz Fischer, *Making Them Like Us: Peace Corps Volunteers in the 1960s* (Washington: Smithsonian Press, 1998), 195.

24. For the original muckraking polemic against the CCF, see Christopher Lasch, "The Cultural Cold War: A Short History of the Congress for Cultural Freedom," in B. J. Bernstein, ed., *Toward a New Past: Dissenting Essays in American History* (New York: Pantheon Books, 1968). For a more recent and dispassionate historical account of the CCF see Frances Stonor Saunders, *The Cultural Cold War: The CIA and the World of Arts and Letters* (New York: New Press, 2000).

25. Edward A. Shils, "The End of Ideology?" *Encounter* 5, no. 5 (1955): 52–58.

26. Daniel Bell, *The End of Ideology: On the Exhaustion of Political Ideas in the 1950s* (New York: Free Press, 1960).

27. Quoted in Pierre Birnbaum, *La Fin du Politique* (Paris: Seuil, 1975), 26.

28. Seymour Martin Lipset, *Political Man* (Garden City, N.Y.: Doubleday, 1960), 416–17.

29. Edward Shils, *The Torment of Secrecy: The Background and Consequences of American Security Policy* (Glencoe, Ill.: Free Press, 1956), 227.

30. John Higham, "The Cult of the 'American Consensus': Homogenizing Our History," *Commentary* 27, no. 2 (1959).

31. Louis Hartz, *The Liberal Tradition in America: An Interpretation of American Political Thought since the Revolution* (New York: Harcourt, Brace, 1955).

32. Daniel Boorstin, *The Genius of American Politics* (Chicago: University of Chicago Press, 1953).

33. Kerr et al., *Industrialism and Industrial Man,* 227.

34. W. W. Rostow, in Millikan and Blackmer, eds., *The Emerging Nations,* xi–xii.

35. Max F. Millikan, W. W. Rostow, and others, *A Proposal: Key to an Effective Foreign Policy* (New York: Harper and Brothers, 1957), 149–50.

36. Bellah, *Beyond Belief,* xvi–xvii.

37. Samuel P. Huntington, "The Change to Change: Modernization, Development, and Politics" (1970) in C. E. Black, ed., *Comparative Modernization: A Reader* (New York: Free Press, 1976), 34. Andrew Janos makes a similar observation by noting that "the Parsonian scheme is not just 'Western' in its orientation; it is peculiarly American in its boundless confidence in the qualities and consequences of modernity" (*Politics and Paradigms: Changing Theories of Change in Social Science* [Stanford: Stanford University Press, 1986], 42).

38. Huntington is sometimes mislabeled a modernization theorist. One reason is that he was a member of the central institutional purveyor of modernization theory in political science, the Social Science Research Council's Committee of Comparative Politics, then chaired by Lucian Pye of CENIS. In addition, Huntington took an exceedingly hawkish stance on the Vietnam War, which coincided tactically with the positions developed by Walt Rostow. Huntington never had any time, however, for the prophetic liberal utopianism of modernization theory.

39. Robert A. Nisbet, *Social Change and History: Aspects of the Western Theory of Development* (New York: Oxford University Press, 1969), 262.

40. Huntington, "The Change to Change," 44.

41. Samuel P. Huntington, "The West: Unique, not Universal," *Foreign Affairs* 75, no. 6 (1996): 37.

42. Michel S. Crozier, Samuel P. Huntington, and J. Watanuki, *The Crisis of Democracy: Report on the Governability of Democracies to the Trilateral Commission* (New York: New York University Press, 1975).

43. John Gretton, "The Double-Barreled Character of Professor Huntington," *Times Educational Supplement,* 29 June 1973: 10. In this article, Huntington is quoted as saying that he was actually a leftist. He claimed that his intellectual mentor was Reinhold Niebuhr, that he favored (the ruthless imposition of) integration, and that he voted for George McGovern in 1972.

44. Samuel Huntington, *Political Order in Changing Societies* (New Haven: Yale University Press, 1968), 1.

45. For a polemical attack on dependency theory and its pernicious effects on the academic politics of Latin American studies and political science, see Robert Packenham, *The Dependency Movement: Scholarship and Politics in Development Studies* (Stanford: Stanford University Press, 1992).

46. Andre Gunder Frank, "The Development of Underdevelopment," *Monthly Review* 18, no. 4 (1966): 17–31.

47. Andre Gunder Frank, "The Sociology of Development and the Underdevelopment of Sociology" (1967), in James Cockcroft et al., eds., *Dependence and Underdevelopment* (Garden City, N.Y.: Doubleday/Anchor, 1972).

48. Colin Leys, *The Rise and Fall of Development Theory* (Bloomington: Indiana University Press, 1996), 11.

49. Michael Latham, *Modernization as Ideology: American Social Science and "Nation Building" in the Kennedy Era* (Chapel Hill: University of North Carolina Press, 2000).

50. Jonathan Nashel, "The Road to Vietnam: Modernization Theory in Fact and Fiction," in Christian Appy, ed., *Cold War Constructions: The Political Culture of United States Imperialism, 1945–1966* (Amherst: University of Massachusetts Press, 2000).

51. Immanuel Wallerstein, "Modernization: Requiescat in Pace," in Lewis A. Coser and Otto N. Larsen, eds., *The Uses of Controversy in Sociology* (New York: Free Press, 1976), 131–32.

52. Daniel Chirot and Thomas D. Hall, "World-System Theory," *Annual Review of Sociology* 8 (1982): 85.

53. Immanuel Wallerstein, *The Modern World System,* 2 vols. (New York: Academic Press, 1974, 1980).

54. *Daedalus* 102, no. 4 (1973).

55. David Lilienthal, *Big Business: A New Era* (New York: Harper and Brothers, 1952).

56. E. F. Schumacher, *Small Is Beautiful* (New York: Harper and Row, 1973).

57. Walt Whitman Rostow, "The American National Style," *Daedalus* 87, no. 2 (1958): 135.

58. Walt Whitman Rostow, "An American Economic Policy in Asia" (1955–56), speech given at the University of Texas, Austin, 12 October 1955, p. 2, Millikan Papers, MIT Archives, box 10, folder 282.

59. David Riesman, "The Dream of American Abundance Reconsidered," *Public Opinion Quarterly* 45, no. 3 (1981): 285–302.

60. John Ehrman, *The Rise of Neoconservatism: Intellectuals and Foreign Affairs, 1945–1994* (New Haven: Yale University Press, 1995), 3.

61. Daniel Bell, *The Cultural Contradictions of Capitalism* (New York: Basic Books, 1975).

62. Robert Bellah went from *Tokugawa Religion: The Values of Pre-industrial Japan* (Glencoe, Ill.: Free Press, 1957) to *Habits of the Heart: Individualism and Commitment in American Life* (Berkeley: University of California Press, 1985); Robert Putnam went from *The Comparative Study of Political Elites* (Englewood Cliffs, N.J.: Prentice-Hall, 1976) to *Bowling Alone: The Collapse and Revival of American Community* (New York: Simon & Schuster, 2000).

63. Etzioni went from *Modern Organizations* (Englewood Cliffs, N.J.: Prentice-Hall, 1964) via *An Immodest Agenda: Rebuilding America before the 21st Century* (New York: New Press, 1983) to *The Spirit of Community: Rights, Responsibilities, and the Communitarian Agenda* (New York: Crown, 1993) and *The New Golden Rule: Community and Morality in a Democratic Society* (New York: Basic Books, 1996). Quote on p. xvii.

64. Expanded to Francis Fukuyama, *The End of History and the Last Man* (New York: Free Press, 1992).

65. Francis Fukuyama, "On the Possibility of Writing a Universal History," in Arthur M. Melzer, Jerry Weinberger, and M. Richard Zinman, eds., *History and the Idea of Progress* (Ithaca: Cornell University Press, 1995), 16.

66. In his presidential address to the American Political Science Association in 1989, Lucian Pye claimed that the collapse of communism proved that modernization theory had been right all along: "Political Science and the Crisis of Authoritarianism: The Vindication of Modernization Theory," *American Political Science Review* 84, no. 1 (1990).

67. Francis Fukuyama, "Illusions of Exceptionalism," *Journal of Democracy* 8, no. 3 (1997): 146.

68. For a comparison of Fukuyama's and Huntington's views of the contemporary global situation, see "The Road to 2050: A Survey of the New Geopolitics," *The Economist,* 31 July 1999.

69. Samuel Huntington, *The Clash of Civilizations and the Remaking of World Order* (New York: Simon & Schuster, 1996).

70. Raymond L. M. Lee, "Modernization, Postmodernism, and the Third World," *Current Sociology* 42, no. 2 (1994): 38.

71. *New York Times,* 13 February 2000: A12.

## FURTHER READING

Almond, Gabriel A., and James Coleman, eds. *The Politics of Developing Areas.* Princeton: Princeton University Press, 1960.

Bell, Daniel. *The Coming of Post-Industrial Society: A Venture in Social Forecasting.* New York: Basic Books, 1973.

Kerr, Clark, et al. *Industrialism and Industrial Man: The Problem of Labor and Management in Economic Growth.* Cambridge: Harvard University Press, 1960.

Lerner, Daniel. *The Passing of Traditional Society: Modernizing the Middle East.* New York: Free Press, 1958.

Lipset, Seymour Martin. *The First New Nation.* New York: Basic Books, 1963.

Pye, Lucian. *Politics, Personality, and Nation-building: Burma's Search for Identity.* New Haven: Yale University Press, 1962.

Rostow, Walt. "The National Style." In Elting E. Morison, ed., *The American Style: Essays in Value and Performance.* New York: Harper and Brothers, 1958.

Shils, Edward A. "Political Development of the New States," *Comparative Studies in Society and History* 2, nos. 3–4 (1960).

# WALT ROSTOW'S STAGES OF ECONOMIC GROWTH: IDEAS AND ACTION

MARK H. HAEFELE

In his first year as president, John F. Kennedy launched a host of new or revised organizations designed to put the people of underdeveloped nations on a trajectory toward U.S.-style modernization.[1] Kennedy's efforts to launch a "Decade of Development" significantly changed U.S. foreign policy and contributed to the globalization of the Cold War. In the early months of 1961, Kennedy created the Alliance for Progress, Food for Peace, and the Peace Corps. Presidential support helped Congress to pass an expanded Foreign Assistance Act by September. In November, Kennedy put U.S. aid programs under his new super-organization, the U.S. Agency for International Development. In its first year, the Kennedy administration increased economic aid to developing nations by at least 24 percent.[2] Between 1960 and 1963, U.S. economic aid to underdeveloped countries increased by one-third.[3] Not only did the administration spend more on development aid than its predecessors, it also provided developing nations with a higher ratio of economic aid to military assistance than any other previous administration.[4] Kennedy's emphasis on the modernization of poor nations also paved the way for America's peculiar strategy in Vietnam, which, according to official policy was "waged in differing ways: to save a country, to build a nation."[5]

To understand Kennedy's policies toward the postcolonial world, it is helpful to examine the impact Walt Whitman Rostow's modernization theories had on Kennedy and his administration. Rostow began to shape Kennedy's thinking on economic development in the late 1950s, before he joined JFK in Washington as deputy special assistant to the president for national security affairs. Although Rostow had spent much of the 1950s developing and promoting his economic theories from his post as an MIT professor, his move to the Kennedy White House was not his first foray into government service. Before moving to Cambridge, Rostow had served as an Army officer, State Department official, and assistant to the executive secretary of the United Nations Economic Commission for Europe. Furthermore, he consulted for the Eisenhower administration and various government agencies during his time at MIT. Rostow would later call his professional life "a counterpoint between the world of ideas and the world of public policy."[6] When he joined the Kennedy administration, he had the intent of converting his economic ideas into policy action.

Although scholars have linked the Kennedy administration's emphasis on global modernization to the production of social scientific theory in America's elite universities, few historians have studied the particular contributions Walt Whitman Rostow made to both social science and Kennedy's conception of economic diplomacy.[7] Rostow's economic theories began to gain influence in the mid-1950s, and by 1960 international conferences of the most prominent Western economists convened to discuss "Rostovian Theory."[8] Even those critical of Rostow's ideas came to acknowledge their gravity. At the height of Rostow's influence, the economic historian Henry Rosovsky claimed, "No other living economic historian occupies a similar position. Indeed, one would probably have to go back to Karl Marx—with whom Rostow likes to compare himself—to find an equally prominent member of our profession, and Marx achieved his greatest fame posthumously."[9] According to Kennedy aide Arthur M. Schlesinger, Jr., many economists from Harvard and MIT contributed to Kennedy's thinking about modernization and foreign aid. Rostow had not invented the idea that "the true role of foreign aid was neither military nor technical assistance but the organized promotion of national development." However, Schlesinger credited Rostow with articulating the definitive purpose of the Kennedy aid program: pushing postcolonial nations "to 'take-off' into self-sustaining growth."[10]

There are at least two reasons Rostow's modernization theories influenced U.S. economic diplomacy, particularly in the Kennedy administration. First, Rostow was able to express his ideas in a popularly accessible manner. Second, he was willing to organize his research around the perceived problems and goals of policymakers. Soon after joining the MIT faculty in 1950, Rostow helped to found the Center for International Studies (CENIS). The goal of Rostow's academic work, and that of CENIS as a whole, was to "undertake no research that does not . . . grow out of the necessity to know something in order to be able to do something."[11] Rostow's research model envisioned a deeply symbiotic relationship between academia and government. Although CENIS was ostensibly an independent academic center, it accepted projects and funding from the CIA.[12] Thus the professor's transition from Cambridge to Washington not only helps us to understand how academic theory influenced Cold War economic diplomacy; it also provides a window onto how the Cold War transformed university research.

## IDEAS

Rostow's most famous contribution to modernization theory was his concept of the "stages of economic growth." The term was first discussed in his 1952 book, *The Process of Economic Growth,* but it took nearly a decade of work and the 1960 publication of *The Stages of Economic Growth: A Non-Communist Manifesto* before his ideas fully matured.[13] Rostow would later claim that he first began to formulate an alternative to Marx's theory of development while a Yale undergraduate.[14] Yet World War II and economic reconstruction in Europe took him away from this task for much of the 1940s. It was during the early 1950s when Rostow perceived the need to return to his work on economic development theory. At that time, some members of America's foreign policy elite were becoming increasingly interested in what they saw as a major weakness in America's Cold War strategy: focusing on developing the ability to counter an overt invasion of Western Europe or Japan when the real threat was "a Communist-led internal revolution in the weaker states of Asia, Africa, and Latin America."[15] According to the economist and Kennedy aide John Kenneth Galbraith, "It was accepted in the 1950s that if the poor countries were not rescued from their poverty, the Communists would take over."[16] The perceived success of the Marshall Plan in Western Europe convinced many policymakers and would-be policymakers that a similar economic aid program could work in the postcolonial world.[17] Support for increasing economic aid to developing nations did not just come from anti-Communists. Others argued that foreign aid could help create markets for American goods, or provide humanitarian relief to lift up the poor and the sick.[18]

In developing his stages of economic growth theory, Rostow paid close attention to policy discussions in Washington. For example, the need to create an alternative to Marx's view that all nations would eventually become Communist was driven home to Rostow at the Princeton Economic Conference of 1954.[19] Here, in a private meeting of the foreign policy elite, he heard their worries about the future of postcolonial nations. CIA chief Allen Dulles, asked, "Do you think we have firmly persuaded the people of that area that it is better to be in our economic orbit than in the Soviet orbit—to put it brutally?"[20] As the conference wore on, the group began to share their deep fears that communism seemed to offer a fast route to material well-being for those frustrated with poverty. It bothered conference participants that the Communists, with their manifestos and Marxian dialectics, had a better theory, or story, about the future. David J. McDonald, president of the United Steel Workers, noted that the United States was fighting an "ideological war" and that the Communist's most powerful weapon was "his idea" that history inevitably led to communism. McDonald declared that the United States needed its own idea to counteract this: "No matter what the basis is, we cannot win unless we have a Manifesto (if that is what you want to call it) or a statement of principles that the people of the world can understand, a Manifesto that we can use to train people to go out and preach, and train them in foreign lands along our way of thinking, so as to put over our ideas in the minds of the people. We must let them know, at least, what our ideas are."[21] Foreshadowing the Peace Corps, McDonald spoke of sending

Americans abroad as a foil to "guys who have been trained to propagandize the communist Manifesto."[22]

Professor Jerome Wiesner of MIT lamented that the United States had not yet developed a modernization ideology to rival that of the Soviet Union: "Unfortunately, we have not found the flame for the torch. That is, we don't have the overt ideological philosophy that we can tell to the natives. . . . We can say such things as 'freedom' and 'economic development,' but we do not have a positive goal which you can talk about, which you can describe how to achieve, etc., in the same sense that the Russians do."[23] For the international banker Robert Garner, the Manifesto had to be "a very good story. . . . We have lost the skill of telling our story."[24]

Rostow was excited by the concept of putting a good story at the core of any modernization ideology the United States hoped to create. He exclaimed, "I am all for it." He saw a Manifesto as "a vivid and meaningful set of ideas that would bite and resist Communist alternatives, it has got to be something which meets their prime problem as they see it. Their prime problem as they see it is the problem of economic growth."[25]

After the Princeton Conference, Rostow sought to simultaneously advance the field of economic development studies and create a non-Communist manifesto. In 1956 he published an academic article, "The Take-Off into Self-Sustained Growth."[26] Here Rostow described the historical evolution of national economies as a three-stage process. The preconditions stage could last a century or more as a nation developed the institutions and culture that formed the basis for the take-off. Take-off was a twenty- to thirty-year process of industrial revolution that led to the final stage, self-sustaining growth.[27] While publishing academic works on the take-off process, Rostow simultaneously coauthored (with Max F. Millikan, CENIS's director) the book *A Proposal: Key to an Effective Foreign Policy,* which used his stage theory as a basis for CENIS's foreign policy recommendations.[28]

During the mid-1950s Rostow and CENIS provided only a few of the voices clamoring for policy initiatives that would increase economic aid for postcolonial nations. However, CENIS's policy recommendations were almost uniquely persuasive because they appeared to flow dispassionately and scientifically from Rostow's stage theory. *A*

*Proposal* garnered contemporary praise and was later called "the most influential contribution by economists" to American foreign policy.[29] The book argued that communism was an aberration in the development process. The Soviet Union and its agents injected this "opportunistic" and "disruptive" disease into societies during the turbulent take-off period.[30] Communists had gained ground by exploiting "the revolution of rising expectations" and convincing people that communism was "the road to social opportunity or economic improvement or individual dignity and achievement."[31] Therefore, the authors argued, the goal of U.S. economic diplomacy should be to hurry nations through the take-off phase, so they would be "inoculated" against communism.

Based on limited macroeconomic data, Rostow argued that he had located economic indicators that defined the transition between the preconditions stage and take-off.[32] He determined that during take-off a country's national investment rate—the proportion of its annual product set aside for investment purposes—went from a preconditional 5 or 6 percent to 15 percent or better.[33] A 1 or 2 percent per capita growth rate maintained for five or more years was another indication that take-off was beginning—if that increase could not be explained by a series of exceptional crops or particularly high export prices.[34] Millikan and Rostow called these quantitative measures "useful rules of thumb" for determining when take-off began.[35] Rostow argued that the quantitative measures he had developed through an examination of past take-offs could be used to predict, and perhaps influence, future take-offs.[36] Applying his quantitative tests to the information available about the Indian economy, he asserted that its take-off was under way, and speculated that it would be "remembered in economic history as the first take-off defined *ex ante* in national product terms."[37]

Rostow's stage theory offered an appealing analytic tool for American policymakers. The increasing number of postcolonial nations entering the global arena threatened to add bewildering complexity to U.S. foreign relations. Rostow provided a system that imposed order on this chaos because, in his model, all nations were merely at different points on the same development path.[38] According to Rostow, "there is emerging from the intensive work of social scientists on the development problem a recognition that there are common elements in the patterns of development of different countries which have implications for development policy everywhere."[39]

Through his use of the stage theory, Rostow claimed to provide an apolitical method of distributing aid where it could be most effectively utilized.[40] By examining a nation's growth rate and national investment rate, economists could determine a country's stage of development.[41] Existing national savings rates could be compared with statistically determined "proper" levels to define a country's development aid requirements.[42] Based on the stage theory, the professors predicted their foreign aid plan would require a maximum U.S. commitment of "about two billion dollars per year, of which over 80 per cent would be loans."[43] This sum, they argued, would be enough to bring postcolonial investment rates into the target range. Assuming other developed nations and private sources could supply an additional $1.5 billion per year, they said, the flow of aid would be sufficient to remove capital requirements as the bottleneck preventing growth in poor nations.[44] While careful to mention that U.S. economic aid would be no guarantee that economic development and the evolution of democratic societies would follow, Rostow also had research which showed that, historically, foreign capital had been a significant take-off stimulator.[45] He made it clear that he expected it could once again promote development in postcolonial nations.[46]

The stage theory also promised Congress and the American public that an upper limit of development-aid funding could be established.[47] Surveying the current progress free world countries had made along the path to self-sustaining growth, the professors projected how much foreign aid these nations could productively absorb. By definition, developing nations would no longer need economic aid once they had achieved the self-sustaining growth stage. Although Rostow had written about the take-off as a twenty- to thirty-year period in his scholarly work, in *A Proposal* he stressed the "decade or two" when the bulk of the take-off was accomplished. This gave a relatively short period of time after which the United States and developing nations could expect aid programs to become unnecessary. The concept of providing aid until nations were "over the hump" in the development process now had more theoretical support.[48] If the professors were correct, the United States could spend a relatively modest amount to make the world safe for democracy.

According to the historian Burton Kaufman, Millikan and Rostow's ideas were based on the unfounded assumption that there was a "causal relationship between development aid and economic development, on the one hand, and between economic development and its political consequences, on the other."[49] They did not consider that "anticommunism, stability, and democracy were not necessarily compatible," and assumed "that the Western experience of economic and political development could easily be transplanted abroad."[50] While these criticisms point to flaws in the arguments behind the stages of economic growth theory, they fail to fully consider that Rostow believed he was fighting an ideological war in which academic research was an important tool. For Rostow, the logical coherence of his arguments was less important than using his theories to fight communism.

## ACTIONS

The Eisenhower administration proved only marginally interested in Rostow's policy proposals.[51] However, in the late 1950s, a young senator from Massachusetts began to take an interest in the professor's work. By 1957, John F. Kennedy was attempting to exploit the subject of economic development as an issue with which he could distinguish his future campaign platform from the policies of the Republican administration. He wanted to position himself as the congressional spokesman for a new internationalism that promoted economic development.[52]

A range of factors motivated Kennedy's interest in foreign aid.[53] However, his main concern in the late 1950s was winning the presidency. Kennedy had to win the election before he could use economic development to reinvigorate America's moral commitment to the Cold War, defeat the Communists, help the poor, or expand American markets. Rostow claimed that Kennedy began to support economic development issues "because he believed they were significant and correct moves in foreign policy and because they were 'liberal' in terms of the political spectrum." Kennedy collaborated with Senator John Sherman Cooper, a Republican from Kentucky, on a resolution to fund Indian economic modernization because it was a "cause with which 'liberals' identified and that was an uncertain and inconstant constituency for him at that time. Conversely those who were opposed would have been opposed to him in any event for a host of reasons."[54] Beyond the strategic and moral importance he placed on Indian development, it was an issue that "marginally might help Kennedy alter his image favorably among the Democratic liberals who were giving him considerable trouble."[55]

Rostow gleaned his observations about Kennedy's foreign aid calculations while serving as one of the senator's "free-lance eggheads." Looking for technical help on economic aid issues, JFK turned to the social scientists clustered along the banks of the Charles River. By his own account, Rostow first met with Kennedy on 26 February 1958 to discuss the testimony the professor would give before the Senate Foreign Relations Committee the next day. As Rostow related it, "From that time, my tie to Kennedy gradually expanded."[56] Among the academics at Harvard and MIT, Kennedy was drawn particularly to Rostow because of the professor's energy and enthusiasm. Rostow gave "quick, tart, specific responses" to all of JFK's inquiries.[57]

A month after Rostow first met the senator in person, he became the primary author of the JFK speech that introduced the Kennedy-Cooper resolution.[58] In "The Choice in Asia—Democratic Development in India," Rostow sounded his refrain that "the two cardinal events in postwar Asia" were the granting of independence in India and the Communist takeover in China.[59] These episodes, occurring within a few years of each other, set the stage for a great proxy battle between the United States and the Soviet Union. The entire postcolonial world was watching to see if the Communists could develop China faster than the capitalists could develop India. Kennedy told the Senate, "India stands as the only effective competitor to China for the faith and following of the millions of uncommitted and restless peoples." If India went Red, "the free world would suffer an incalculable blow."[60] Furthermore, beyond the problems in India, other postcolonial nations were entering the take-off phase. Thus, they too would be ripe for Communist subversion. Signaling his commitment to the domino theory, Kennedy declared, "We dare not give any up as lost."[61]

In the race to win the hearts and minds of the postcolonial regions, Kennedy warned that the Communists had some major advantages. For example, they provided an alternative to colonialism "with the glamour of novelty." Communism seemed "to offer a disciplined, coherent and irresistible answer to the overwhelming problems of economic mobilization and takeoff."[62] On the other hand, the United States had its tremendous economic power, which might be harnessed to meet the Soviet challenge. Kennedy's speech went on to suggest that the United States could be more efficient in distributing aid to India than it had been during the Marshall Plan. Advancements in economic theory, like the CENIS measure of "absorptive capacity," could better gauge how much economic aid would be required by the developing nations.[63]

By writing speeches for Kennedy, Rostow inserted his terminology and concepts into the candidate's foreign policy strategy. Kennedy now spoke of India as having "passed the point of economic take-off," and "launched upon an effort which will by the end of the century make her one of the big powers of the world, with a population just under one billion and capable of harnessing all the resources of modern science, technology and destruction."[64] Rostow's writings for Kennedy demonstrated the professor's skill at crafting modern jeremiads. According to Rostow, the United States—which had once so successfully fought the evils of communism with economic aid—had lost its way. As the judgment day in the developing world was drawing near, America had to return to the path of righteousness. Rostow suggested in no uncertain terms that the future of the free world hinged on passing the Kennedy-Cooper aid to India. In doing so, Rostow had engineered for JFK a vital anti-Communist issue to stump. Now the Democrat could charge that the Republicans were soft on communism.

In terms of Kennedy's political career, Rostow had crafted a speech that tied support for economic development programs into the larger theme of the Kennedy campaign. The unsolved problems in the developing world became symbolic of a Republican administration that was on automatic pilot. According to Kennedy, "Our sense of drift, our gnawing dissatisfaction, our seemingly hopeless predicament in reaching but the fringes of a great crisis is nowhere more evident than in our search for policies adapted effectively and concretely to the new and generally uncommitted nations which run from Casablanca to the Celebes."[65] Just as Rostow had himself suggested, Kennedy was arguing that the solution to the sense of domestic drift lay in promoting a liberal agenda abroad. This indeed, was why Kennedy would also adopt as his campaign slogan another Rostowism, "The New Frontier."

In using this phrase, Kennedy was invoking the frontier as an epochal, character-forming event and place for the American nation.

Despite Rostow's "Choice in Asia" speech, the Kennedy-Cooper resolution stalled in 1958. Yet Congress would become more interested in development aid programs as a series of crises drew international attention to postcolonial regions. The following year the resolution passed, after another Rostow-written Kennedy-delivered speech in the Senate. When Kennedy read his speech on the "economic gap," in February 1959, he reaffirmed his commitment to an economic aid program based on Rostow's unproven stage theory.[66] The economic gap that Kennedy announced to the nation was the "gap in living standards and income and hope for the future" between "roughly speaking, the top half of our globe and the bottom half." Here, Kennedy declared, was the "most critical challenge" facing the United States. The desire of poor nations to develop was "altering the face of the globe, our strategy, or security and our alliances, more than any current military challenge."[67]

The economic gap speech played on Kennedy's direct hit with the "missile gap." During that sensational 14 August 1958 speech in the Senate, Senator Homer Capehart threatened to have the galleries cleared when Kennedy questioned the validity of the assumption that nuclear weapons were the "ultimate deterrent" against Soviet aggression. Kennedy claimed that Soviet advances in nuclear capabilities made brinkmanship an inadequate means of protecting national security. He argued that America had to increase its nuclear arsenal and move to a more flexible way of responding to the Soviet threat.[68] Historians have recognized Kennedy's erroneous implication that the United States was falling behind the Russians in missile development as a calculated political move.[69] However, Kennedy's follow-up "economic gap" speech, which spuriously implied that America was falling behind the Russians in providing development aid, has been largely overlooked.[70] Kennedy portrayed the economic gap as an equally serious and more immediate danger to national security than the missile gap. For, if postcolonial regions turned to communism, JFK feared, "no amount of space satellites or nuclear-powered planes or atomic submarines could ever save us."[71] He warned that the crisis in postcolonial nations had only gotten worse since he delivered "The Choice in Asia" speech. China's economic growth in 1958 was reportedly three times that of India's, giving communism great prestige in developing areas.[72] Now India faced the turning point—1959 "could be the year of their economic downfall—or the year of their economic 'takeoff,' enabling them to get ahead of their exploding population, to stabilize their economies, and to build a base for continuing development and growth."[73] Quoting Rostow's theories about necessary investment rates as if they were scientific fact, Kennedy laid out a proactive plan for long-term aid.[74]

According to David Halberstam, while the early relationship between Rostow and Kennedy was good, it grew more distant after Rostow returned from his 1958–59 academic year in England.[75] By late 1959 the relationship had changed as full-time campaign organizers and strategists moved into JFK's inner circle. However, despite the new layer between Kennedy and the freelance academics, Rostow remained important to the team as a talented writer and increasingly famous scholar. Upon returning from England, he once again proved his usefulness by giving the Kennedy the slogan "Let's get this country moving again," which JFK first used in the Oregon primaries.[76] After the 1960 Democratic convention, Rostow topped the list of scholars that the Kennedy team wanted to tap for speech writing.[77] As Kennedy refined his policy initiatives before the election, Rostow had a hand in the evolution of the Alliance for Progress and the Peace Corps.[78]

During the campaign Kennedy talked about the "danger that history will make a judgment that these were the days when the tide began to run out for the United States. These were the times when the Communist tide began to pour in."[79] As his administration unfolded, such statements proved to be more than high-octane campaign rhetoric. By early 1961 the speeches that Rostow had drafted for Kennedy, which foretold of the postcolonial regions becoming the next major Cold War battleground, seemed remarkably prescient. In the first week of January, Khrushchev threatened Soviet support for "wars of national liberation" in developing countries. Kennedy would later call this speech "possibly one of the most important speeches of the decade," and a clear sign of Soviet intentions.[80] Kennedy began his administration with serious concerns about the nation's security. In his 29 January 1961 State of the Union, he used language similar to the wartime language of Abraham Lincoln in the Gettysburg Address: "Before my term has ended, we shall have to test anew whether a nation organized and governed such as ours can endure. The outcome is by no means certain. The answers are by no means clear."[81]

In the oft-quoted story, it was six days after the inauguration when Rostow had the dubious honor of introducing Kennedy to the problem of Vietnam.[82] After Rostow had the president read a report written by the counterinsurgency specialist Edward Lansdale, "Kennedy looked up and said: 'This is the worst one we've got, isn't it?' He had been briefed by Eisenhower on Laos, Congo, and Cuba; on the missile business—on all of these things—but not on Vietnam."[83] Magnifying concerns about Vietnam, by February 1961 Laos was on the brink of falling to communism.[84] By April the Bay of Pigs fiasco seemed to damage American credibility worldwide.

Administration concerns about a growing Communist threat in postcolonial regions had some basis in fact. According to Vladislav Zubok and Constantine Pleshakov, "On July 29, KGB chief Shelepin sent a memorandum to the Chairman [Khrushchev] containing a vast array of proposals to create 'a situation in various areas of the world that would favor dispersion of attention and forces by the United States and their satellites, and would tie them down during the settlement of the question of the German peace treaty and West Berlin.' "[85] Khruschev was attempting to use a "blend of disinformation, nuclear bluffing, and the utilization of the 'movements of national liberation' around the globe, including in the United States' back yard, Latin America" to "create a preponderance of power for the U.S.S.R."[86]

Kennedy's personality and his assessment of the geopolitical situation meant that he would try to create bold new initiatives to deal with America's strategic problems. JFK would rather try something new and fail than wonder what might have been. While campaigning, he said, "Governments can err, Presidents do make mistakes, but the immortal Dante tells us that Divine Justice weighs the sins of the cold-blooded and the sins of the warmhearted in a different scale. Better the occasional faults of a government living in the spirit of charity than the consistent omissions of a government frozen in the ice of its own indifference."[87] To help boost American prestige and focus the world on positive tasks, Kennedy's first grand initiative for the decade—announced before the Apollo space program—was sponsoring economic development in postcolonial regions.

After Kennedy entered the White House, economic aid programs could have ended up on the list of campaign promises that later proved too impractical to execute. He could have listened to the mounting chorus of academics finding fault with Rostow's stage theory. From within the administration Galbraith was soon voicing his opinions about the limits of development aid. In a 1961 *Foreign Affairs* article Galbraith used Rostow's terminology—writing about nations and their "stage of development."[88] However, he seriously questioned America's ability to modernize other nations by providing economic capital. He admitted that it was "doubtful that many of us, if pressed, would insist that economic development was simply a matter of the external aid." Galbraith believed that economic aid had been touted as a panacea because "nothing could be more convenient than to believe this, for once we admit that it is not the case, we become trapped in a succession of previously complex problems."[89] Given the crisis mentality in the administration, Galbraith's comment that it would be "convenient" to believe in the redemptive power of U.S. aid was an understatement. It seemed to be a national security imperative to make underdeveloped nations buy into something like the stages of growth theory—even if economists within the administration did not believe in it. When Rostow sold his plan for a "Decade of Development" to Kennedy, he reminded the president of the crises in "the Congo, Cuba, Laos, Viet-Nam, Indonesia, Iran, etc." and advised, "we shall need some such big new objective in the underdeveloped areas to keep them [the Communists] off our necks as we try to clean up the spots of bad trouble."[90]

Rostow's 2 March 1961 memo on the Decade of Development effectively restated his case for using the stages of economic growth as a launch point for Kennedy's economic development policy.[91] He calculated that "a good many countries in the underdeveloped world will, during the 1960's, either complete the take-off process or be very far advanced in it." Rostow wrote, "It should be possible, if we all work hard, for Argentina, Brazil, Colombia, Venezuela, India, the Philippines, Taiwan, Turkey, Greece—and possibly Egypt, Pakistan, Iran and Iraq—to have attained self-sustaining growth by 1970."[92] He hoped that a presidential speech and congressional funding for economic aid might have a beneficial worldwide propaganda effect. If the United States made a substantial commitment to change in the developing world, it might help win hearts and minds for the West. By giving "such a concrete goal for the 1960's," Rostow claimed the plan "could have enormous power in catching the public imagination in all countries."[93]

Rostow also stressed the use of his "take-off" into "self-sustaining growth" terminology as a crucial element of the administration's sales pitch. He continued to provide advice on why his ideas made good politics. In this case he reminded the president that his theory allowed the recipient nations and the Congress to believe that U.S. intervention was only temporary. According to Rostow, talking in terms of reaching self-sustaining growth "should also reassure the Congress that we are not getting onto an endlessly expanding demand for American resources for development purposes."[94] Again, Kennedy took up Rostow's recommendations.

On 22 March 1961, Kennedy asked members of Congress for economic development funding. Rostow had drafted the crucial parts of the speech.[95] Kennedy told his former colleagues on Capitol Hill, "Many of these less-developed nations are on the threshold of achieving sufficient economic, social and political strength and self-sustained growth to stand permanently on their own feet. The 1960's can be, and must be, the crucial 'Decade of Development'; the period when many less-developed nations make the transition to self-sustained growth."[96] Rostow's words helped move the Congress. By the fall Kennedy had the funds to expand development aid and had created most of the new agencies that he tasked with bringing about a Rostovian transformation of postcolonial regions.

By working with Kennedy as an adviser during the campaign and as deputy special assistant in 1961, Rostow was able to have an impact on Kennedy's economic diplomacy. However, it was a great irony of Rostow's career that, as the power of the stages of economic growth idea grew within the Kennedy administration, the personal power of its author began to diminish. Kennedy soon began to differ with Rostow about how his ideas should be translated into action. For example, Rostow grew increasingly sure of the need for military efforts to combat the Communist insurgency in Vietnam. Kennedy, on the other hand, was anxious to rely more heavily on modernization to turn the tide. In August 1961, JFK sent a secret telegram to South Vietnamese President Ngo Dinh Diem emphasizing that "Military operations will not achieve lasting results unless economic and social programs are accelerated." Therefore, Kennedy wanted to "accelerate measures to achieve a self-sustaining economy and a free and peaceful society in Viet-Nam."[97] Kennedy supported Ambassador Frederick Nolting's plan to develop rural health plans, education programs, agricultural credits, new roads, and communication networks to tie villages into "the life of the nations" and improve "living conditions in the countryside."[98] Rather than trying to defeat Communist insurgencies with the level of military force recommended by his generals, Kennedy chose a two-pronged approach to Vietnam, mixing military efforts with modernization aid. In what became known as the 1961 "Thanksgiving Day Massacre," JFK helped solidify his Vietnam strategy by moving the increasingly hawkish Rostow out of the White House and into the State Department.

As Kennedy and his successor, Lyndon Johnson, agonized over increasing military commitments in Vietnam, their administrations continued to hope that economic modernization could serve as a moral equivalent to war.[99] This was wishful thinking, but it so permeated America's views that some have claimed modernization became a defining American ideology during the 1960s.[100] By 1966 an internal study by U.S. AID reported that, somehow, the United States had "moved to the thesis that grass roots economic and social improvements are decisive ingredients in blunting the force of and defeating insurgencies." Yet, the study pointed out, after five years of heightened U.S. attempts to launch Vietnam into the take-off phase "there is no empirical evidence that grass roots economic programs or any other design of economic development programs can be decisive in wars of insurgency of the type we face in Asia."[101]

Although modernizing Vietnam remained a priority for the Johnson administration, LBJ also found himself increasing America's military commitments to Southeast Asia.[102] In a second irony of Rostow's career, the hawkish views that had cost him his White House job in 1961 brought him back to Pennsylvania Avenue in 1966. That year Johnson named Rostow his top foreign policy adviser and chief spokesman for the war effort.

Walt Rostow's stages of economic growth theory grew, in part, out of a conscious attempt to create a modernization ideology—although it was intended to be more influential among the "natives" than inside the U.S. government.[103] Despite academic criticism of Rostow's theory, its perceived efficacy as a psychological and political Cold War weapon ensured its dissemination beyond the ivory tower. Following the development of the stages theory illuminates how the study of modernization in American social science departments shaped U.S. foreign policy. However, Rostow and his ideas also illustrate how the production of knowledge at America's elite universities was itself deeply influenced by the government's Cold War agenda.

## NOTES

1. In this essay I use the terms "economic development" and "modernization" interchangeably. "Modernization" is primarily an American term, developed by American social scientists in the period after World War II and reaching the height of its popularity in the 1960s. Dean C. Tipps, "Modernization Theory and the Comparative Study of Societies: A Critical Prospective," *Comparative Studies In Society and History* 15, no. 2 (March 1973): 208. As defined by the *International Encyclopedia of the Social Sciences* (1968), "modernization" is "the current term for an old process—the process of social change whereby less developed societies acquire characteristics common to more developed societies." Daniel Lerner, "Modernization," *International Encyclopedia of the Social Sciences* (New York: Macmillan, 1968), 10:386. By modernization theory I mean the theory that economic aid for modernization—which was often called development aid—could be used to transform societies so that they politically, ideologically, and economically harmonize with the United States of America.

2. Organization for Economic Co-operation and Development, *The Flow of Financial Resources to Less-Developed Countries 1961–1965* (Paris, 1967), 34. Rostow claimed that, including U.S. contributions to the World Bank, International Development Association, and other organizations, U.S. development aid increased by one-third. Rostow, *Eisenhower, Kennedy, and Foreign Aid* (Austin: University of Texas Press, 1985), 183.

3. Agency for International Development, Statistics and Reports Division, *U.S. Overseas Loans and Grants and Assistance from International Organizations* (Washington: Agency for International Development, 1970).

4. R. D. McKinlay and A. Mughan, *Aid and Arms to the Third World: An Analysis of the Distribution and Impact of U.S. Official Transfers* (London: St. Martin's Press, 1984), 41.

5. Department of State, "Quiet Warriors: Supporting Social Revolution in Viet-Nam" (Washington: Department of State, 1966), 34.

6. Rostow, "Ideas and Action," 11 June 1962, Address at Carnegie Institute of Technology, *Department of State Bulletin*, 9 July 1962: 59. See also Schlesinger, on how Kennedy men acted on the president's behalf "to bring the world of power

and the world of ideas together in alliance—or rather, as he himself saw it, to restore the collaboration between the two worlds which had marked the early republic." Arthur M. Schlesinger, Jr., *A Thousand Days: John F. Kennedy in the White House* (Boston: Houghton Mifflin, 1965), 109.

7. On modernization theory and Kennedy diplomacy see Michael E. Latham, *Modernization as Ideology: American Social Science and "Nation Building" in the Kennedy Era* (Chapel Hill: University of North Carolina Press, 2000). Economists have more fully explored Rostow's impact on economic theory than historians have examined his impact on Cold War diplomacy. See for example his inclusion in such works as Michael Szenberg, ed., *Eminent Economists: Their Life Philosophies* (New York: Cambridge University Press, 1992), 222–35, and J. A. Kregel, ed., *Recollections of Eminent Economists* (New York: New York University Press, 1989), 2, 163–95. Charles P. Kindleberger and Guido di Tella, eds., *Economics in the Long View: Essays in Honour of W. W. Rostow*, 3 vols. (New York: New York University Press, 1982), is a collection of essays about Rostow's economics that avoids his government work. For a conscious and scholarly attempt at examining the intersection between Rostow's economic and government career—by an author other than Rostow—see John Lodewijks, "Rostow, Developing Economies, and National Security Policy," in Craufurd D. Goodwin, ed., *Economics and National Security* (Durham: Duke University Press, 1991). Rostow has written a six-volume series of books, Ideas and Action, and a quasi-memoir. See Rostow, *Eisenhower, Kennedy, and Foreign Aid*, and Rostow, *The Diffusion of Power: An Essay in Recent History* (New York: Macmillan, 1972).

8. P. H. Baran and E. J. Hobsbawm, "The Stages of Economic Growth," *Kyklos* 14 (1961): Fasc. 2, 236.

9. Henry Rosovsky, "The Take-Off into Sustained Controversy," *Journal of Economic History* 25, no. 2 (June 1965): 271.

10. Schlesinger, *A Thousand Days*, 588.

11. George Rosen, *Western Economists and Eastern Societies: Agents of Change in South Asia, 1950–1970* (Baltimore: Johns Hopkins University Press, 1985), 29.

12. Rostow, "Development: The Political Economy of the Marshallian Long Period," in Gerald M. Meier and Dudley Seers, eds., *Pioneers in Development* (New York: Oxford University Press, 1984), 241n.

13. Rostow, *The Process of Economic Growth* (New York: Norton, 1952). Rostow, *Stages of Economic Growth: A Non-Communist Manifesto* (New York: Cambridge University Press, 1960).

14. Rostow, *Pioneers in Development*, 229.

15. Richard M. Bissell, Jr., with Jonathan E. Lewis and Frances T. Pudlo, *Reflections of a Cold Warrior: From Yalta to the Bay of Pigs* (New Haven: Yale University Press, 1996), 76.

16. John Kenneth Galbraith, *The Nature of Mass Poverty* (Cambridge: Harvard University Press, 1979), 31–32.

17. Bissell, *Reflections of a Cold Warrior,* 71.

18. Galbraith, *Nature of Mass Poverty,* 30; James C. Thomson, Jr., Peter W. Stanley, and John Curtis Perry, *Sentimental Imperialists: The American Experience in East Asia* (New York: Harper & Row, 1981), 310; Rosen, *Western Economists,* 4; Franz Schurmann, *The Logic of World Power: An Inquiry into the Origins, Currents, and Contradictions of World Politics* (New York: Pantheon, 1974), 52–53; H. W. Arndt, *Economic Development: The History of an Idea* (Chicago: University of Chicago Press, 1987), 56.

19. According to the Princeton Economic Conference transcript, the participants were, Samuel W. Anderson, Assistant Secretary of Commerce; George B. Baldwin, MIT Center for International Studies; Lloyd V. Berkner, President, Associated Universities, Inc.; Robert Cutler, Special Assistant to the President; Allen W. Dulles, Director, Central Intelligence Agency; Arthur Flemming, Director, Office of Defense Mobilization; Robert Garner, Vice-President, The International Bank; Gabriel Hauge, Administrative Assistant to the President; C. D. Jackson, Time, Inc.; John K. Jessup, Time, Inc.; Edward S. Mason, Harvard University; David J. McDonald, President, United Steelworkers of America; John MacKenzie, Atomic Energy Commission; Thomas McKittrick, Chase National Bank; Max Millikan, Director, Center for International Studies, MIT; H. Chapman Rose, Assistant Secretary of the Treasury; Walt W. Rostow, Center for International Studies, MIT; Harold E. Stassen, Director, Foreign Operations Administration; Charles L. Stillman, Vice-President, Time, Inc.; Abbott Washburn, U.S. Information Agency; and Jerome Wiesner, MIT. Dulles, Stassen, and Cutler did not stay for the Sunday session, while Jessup and Rose did not arrive until Sunday morning. Princeton Economic Conference Transcript, (1) 1–2, C. D. Jackson Papers, Eisenhower Library, box 83, 217.

20. Allen Dulles, Princeton Economic Conference, 70.

21. McDonald, ibid., 95.

22. Ibid., 97–98. On Millikan, Rostow, and the formation of the Peace Corps see James Killian, *The Education of a College President* (Cambridge: MIT Press, 1985), 68.

23. Wiesner, Princeton Economic Conference, 102.

24. Garner, ibid., 118.

25. Rostow, ibid., 113.

26. Walt W. Rostow, "The Take-Off into Self-Sustained Growth," *Economic Journal* 66 (1956): 25–48.

27. Ibid., 25.

28. Max F. Millikan, W. W. Rostow, and others, *A Proposal: Key to an Effective Foreign Policy* (New York: Harper, 1957).

29. Ian M. D. Little, *Economic Development: Theory, Policy, and International Relations* (New York: Basic Books, 1982), 112.

30. Millikan and Rostow, *A Proposal,* 151. On the concept of communism as a

disease of the transition, see Rostow to Jackson, 5 November 1958, Rostow, Walt W., 1958, C. D. Jackson Papers, Eisenhower Library, box 6, 2–3.

31. Millikan and Rostow, *A Proposal,* 151.

32. Rostow, "The Take-Off," 30–31.

33. Millikan and Rostow, *A Proposal,* 49. Rostow defined the beginning of the take-off period as most often associated with three factors: (a) a rise in the rate of productive investment, (b) the development of a leading industry that was rapidly growing, and (c) the existence of a political and social framework compatible with growth. Rostow, "The Take-Off," 32.

34. Rostow, "The Take-Off," 30. Millikan and Rostow, *A Proposal,* 49.

35. Millikan and Rostow, *A Proposal,* 49.

36. Rostow, "The Take-Off," 30–31.

37. Ibid., 37.

38. Millikan and Rostow, *A Proposal,* 43.

39. Ibid., 43–44.

40. Eugene Staley, "International Law and Relations," *American Political Science Review* 52, no. 3 (September 1958): 891.

41. The professors conceded that numbers alone did not give a full picture of a society, but left the other criteria with which they determined the development stage vague: Millikan and Rostow, *A Proposal,* 48–49.

42. Ibid., 49.

43. Ibid., 106.

44. Ibid.

45. Rostow, "The Take-Off," 41.

46. Millikan and Rostow, *A Proposal,* 1.

47. Rostow acknowledged the importance Congress placed on making certain that aid funding would not go on forever: Rostow, Interview with the author, March 1998, College Station, Tex.

48. Millikan and Rostow, *A Proposal,* 53.

49. Burton I. Kaufman, *Trade and Aid: Eisenhower's Foreign Economic Policy, 1953–1961* (Baltimore, 1982), 98.

50. Ibid.

51. Rostow, *Aid,* 320.

52. John F. Kennedy, "A Democrat Looks at Foreign Policy," *Foreign Affairs* 36, no. 1 (October 1957): 53.

53. Latham, *Modernization as Ideology,* 13–17.

54. Rostow, *Aid,* 68–69.

55. Ibid., 69. See also, Rostow, John F. Kennedy Library Oral History Program, Kennedy Library, 4.

56. Rostow, *Aid,* 71.

57. David Halberstam, *The Best and the Brightest* (New York, 1972), 195.

58. Kimber Charles Pearce, "Walt Whitman Rostow's Rhetoric of Moderniza-

tion: Cold War Economics, Foreign Policy Advocacy, and Social Scientific Argumentation," Diss., Penn State University, 1997, 142n.

59. John F. Kennedy, *A Compilation of Statements and Speeches Made during His Service in the United States Senate and House Of Representatives* (Washington: U.S. Government Printing Office, 1964), 594.

60. Ibid., 596–97.

61. Ibid., 593.

62. Ibid. Besides using such unmistakable Rostovian terminology as "takeoff," the speech contained other Rostow flourishes.

63. Ibid., 598.

64. *Congressional Record,* 85th Congress, 2d sess., 104, pt. 4: 5246–53.

65. Kennedy, *A Compilation,* 592.

66. Kennedy, *The Strategy of Peace* (New York, 1960), 45–54.

67. Ibid., 45–47.

68. Ibid., 33–45.

69. Richard N. Current et al., *American History: A Survey* (New York: McGraw-Hill, 1983), 820. On 7 February 1961, the *New York Times* carried a story that asserted that studies made by the Kennedy administration since inauguration day showed tentatively that no "missile gap" existed in favor of the Soviet Union.

70. Between 1955 and 1958, U.S. economic aid contributions to Near Eastern and Asian countries exceeded that of the Sino-Soviet bloc by nearly $1 billion: Rostow, *Aid,* 18.

71. Kennedy, *Strategy of Peace,* 47.

72. Ibid., 48. At the time he gave this speech, the disastrous results of the Great Leap Forward were not yet know in the West.

73. Ibid., 47.

74. Ibid., 49–52.

75. Halberstam, *Best and the Brightest,* 195. By Rostow's own account, he stayed in close contact with Kennedy through Fred Holborn: Rostow, John F. Kennedy Library Oral History Program, 16.

76. Rostow, Recorded interview by Jean W. Ross, 4 September 1981, in *Contemporary Authors,* New Revision Series, 8:430. See also Rostow, John F. Kennedy Library Oral History Program, 21–22.

77. Richard Goodwin, as cited in Pearce, "Walt Whitman Rostow's Rhetoric of Modernization," 151.

78. Lincoln Gordon, "The Alliance at Birth: Hopes and Fears," in L. Ronald Scheman, ed., *The Alliance for Progress: A Retrospective* (New York: Praeger, 1988), 74–75. Kennedy to Rostow, 16 November 1960, Papers of Max F. Millikan, "Correspondence, 1959–1961," box 1, Kennedy Library.

79. Kennedy in Lloyd C. Gardner, *Pay Any Price: Lyndon Johnson and the Wars for Vietnam* (Chicago: I. R. Dee, 1995), 33.

80. Kennedy to National Security Council, 18 January 1962, *Foreign Relations of the United States, 1961–1963,* 8:240.

81. Kennedy, "State of the Union Message, 29 January 1961," text in John W. Gardner, ed., *To Turn the Tide* (New York: Harper, 1962), 43.

82. Rostow, John F. Kennedy Library Oral History Program. John M. Newman, *JFK and Vietnam: Deception, Intrigue, and the Struggle for Power* (New York: Warner Books, 1992), 3. Rostow, Recorded interview by Paige E. Mulhollan, 21 March 1969, Lyndon B. Johnson Library Oral History Program, 64.

83. Rostow, John F. Kennedy Library Oral History Program, 44.

84. Newman, *JFK and Vietnam,* 10.

85. Vladislav Zubok and Constantine Pleshakov, *Inside the Kremlin's Cold War: From Stalin to Khrushchev* (Cambridge: Harvard University Press, 1996), 253.

86. Ibid., 255.

87. John F. Kennedy, 5 September 1960, as quoted in Patrick Hatcher, *Suicide of an Elite: American Internationalists and Vietnam* (Stanford: Stanford University Press, 1991), 112.

88. John Kenneth Galbraith, "A Positive Approach to Economic Aid," *Foreign Affairs* 39 (April 1961): 448.

89. Ibid., 449. By 1962, J. P. Lewis asserted that lack of outside capital was not the principal impediment to rapid economic growth. John P. Lewis, *Quiet Crisis in India* (Washington: Brookings Institution, 1962), 56.

90. Rostow to Kennedy 2 March 1961, NSF, Kennedy Library, box 64a, 1.

91. Rostow gave Richard Goodwin credit for coming up with the "Decade of Development" phrase. Rostow to Kennedy, 2 November 1961, NSF, Kennedy Library, box 64a, 2.

92. Ibid.

93. Ibid., 1–4.

94. Ibid., 4.

95. Rostow, John F. Kennedy Library Oral History Program, 51.

96. Kennedy, "Special Message to the Congress on Foreign Aid, 22 March 1961," in Gardner, ed., *To Turn the Tide,* 144.

97. Kennedy to Diem, 3 August 1961, NSF, Kennedy Library, box 193.

98. Nolting to Rusk, 10 August 1961, NSF, Kennedy Library, box 193. On strategic hamlets, see also Latham, *Modernization as Ideology,* 196–263.

99. Gardner, ed., *To Turn the Tide,* 6–9.

100. Latham, *Modernization as Ideology,* 7.

101. Solomon Silver, "Counter-Insurgency and Nation Building: A Study with Emphasis on Southeast Asia," United States Agency for International Development, 1967, AID Library; National Security Archive, 1994, Fiche number 00182, 46.

102. When LBJ expanded the war, he "clung all the harder to an abstract vision of Vietnam transformed, just as the Texas hill country had been transformed. 'I

want to leave the footprints of America in Vietnam,' he said in 1966. 'I want them to say when the Americans come, this what they leave—schools, not long cigars. We're going to turn the Mekong into a Tennessee Valley.' " As quoted in Gardner, ed., *To Turn the Tide,* 197.

103. Wiesner, Princeton Economic Conference, 102.

## FURTHER READING

Kindleberger, Charles P., and Guido di Tella, eds. *Economics in the Long View: Essays in Honour of W. W. Rostow.* New York: New York University Press, 1982.

Lodewijks, J. "Rostow, Developing Economies, and National Security Policy." In Craufurd D. Goodwin, ed., *Economics and National Security.* Durham: Duke University Press, 1991.

Millikan, Max, Walt W. Rostow, and others. *A Proposal: Key to an Effective Foreign Policy.* New York: Harper, 1957.

Rostow, Walt W. *The Diffusion of Power: An Essay in Recent History.* New York: Macmillan, 1972.

———. *Eisenhower, Kennedy, and Foreign Aid.* Austin: University of Texas Press, 1985.

———. *The Stages of Economic Growth: A Non-Communist Manifesto.* Cambridge: Cambridge University Press, 1960.

# PART II

# CELEBRATING MODERNIZATION

# SELLING CAPITALISM: MODERNIZATION AND U.S. OVERSEAS PROPAGANDA, 1945–1959

LAURA BELMONTE

In an age where Tibetan sherpas wear Nike clothing and watch CNN atop Mount Everest, global capitalism is an omnipresent reality. While scholars debate the ramifications and meanings of the "triumph of capitalism," it is valuable to revisit an era when the battle between capitalism and communism still raged.[1] In 1960 economist Walt Whitman Rostow published *The Stages of Economic Growth: A Non-Communist Manifesto.* Explicitly challenging Karl Marx's portrait of capitalism as an oligarchic and unstable system, Rostow defended capitalism as the surest path to political freedom, personal fulfillment, and economic security. He outlined an economic progression in which "traditional" societies reached a "take-off," attained "maturity," and then entered an "age of high mass-consumption." Not surprisingly, Rostow identified the United States as the exemplar of enlightened modernity and democratic values.[2]

Like most of his contemporaries, Rostow fervently believed in American exceptionalism. Americans have long viewed themselves as a free and prosperous people whose nation inspires admiration throughout the world. They are convinced that the United States can spread its vision of democratic capitalism abroad without imperiling the standards of living and political liberties making America special. In the words of the historian Michael Hunt, the United States can "transform the world without itself being transformed."[3]

Such views pervaded U.S. foreign policy during the early Cold War. U.S. officials like Rostow preached a gospel of modernization in which economic development fostered political and social freedoms. They fused a benevolent conception of American national identity to the pursuit of U.S. economic and political objectives abroad. Assuming that all foreign peoples would embrace capitalism if given the opportunity to do so, U.S. policymakers claimed that democratic capitalism was the only sure path to peace, prosperity, and freedom. While denying imperialistic ambitions, they declared that all nations could attain the superior way of life found in the United States.

There are striking parallels between *The Stages of Economic Growth* and U.S. propaganda materials produced during the early Cold War. While U.S. information officials did not use the term "modernization," their efforts to promote democratic capitalism echoed modernization theorists. This is not surprising given that many social scientists who espoused modernization theory, including Rostow, Alex Inkeles, and Daniel Lerner, worked as consultants to America's psychological warfare and propaganda programs. Drawn together by a collective vision of American national greatness, public and private individuals crafted propaganda that claimed that the United States not only could but should lead the world to modernity, liberalism, democracy, and capitalism. Through linking the social, spiritual, and political benefits of capitalism to its economic advantages, they offered a powerful alternative to communism. Propagandists and modernization theorists worked separately to achieve the shared goal of a global order governed by American standards of freedom, productivity, and rationality.[4]

At the end of World War II, the United States was poised to make itself the world's political, economic, cultural, and strategic superpower. Many foreigners viewed the United States as the epitome of modernity. America's industry, technology, mass culture, efficiency, consumerism, and progress were widely admired and occasionally feared by international business people, intellectuals, and mass audiences.[5] U.S. officials worried that less fortunate countries would resent—and perhaps sabotage—America's economic and political success. In order to avert such suspicion and resistance, U.S. policymakers dedicated themselves to explaining the U.S. economic system to foreign audiences. From the inception of the postwar information program, American propagandists linked the defense of liberal capitalism to the preservation of world peace and freedom. In articulating the material and immaterial values democratic capitalism accorded individuals, they defined American national identity and defended U.S. strategic interests to a world facing the threat of communism.[6] This essay examines some of these attempts to make modernization appealing internationally.[7]

In the aftermath of World War II, U.S. officials expressed dismay at the distorted and unfavorable picture of the United States being propagated by the Soviet Union. On 20 January 1946, Averell Harriman, the U.S. ambassador to the USSR, described widely disseminated Communist accounts of strikes, unemployment, crime, and racial discrimination in the United States. The Soviets saw communism, not democratic capitalism, as the most progressive political and economic system in the world. Rather than attacking the Soviet government—a strategy that risked sparking an anti-American backlash—Harriman urged his superiors to embark on a "vigorous and intelligent" American information program which explained the virtues of the American way of life to foreign audiences, especially those in Communist countries.[8]

Other U.S. officials made similar recommendations. In November 1947, General Walter Bedell Smith, Harriman's successor, warned that "the myth of Communist paradise" was impeding U.S. attempts to promote the Marshall Plan. Smith offered detailed instructions for countering Soviet propaganda. He suggested publicizing the regimentation of the Soviet economy in which "labor loses individuality and becomes like a draft animal to be used where boss thinks best." He pointed to child labor, low productivity, and the poor standard of living as further ways to undermine communism. Giving a factual account of American working conditions and the realities of capitalism, Smith argued, would generate support for the Marshall Plan among Europeans.[9]

As the ideological battle between capitalism and communism intensified, U.S. information leaders escalated their efforts to promote the American economic system abroad. Like Rostow and other modernization theorists, American propagandists insisted that the United States did not view itself as a model for all nations. A 1959 United States Information Agency (USIA) policy paper read, "The Agency does not attempt to 'sell' the American economic system as a blueprint for other countries to follow."[10] This disingenuous disclaimer notwithstanding, U.S. information officials and modernization theorists were quite willing to advocate American economic ideals and to extol the virtues of life in a capitalist democracy. They viewed the American standard of living and mass consumption as evidence that the U.S. economic system represented the pinnacle of economic development and modernity.

U.S. information authorities hoped to capitalize on the high level of international curiosity about living conditions in the United States. Consequently, they carefully constructed programs which stressed three basic elements of the American economy: free competitive enterprise, free trade unionism, and limited government intervention. In creating this picture of capitalism, USIA administrators emphasized that the American economic system, unlike socialism or communism, did not leave laborers beholden to an uncaring bureaucracy. "We *do* insist," information leaders asserted, "that the economy should exist for the benefit of the citizen, not for the state." Therefore, their portrayal of the American economy emphasized "related themes" such as the quest for social justice, the equitable distribution of income, "the growing classlessness of our society," the potential growth of the U.S. economy, and the thriving culture of the United States.[11]

U.S. information strategists meticulously interwove the economic and social benefits capitalism could produce.[12] Information packets prepared for distribution in all American embassies featured stories like "Labor's Drive for Guaranteed Annual Wages," "Union Plan Opens New Careers for Disabled Miners," "Wider Employment Opportunities for Women," and "Profit-Sharing Plans in U.S. Industry." Overall, U.S. propagandists accented harmonious labor and management relations, movement toward racial and gender equality in the workplace, and the material benefits capitalism afforded the typical worker, especially when juxtaposed to his or her Soviet counterpart.[13]

In advocating the American economic system, U.S. policymakers had to overcome negative international perceptions of capitalism. Soviet propagandists bombarded foreign audiences with reports of widespread labor unrest, insoluble social problems, economic instability, and high unemployment in the United States.[14] These accounts resonated abroad. Even after war-torn nations began to recover, American officials noted that misconceptions about the U.S. economy persisted. In early 1951, State Department analysts described how European "managerial elites" were exploiting loopholes in their national tax and trust laws. Although the United States forbade similar practices, the officials reported, much of the European populace linked the abuses to the American free enterprise system.[15]

In some nations, conceptions of capitalism remained those put forth by Marx in the 1848 political treatise *The Communist Manifesto*. Using Great Britain as a case study, Marx declared that capitalism led to poverty, instability, and exploitation. Over a century later, American propagandists in the State Department and the USIA found themselves struggling to disprove Marx's charges. For example, a 1956 survey of 1,665 entrepreneurs in India revealed generally unfavorable attitudes, characterizing capitalism as a system marked by worker exploitation, high unemployment, oligarchy, and "a general lack of social responsibility." For these reasons, Indian businessmen concluded that capitalism was not an acceptable system for their nation.[16]

U.S. information leaders addressed these criticisms by differentiating U.S. capitalism from its European "cartel-like or feudalistic" variations. They praised the American "mixed economy" characterized by federal regulations, individual freedom, collective bargaining, and economic competition. They stressed the purchasing power of the American consumer and his or her ability to choose among competing goods and services.[17] They emphasized the stability and productivity of the U.S. economy.[18] Yet even some USIA officials resisted this portrayal. One complained, "I don't think you're going to get any successful preaching of that point because the average government employee, the average bureaucrat, no matter how sincere, would not" accept a completely affirmative version of U.S. capitalism.[19]

The Communists of course flatly rejected this vision. Determined to defeat capitalism, Soviet propagandists derided the American economy as immoral, imperialist, and materialistic. Communist officials claimed that the "socialist" system of the Sino-Soviet bloc provided the "only pattern for rapid industrialization and economic growth which will benefit the many instead of a select few."[20] Soviet authorities contended that the average U.S. worker stood powerless in the face of pervasive malnutrition, severe unemployment, and an oligarchic political system. Furthermore, they claimed Wall Street financiers intensified the arms race "for the purpose of reinforcing the dictatorship of monopoly capital" and "to convince workers that a militarized economy means full employment." Capitalism, in short, fueled the Cold War.[21]

In response to such attacks, U.S. information experts assailed the Soviet "worker's paradise." When State Department analysts identified the principal weaknesses of the Soviet economy, they argued: "While all labor in the Soviet Union is in effect forced since 'the happy workers' cannot leave the country and must work, the concentration camp system as such probably constitutes the Soviet Union's principal psychological vulnerability since it runs entirely counter to Russian ideals of solidarity and fraternity and since it is the living proof of the evils inherent in trying to force an unworkable system to work." Furthermore, the analysts suggested publicizing the low standard of living and poor housing conditions in the USSR. They recommended emphasizing the economic disparity between the average Soviet citizen and Communist bureaucrats who enjoyed "dachas, good clothes, good food and other luxuries."[22]

U.S. propagandists stressed the impact of communism on individuals and families. Some U.S. Information Service (USIS) publications, such as *The Truth Crushes Commie Lies,* bluntly attacked Communist labor laws. "Communism means no freedom for workers," the pamphlet declared. The text pointed out that Soviet workers could not bargain collectively, choose or quit their jobs, strike, or form their own unions.[23] The provocative USIS comic book *It Happened to Us!* portrayed communism's deleterious effect upon a Soviet family. One of the cartoons depicts the young daughter, Louise, at a Communist indoctrination center. A matronly teacher tells her, "Home-making and raising children are inferior occupations." Not yet modern enough to embrace nontraditional gender roles, the USIA implied that only an economically backward nation created women who valued careers more than motherhood.[24] U.S. information officials frequently criticized slave labor in the USSR. Through stories like "Slave Labor

Follows the Russian Flag" and "The New Slavery," they contrasted oppressive working conditions in Communist nations with the freedom and prosperity found among American laborers.[25] Communism, U.S. information officials maintained, destroyed families and devalued workers.

Capitalism, however, enabled individuals to fulfill their career ambitions and to live in comfort. In the early 1950s the USIS distributed over one million copies of *Meet Some Americans at Work*, a lengthy pictorial essay portraying a variety of U.S. workers. All appeared content. Not a word about racial and gender discrimination, wage inequities, or labor unrest accompanied the photographs.[26] In October 1955, USIA guidelines on the American economy stressed the salary increases, investment opportunities, and fringe benefits available to productive U.S. workers.[27] In 1957, the USIA pamphlet *Thomas Brackett* emphasized the lifestyle of the average American. Brackett, a Ford Motor Company employee, owned a house stocked with appliances and a car. He planned to send his four children to college. His high wages enabled his wife to remain at home. "There are millions of American capitalists like the Bracketts," the booklet concluded.[28]

Juxtaposing the gains in wages and benefits won by American unions to the existence of forced labor camps behind the Iron Curtain, USIA administrators sought to define unions as the force protecting the typical American worker.[29] The USIS booklet *American Labor Unions: Their Role in the Free World* exemplifies these efforts, asserting: "American workers know how difficult is the struggle for security and justice. Through their unions, they triumphed after many failures. . . . Capitalism in a democracy uses its forces not in a negative way, to depress and exploit the masses, but to expand production, to create new ideas and new wealth."[30] USIA authorities frequently cited American labor leaders in order to demonstrate widespread domestic support for the objectives espoused by the U.S. information establishment.[31] They pointed to union programs for women and African Americans as examples of progressive, democratic attitudes.[32]

The role of organized labor, however, formed only a portion of the larger image of the American worker crafted by the USIA. Rarely focusing on white-collar workers, the agency usually highlighted factory workers in materials directed at foreign laborers. For example, a December 1955 article called "An American Worker's Family" featured

Ray Bellingham, a mill operator at General Electric's locomotive and car equipment department in Erie, Pennsylvania. The Bellinghams discussed Ray's wages, mortgage payments, workday, and taxes. His wife, Helen, described her attempts to maintain a budget while feeding and clothing their family of six.[33]

The Bellinghams exemplified how the "classlessness" of U.S. society enabled individuals to reap the benefits of capitalism. These gains, the USIA showed, extended beyond corporate executives and reached even manual laborers. Profit-sharing, paid vacations, company-sponsored scholarships, and health insurance provided additional examples. Job security, workman's compensation, and unemployment stipends demonstrated the existence of an American social welfare system.[34] Like the modernization theorists, U.S. propagandists attacked the Marxist claim that capitalism benefited only the wealthy.

In contrast to the dignity and decent standard of living accorded American workers, USIA materials showed "Soviet drones" locked in an despotic system plagued by sinecures, forced labor camps, and oppressive working conditions.[35] Communist unions, American information officials alleged, existed only to ensure worker discipline and production quotas set so high that no worker could ever meet them.[36] Simple factual accounts of Communist slave labor camps provided USIA policymakers with propaganda more effective than anything they could create.[37]

But countering Communist allegations that capitalism served only rich white men was a great challenge for USIA officials, who considered racial issues "America's major point of vulnerability, especially when dealing with non-white peoples."[38] USIA information packets frequently included stories acclaiming an African American for his or her achievements in order to demonstrate that racial discrimination did not impede careers.[39] They also emphasized the progress made by U.S. companies in eradicating racial inequities.[40] By "put[ting] the Negro problem in perspective," USIA officials could focus on advantages of democratic capitalism.[41]

These advantages, they argued, included a better life for women and children. U.S. information administrators exposed the Soviet "Workers' Paradise" as one in which women operated drop forges and worked as stevedores while their children languished in state-run day care. U.S. propagandists hoped to shatter Communist claims of gender equity and equality of opportunity.[42] USIA women's packets often featured stories about the economic status of women behind the Iron Curtain. In August 1953, June S. McIlvaine, an American journalist, recounted her recent visit to the USSR. In a tour of the Stalin Auto Works, McIlvaine recalled: "I saw many women working in the foundry. Without goggles, fireproof gloves or any of the safety devices Americans would regard as essential, they were pouring molten metal. . . . I saw girls who didn't look more than 14 years old mopping floors in the subway, laying bricks and even lugging loads of bricks up ten flights of steps."[43] True concern for the role of women, U.S. information officials implied, necessitated protecting their roles as homemakers and mothers, not as manual laborers. USIS materials stressed U.S. laws safeguarding women from hazardous jobs. Most important, they emphasized that the high wages earned by American men allowed mothers to raise their children at home.[44]

This emphasis on domesticity created some fascinating contrasts between Communist and American propaganda. Using articles like "Help for Housewives with Heart Disease" and omitting women perceived as too career-oriented from agency materials, USIA officials countered Soviet portrayals of American working women as immoral and greedy.[45] By presenting women like Mrs. Gail Foster of Philadelphia as typical Americans, U.S. information leaders hoped to instill images of selflessness and devotion extending beyond the family. In an April 1953 USIA packet aimed at foreign women, Mrs. Foster described not only her child-rearing activities and household chores, but also her involvement with her church and a community housing committee.[46] American women best typified agency ideals by achieving in the home, not at the workplace.

In addition to written materials and radio programs, international trade fairs highlighted the U.S. economy. American displays often featured a typical furnished house, manufactured goods and appliances, and mail-order catalogs, as well as television and motion-picture shows. Representatives of the Department of Commerce and private U.S. firms explained conditions of living in the United States to thousands of visitors.[47] The exhibits usually accented U.S. consumer goods. At the Barcelona International Samples Fair in June 1956, workers at the American Pavilion distributed doughnuts, ice cream cones, cups of milk, samples of cheese, baked goods made from prepared mixes, and cigarettes. Other aides staged a continuous fashion show featuring nine models wearing the latest American designs. The items proved highly popular with both men and women.[48]

Nonetheless, U.S. policymakers recognized that American material wealth was not necessarily a propaganda asset. Communist propagandists often seized on international displays of U.S. consumer goods as evidence of materialism and immorality in the United States. To deflect such distortions, U.S. propagandists linked the success of the American economy to its democratic system. Communism, they insisted, destroyed individual initiative.[49] On 23 April 1953, William L. Grenoble, an administrator of the International Motion Picture Service, explained: "One of our biggest jobs—this is of course directly related in antipathy to the Communist line—is to demonstrate that although the average American has a good deal more of the material things of life than many people throughout the world, he has attained those by the application of hard work and ingenuity, and other people can do the same."[50] Americans, in short, were not lazy. They had earned their possessions by performing well in an economy that valued productivity and creativity. Such arguments also implied that nations that did not emulate American modernization were inferior.

Because foreign audiences often noticed these value judgments, even accurate portrayals of typical U.S. workers could produce undesirable results. Although broadcasts extolling capitalism generated fan mail, some of the letters contained sarcastic comments like, "I listen to the Voice of America everyday. Please send me a Buick automobile. Yours sincerely."[51] Rather than asking for American consumer goods, other audience members were intimidated by accounts of American economic performance. In December 1954, Clifton B. Forster, the public affairs officer of the USIA post in Fukora, Japan, recounted his difficulties in reaching Japanese laborers. When presented with factual representations of "the daily activity of an American laborer which show him driving to work in his own car, eating a steak by a Westinghouse Refrigerator, etc.," Foster explained, the Japanese expressed strong resentment and feelings of inferiority. "You are much too advanced over there," one labor leader commented.[52]

Yet foreigners were fascinated by U.S. consumer goods. Mail-order catalogs from U.S. stores ranked among the most popular materials at USIS libraries. In Finland, U.S. embassy officials claimed back issues of the Sears, Roebuck & Company catalog "have been worn out through use, rebound with stronger covers and put back into circulation." In West Berlin, USIS authorities chained the catalogs to the tables as Germans crowded four deep to glimpse the illustrations. An airport bookstore in Djakarta, Indonesia, reported selling the catalogs for $20 each despite currency restrictions that prevented Indonesians from ordering the items featured.[53]

Such popularity encouraged U.S. propagandists to respond assertively to Soviet distortions of the American economy. Certain that the Soviet Union could not match U.S. levels of productivity, State Department analysts expressed little concern over improvements in the Soviet standard of living.[54] USIS materials emphasized the comparative worktime required to buy certain items in the United States and the Soviet Union. For example, an April 1953 pamphlet featured a chart showing the buying power of an average Moscow worker as far lower than that of a laborer in New York. "For a pound of bread, he has to work twice as long as the American worker; for potatoes, he has to work about three times as long; for beef, 5 times; for eggs, about 7 times; and for sugar, 25 times."[55] USIA researchers noted clothing, housing, and food shortages in the USSR.[56]

Nothing exemplifies the U.S. effort to promote democratic capitalism and modernization better than the "People's Capitalism" campaign. In August 1955, after completing a six-month tour of USIA facilities worldwide, T. S. Repplier, president of the Advertising Council and an adviser to President Dwight D. Eisenhower, claimed that the United States needed propaganda to counter Communist gains in the underdeveloped world. Intentionally appropriating Communist rhetoric, Repplier suggested "People's Capitalism" as the campaign's slogan. Impressed with Repplier's recommendations, Eisenhower ordered U.S. information strategists to plan an unprecedented global effort to explain capitalism to foreign peoples. In conjunction with private citizens in the advertising and public relations fields, American officials carefully designed written texts, films, trade fairs, and exhibitions that debunked Marxist rhetoric and promoted democratic capitalism.[57]

Privately, the creators of "People's Capitalism" expressed deep faith in democratic capitalism and modernization. On 28 November 1955, USIA Research Officer Henry Loomis argued that capitalism allowed individual nations to progress without violent revolution.[58] In January 1956, while explaining the campaign to the U.S. Department of Commerce, USIA Deputy Director Abbott Washburn praised "People's Capitalism" for emphasizing that "the people own the capital and the people share the benefits."[59]

At the same time, propaganda advisers tested the themes of "People's Capitalism" before American audiences. On 27 October 1955, Repplier spoke to the Business Paper Editors of America and stressed the urgency of finding a way to explain "the American way of life." After candidly admitting that "People's Capitalism" sounded "Russian," Repplier asserted:

> like "democracy," "freedom" and other words which were bequeathed to us in the founding documents, the word "people's" has been kidnapped by the Russians. Yet no word is more American. The U.S. Constitution begins with "We, the people," and an immortal and inspired definition of democracy is Abraham Lincoln's "government of the people, by the people, and for the people." It is high time we liberated this noun from the Russians. We cannot let the Soviets steal all our good words. At long last, let us turn the tables on them. Let us take back a word as American as apple pie.[60]

A few weeks later, Sherman Adams, another of Eisenhower's advisers, made a similar appeal on the Mutual Broadcasting System radio network.[61]

Before sending "People's Capitalism" abroad, USIA leaders held a public preview of the exhibit. On 14 and 15 February 1956, almost 25,000 people, including 100 invited foreign journalists, filed through the main hall of Washington's Union Station to preview "People's Capitalism." Celebrated as a "means of bringing information about America to the world and counteracting the falsehoods of communism," the display highlighted two homes: the common dwelling in 1776 and a modern, prefabricated steel house stocked with new furniture and labor-saving appliances. Visitors learned that "people's capitalism," unlike previous economic systems, enabled most workers to own property and to benefit from the results of increased productivity through higher wages and greater availability of consumer goods. "The people themselves," the exhibit declared, "are the capitalists."[62]

But "People's Capitalism" meant different things to different people. Visitors to the exhibit offered their opinions. President Eisenhower suggested the incorporation of additional material on the religious and cultural life of the typical U.S. worker in order to illustrate that capitalism fostered freedoms beyond the workplace. Others remarked that the homes "looked too good" to represent typical workers. After evaluating the comments made by USIA officers and visitors to the exhibit, the agency made minor revisions.[63] In an attempt to evoke more humble Americana, a revised version of the display used a log cabin similar to Abraham Lincoln's childhood home. And, striving to achieve a more "lived-in" look, USIA officials replaced the new furniture and appliances in the modern house with used ones.[64]

The revised script for "People's Capitalism" offers cogent insights into the methods and motives for the campaign. Bold-faced titles alerted visitors to important themes including "THE REWARDS WERE SHARED WITH THE WORKERS," "AMERICA BECAME A MIDDLE-INCOME NATION," "ALMOST EVERYBODY BECAME A CAPITALIST," and "WEAKNESSES TEND TO BE ONLY TEMPORARY." Anticipating many of the points later made by Rostow, the exhibit defined capitalism as much more than an economic system. Contrary to Marx's economic determinism, "People's Capitalism" encompassed political, spiritual, and cultural elements as well as economics. Although Communists presented themselves as the guardians of working people, only capitalist nations gave their citizens "*complete freedom* to choose their jobs, to work where they wished, to invest, to start a business or a labor union." Where Marx predicted monopolies, instability, and low wages, "People's Capitalism" proved the vitality of capitalism. Under a competitive economic system, American wages *increased*. Instead of concentrating property in the hands of a few, U.S. capitalism made it possible for almost everyone to own property. Rather than abusing their workers, U.S. companies protected them through generous insurance policies and pension plans. In contrast to Communist censorship of culture and religion, Americans enjoyed rich intellectual and spiritual lives. USIA leaders were certain this portrait of democratic capitalism could counter even the most strident Communist propaganda.[65]

In November 1956, "People's Capitalism" opened in Bogotá, Columbia. During two weeks, 235,000 people attended the exhibit. When the display reached Guatemala City, 94,000 people, a third of the city's population, came. After making stops in Chile and Bolivia, "People's Capitalism" traveled to Ceylon, where another 50,000 people saw the exhibit. But while the USIA considered "People's Capitalism" a smash hit, budgetary and logistical problems forced the agency to suspend the exhibits for 1957.[66]

Although "People's Capitalism" drew impressive crowds, it is difficult to assess whether it changed foreign perceptions of capitalism. Throughout the campaign, audiences complained that USIA officials did not adequately acknowledge economic problems in the United States. This criticism was well founded. At a time when one in five Americans lived in poverty, the "People's Capitalism" pamphlet proclaimed that the United States "has left far behind the indifference to the public, the lack of concern for the workers, the ruthless preoccupation with profits which many critics in the past considered inevitable in a capitalist society."[67] Such explanations rang hollow even in foreign nations allied with the United States. In December 1956, USIA officials reported that a majority of 4,205 Western Europeans surveyed did not believe that U.S. capitalism provided great opportunities for individual advancement or economic security for the elderly. While they lauded the productivity of the American economy, they expressed skepticism that capitalism was the sole reason for U.S. efficiency and standards of living.[68]

Convinced that they could not answer such criticism directly without undermining "People's Capitalism," U.S. information officials tried to divert attention to the positive features of democratic capitalism. In March 1957, responding to an official Soviet request for information about the "People's Capitalism" exhibit, USIA Director Arthur Larson ordered his staff to prepare materials on unemployment, installment buying, and Wall Street capitalists. To correct Soviet distortions of U.S. unemployment, Larson urged USIA officials to emphasize the number of vacant jobs, the seasonal nature of some jobs, and the existence of unemployment compensation. Because of the social welfare programs in America, Larson reminded his colleagues, unemployment "quite definitely should not and does not necessarily mean breadlines, soup kitchens, squalor, starvation."[69] To counter Communist accusations that financiers controlled the United States,

USIA officials explained the benefits and liabilities of the use of credit, the structure of American corporations, and the buying power of American consumers.[70]

Larson and other USIA administrators claimed that the charge of materialism directed at Americans was not usually an emotionally significant one for those critiquing the United States. Consumerism therefore remained a prominent feature of American international information programs. USIA officials remained confident that as long as depictions of luxury items were omitted, international audiences found purchasing power an important factor distinguishing American and Soviet workers.[71] At the 1958 Brussels World's Fair, U.S. propagandists claimed that the Soviet industrial exhibits stressed scientific advances and heavy machinery in order "to divert attention from the area of communist economic weakness—[the] production of consumer goods." U.S. information leaders criticized "the well-advertised Soviet posture that the USSR can serve as both a model for industrialization of the underdeveloped countries and a source of aid without strings."[72] Foreshadowing Rostow's emphasis on mass consumption as evidence of economic maturity, U.S. propagandists maintained that consumerism improved Americans' daily lives without eroding their social values. They shared Rostow's belief that no society lacking genuine social welfare programs, mass consumption, and social and political freedom was a good model for modernization.

"People's Capitalism" signified a more fulfilling, comfortable life for the individual. In choosing the word "people's," U.S. propagandists sought to appropriate Communist discourse in showing how the American economy allowed individuals to flourish as citizens and consumers. Capitalism accorded the average worker dignity as embodied in personal buying power and fringe benefit programs. American information officials had little difficulty making the image of a typical U.S. housewife more attractive than that of a Soviet woman working on the railroad or the Communist man suffering in a labor camp. Through skillful crafting of propaganda materials, they placed less appealing aspects of American society in a better light. In articulating the material advantages and intangible values of modernization, U.S. officials fused their notions of national identity to the imperatives of national security.

## NOTES

1. There is a burgeoning literature on the implications of globalization in the post–Cold War world. Important examples include: Robert Heilbroner, "The Triumph of Capitalism," *New Yorker*, 23 January 1989: 98–109; Richard Ned Lebow and Janice Gross Stein, *We All Lost the Cold War* (Princeton: Princeton University Press, 1994); Thomas J. McCormick, "Troubled Triumphalism: Cold War Veterans Confront a Post–Cold War World," *Diplomatic History* 21 (summer 1997): 481–92; Walter LaFeber, "The Tension between Democracy and Capitalism during the American Century," *Diplomatic History* 23, no. 2 (spring 1999): 263–84; Thomas Friedman, *The Lexus and The Olive Tree* (New York: Farrar, Straus & Giroux, 2000); and William Greider, *One World, Ready or Not: The Manic Logic of Global Capitalism* (New York: Simon and Schuster, 1997).

2. W. W. Rostow, *The Stages of Economic Growth: A Non-Communist Manifesto* (New York: Cambridge University Press, 1960).

3. Michael Hunt, *Ideology and U.S. Foreign Policy* (New Haven: Yale University Press, 1987), 42. See also Anders Stephanson, *Manifest Destiny: American Exceptionalism and the Empire of Right* (New York: Hill and Wang, 1995).

4. On modernization, see Michael E. Latham, *Modernization as Ideology: American Social Science and "Nation Building" in the Kennedy Era* (Chapel Hill: University of North Carolina Press, 2000). On connections between the U.S. foreign policy establishment and private citizens, see Scott Lucas, *Freedom's War: The American Crusade against the Soviet Union* (New York: New York University Press, 1999); Allen Needell, " 'Truth Is Our Weapon': Project TROY, Political Warfare, and Government-Academic Relations in the National-Security State," *Diplomatic History* 17 (summer 1993): 399–420; and Christopher Simpson, ed., *Universities and Empire: Money and Politics in the Social Sciences during the Cold War* (New York: Free Press, 1998).

5. There is an enormous literature supporting these contentions. Examples include: Emily Rosenberg, *Spreading the American Dream: American Economic and Cultural Expansion, 1890–1945* (New York: Hill and Wang, 1982); Frank Costigliola, *Awkward Dominion: American Political, Economic, and Cultural Relations with Europe, 1919–1933* (Ithaca: Cornell University Press, 1984); and Mary Nolan, *Visions of Modernity: American Business and the Modernization of Germany* (New York: Oxford University Press, 1994).

6. My understanding of national identity and narrative has been profoundly influenced by Benedict Anderson, *Imagined Communities: Reflections on the Origin and Spread of Nationalism*, rev. ed. (New York: Verso, 1991), 6–7.

7. Standard accounts of the USIA focus on the bureaucratic structure, rather than the content, of the U.S. information program. See Robert E. Elder, *The Information Machine: The USIA and American Foreign Policy* (Syracuse: Syracuse University Press, 1968); Leo Bogart, *Premises for Propaganda: The United States*

*Information Agency's Operating Assumptions in the Cold War* (New York: Free Press, 1976); Wilson P. Dizard, *The Strategy of Truth: The Story of the U.S. Information Service* (Washington: Public Affairs Press, 1961); and John W. Henderson, *The United States Information Agency* (New York: Praeger, 1969).

8. Harriman to Secretary of State, 20 January 1946, *Foreign Relations of the United States, 1946,* 6:676–78 (hereafter cited as *FRUS*).

9. Smith to Secretary of State, 15 November 1947, *FRUS, 1947,* 6:619–21.

10. U.S. Information Agency Basic Guidance and Planning Paper No. 11, "The American Economy," 16 July 1959, Subject Files on Policy, United States Information Agency Archives, Washington, D.C. (hereafter cited as USIAA).

11. U.S. Information Agency Basic Guidance and Planning Paper No. 11, "The American Economy," 16 July 1959, Subject Files on Policy, USIAA.

12. For more on attempts to influence international labor, see Ray Godson, *American Labor and European Politics: The AFL as a Transnational Force* (New York: Crane, Russak, 1976); Anthony Carew, *Labour under the Marshall Plan: The Politics of Productivity and the Marketing of Management Science* (Manchester: Manchester University Press, 1987); and Michael J. Hogan, *The Marshall Plan: America, Britain, and the Reconstruction of Western Europe, 1947–1952* (New York: Cambridge University Press, 1987).

13. See Feature Packets on Labor, RG 306, Feature Packets, Recurring Themes, boxes 7–14, National Archives II, College Park, Maryland (hereafter cited as NA2).

14. See, for example, "The U.S. Labor and Social Scene as Viewed by the Labor Press in the USSR," RG 59, Records Relating to International Information Activities, 1938–53, Lot 52D389, box 42, NA2. See also Draft Statement for Secretary of State George Marshall on the United States International Information and Cultural Relations Program for his Budget Presentation before the House Appropriations subcommittee, 27 January 1947, RG 59, Lots 587 and 52–48, Records of the Assistant Secretary of State, 1945–50, Office Symbol Files, 1945–50, box 4, NA2.

15. Part III, Notes on Target Areas, Chapter V: Europe in Project Troy Report to the Secretary of State, 1 February 1951, Volume I, RG 59, Lot 52–283, Records of Relating to Project Troy, 1950–51, box 1, NA2.

16. The Indian Image of the United States, A Preliminary View: Part II: The American Way of Life, RG 306, Office of Research, Production Division Research Reports, 1956–59, box 5, NA2.

17. Information Policy on the American Economy, 3 October 1955, Subject Files on Exhibits and Fairs–People's Capitalism, USIAA; Western European Attitudes Related to the People's Capitalism Campaign, 31 December 1956, ibid.; and Japanese Attitudes Related to the People's Capitalism Campaign, 7 October 1957, ibid. See also Themes on American Life and Culture, Basic Guidance and Planning Paper No. 10, 14 July 1959, Subject Files on Policy, USIAA.

18. *A Primer on the American Economy,* USIA Pamphlet Files, USIAA.

19. *A Summary of USIA Operating Assumptions*, Volume 3, RG 306, Office of Research, Special Reports, 1953–63, box 7, PA 3–4, NA2.

20. Basic Guidance and Planning Paper No. 11, "The American Economy," Subject Files on Policy, USIAA; Refutation of Soviet Contention that Socialism Is Higher System than Capitalism, RG 306, Requestor Only Reports, 1956–62, box 2, NA2.

21. See, for example, Notes from the Soviet Provincial Press, October 1956, RG 306, Office of Research, Production Division Research Reports, 1956–59, box 3, NA2. The USIS analyses *Iron Curtain Radio Comment on Voice of America* provide numerous examples. For these reports, see RG 306, Reports and Related Studies, 1948–53, boxes 8 and 9, NA2. On the American military-industrial complex, see Nikita Khrushchev, Speech at Jubilee Session of Supreme Soviet of USSR, 6 November 1957, *Speeches and Interviews on World Problems,* Moscow 1958, found in Selected Statements from Khrushchev's Speeches, Writings, and Interviews (1938–59), RG 306, Office of Research, Special Reports, 1953–63, box 16, NA2.

22. "An Analysis of the Principal Psychological Vulnerabilities in the USSR and of the Principal Assets Available to the US for Their Exploitation," undated, RG 59, Lot 52D432, Bureau of Public Affairs, Office Files of Assistant Secretary Edward W. Barrett, 1950–51, box 5, NA2.

23. *The Truth Crushes Commie Lies,* RG 59, Lot 52D365, Records Relating to International Information Activities, 1938–53, box 61, NA2.

24. *It Happened to Us,* USIA Pamphlets, USIAA.

25. See, for example, Labor Packet–June 1953, RG 306, Feature Packets, Recurring Themes, box 7, NA2; "The New Slavery," USIA Pamphlets, USIAA.

26. *Meet Some Americans at Work,* USIA Pamphlets, USIAA.

27. Information Policy on the American Economy, 3 October 1955, USIA Subject Files on Exhibits and Fairs–People's Capitalism, USIAA.

28. *Thomas Brackett,* USIA Pamphlet Files, USIAA.

29. "Workers Win 10–Year Fight Against Forced Labor," Labor Packet–July 1957, RG 306, Feature Packets, Recurring Themes, box 14, NA2; *The All Union Family,* an AFL-CIO publication included in Labor Packet–February 1957, RG 306, Feature Packets, Recurring Themes, box 11, NA2; *If You Were a Soviet Worker,* USIA Pamphlet Files, USIAA.

30. *American Labor Unions: Their Role in the Free World,* USIA Pamphlets, USIAA.

31. See, for example, George Brown's "Why Should We Be Interested in International Affairs?" Labor Packet–May 1957, RG 306, Feature Packets, Recurring Themes, box 14, NA2. Labor leaders also provided congressional testimony in behalf of the USIA. See the comments of Boris Shishkin, Director of Research, American Federation of Labor, Hearings before a Subcommittee of the Committee on Foreign Relations, United States Senate, 83d Congress, 1st sess., *Overseas Information Programs of the United States,* 1953, 731–43. The State Department also

consulted union leaders. See Briefing for Labor Advisory Committee, 19 December 1950, RG 59, Lot 52D365, Records Relating to International Information Activities, 1938–53, box 61, NA2.

32. "U.S. Labor Unions Promote Political Education for Women," Women's Packet–October 1954, RG 306, Feature Packets, Recurring Themes, box 19, NA2; "Visitor Finds Negroes Active in U.S. Labor Movement," 2 January 1952, *Air Bulletin*, RG 306, *Air Bulletin*, box 2, NA2; William Green, "Organized Labor and the Negro," 16 January 1952, *Air Bulletin*, ibid.

33. "An American Worker's Family," Labor Packet–December 1955, RG 306, Feature Packets, Recurring Themes, box 12, NA2; "Living and Working in a Free Enterprise System," Labor Packet–July 1957, RG 306, Feature Packets, Recurring Themes, box 14, NA2.

34. "Manual Workers Gaining Over White Collar Groups," Labor Packet–October 1956; "Revolution in Income Distribution in the United States," Labor Packet–November 1956; "The Growth of Profit Sharing in the United States," Labor Packet–January 1957; "Low Cost Vacations for American Wage Earners," Labor Packet–July 1956; "American Industry Supports Higher Education," Labor Packet–August 1956; "Fringe Benefits Increase Among American Workers," Labor Packet–December 1956; all found in RG 306, Feature Packets, Recurring Themes, box 14, NA2.

35. Albert Parry, "Soviet Drones," *Wall Street Journal*, 29 July 1954 included in Labor Packet–September 1954, RG 306, Feature Packets, Recurring Themes, box 9, NA2.

36. "Hardships of Workers Behind the Iron Curtain Disclosed," *Air Bulletin*, 23 January 1952, RG 306, *Air Bulletin*, box 2, NA2.

37. "Refugee Returns from Grave of Communist Labor Camps," Women's Packet–November 1954, RG 306, Feature Packets, Recurring Themes, box 19, NA2; Matthew Woll, "Slave Labor Behind the Iron Curtain," *Air Bulletin*, 7 March 1951, RG 306, *Air Bulletin* files, box 2, NA2.

38. *A Study of USIA Operating Assumptions*, Volume 3, RG 306, Office of Research, Special Reports, 1953–63, box 7, TC 19–20, NA2.

39. See, for example, "Wilkins Appointment Highlights Progress of American Negro," Labor Packet–April 1953, RG 306, Feature Packets, Recurring Themes, box 8, NA2.

40. See David Sarnoff, "RCA's Policy of Nondiscrimination in Employment," Labor Packet–December 1955, RG 306, Feature Packets, Recurring Themes, box 12, NA2.

41. "Communicating with the Soviet People: Suggestions for American Tourists and Students," RG 306, Office of Research, Special Reports, 1953–63, box 19, NA2.

42. "East German Women Tell of Privations," Women's Packet–October 1953, RG 306, Feature Packets, Recurring Themes, box 17, NA2; "Women in East Germany," June 1953, ibid.

43. Rare Visitor to USSR Reports on Soviet Woman's Status, August 1953, RG 306, Women's Packet no. 6, RG 306, Feature Packets, Recurring Themes, box 17, NA2.

44. An Analysis of the Principal Psychological Vulnerabilities in the USSR and of the Principal Assets Available to the US for Their Exploitation, undated, RG 59, Lot 52D432, Bureau of Public Affairs, Office Files of Assistant Secretary Edward W. Barrett, 1950–51, box 5, NA2.

45. USIA Policy guidelines asserted, "Since the wage earner role offers the greatest opportunity for distortion overseas, . . . information showing the important place of women in America's labor force should not be presented in isolation from facts showing them first as women." See Basic Guidance and Planning Paper No. 12 on Women's Activities (Part II), 13 August 1959, Subject Files on Policy, USIAA. For more on "the right and wrong way of housework," see "Help for Housewives with Heart Disease," Women's Packet–April 1954, RG 306, Feature Packets, Recurring Themes, box 18, NA2. On Soviet characterizations of American women, see Unsigned letter to Alice K. Leopold, Assistant to the Secretary of Labor, 2 March 1960, RG 306, Requestor Only Reports, 1956–62, box 2, NA2.

46. "A Visit with Mrs. Foster," Women's Packet–April 1953, RG 306, Feature Packets, Recurring Themes, box 16, NA2.

47. For an explanation of the objectives of U.S. trade exhibits, see House Committee on Foreign Affairs, *Strengthening International Relations Through Cultural and Athletic Exchanges and Participation in International Fairs and Festivals,* 84th Congress, 2d sess., 22 June 1956, Committee Print.

48. USIS Madrid to USIA Washington, 5 July 1956, RG 306, Office of Research, Country Project Correspondence, Spain, 1952–63, box 19, NA2.

49. The USIS pamphlet *Sinews of America* provides a cogent example. See USIA Pamphlet Files, USIAA.

50. Testimony from 23 April 1953, *Overseas Information Programs of the United States,* Hearings before a Subcommittee of the Committee on Foreign Relations United States Senate, 83d Congress, 1st sess., pt. 2, 986–87.

51. See the testimony of John A. Nalley, 12 May 1953, *Overseas Information Programs of the United States,* Hearings before a Subcommittee of the Committee on Foreign Relations United States Senate, 83d Congress, 1st sess., pt. 2, 1298–99.

52. USIS Tokyo to USIA Washington, 14 December 1954, RG 306, Office of Research, Country Project Correspondence, 1952–63, box 13, NA2.

53. "Mail Order Catalogues a Hit around the World," *New York Times,* 5 October 1955; *Christian Science Monitor,* 13 April 1956; Frank Sullivan, "Our Best Seller Abroad," *New York Times Magazine,* 13 November 1955.

54. See, for example, Memorandum by W. K. Schwinn and A. A. Micocci, 7 April 1950, RG 59, Lot 53D48, International Information Director's Office, Subject Files, 1949–51, box 115, NA2. See also Emergency Plan for Psychological Offensive (USSR), 11 April 1952, RG 59, Lot 52D432, Bureau of Public Affairs, Office Files of Edward W. Barrett, 1950–51, box 5, NA2.

55. Labor Packets, August 1953 and March-April 1954, RG 306, Feature Packets, Recurring Themes, boxes 7 and 10, USIAA.

56. See, for example, Notes from the Soviet Provincial Press, May and June 1956, RG 306, Production Division Research Reports, 1956–59, box 1, NA2.

57. Walter Hixson, *Parting the Curtain: Propaganda, Culture, and the Cold War, 1945–61* (New York: St. Martin's Press, 1997), 133.

58. Loomis to Washburn, 28 November 1955, RG 306, Office of Research Multi Area (World) Project Files, 1953–63, box 1, NA2.

59. Washburn to McClellan, 3 January 1956, RG 306, Office of the Director, Director's Chronological Files, 1953–64, box 1, microfilm reel 10.

60. Extract of Speech by Theodore S. Repplier, 27 October 1955, RG 306, Office of Research, Multi Area (World) Project Files, 1953–63, box 1, NA2.

61. Excerpt from Speech by Honorable Sherman Adams, 1 December 1955, ibid.

62. *New York Times,* 14–15 February 1956. For the revised text of the "People's Capitalism" exhibit, see USIA Subject Files on Exhibits and Fairs, "People's Capitalism," USIAA.

63. See, for example, "Agency Comments on People's Capitalism Exhibit," 6 March 1956, RG 306, Office of Research Files, Multi Area (World) Project Files, 1953–63, box 1, NA2; "Non-Agency Comments on People's Capitalism Exhibit," 15 March 1956, ibid.

64. *New York Times,* 19 August 1956, 3 September 1956.

65. Streibert to All USIS Posts, 12 June 1956, Subject Files on Exhibits and Fairs–People's Capitalism, USIAA.

66. *Washington Post,* 2 September 1958.

67. *People's Capitalism: The United States Economy in Evolution,* USIA Pamphlet Files, USIAA.

68. The nations surveyed were Great Britain, France, Italy, West Germany, and the Netherlands. See West European Attitudes Related to the People's Capitalism Campaign, 31 December 1956, RG 306, Office of Research, Program and Media Studies, 1956–62, box 1, NA2.

69. Larson to USIS Posts, 1 March 1957, Subject Files on "Disinformation," USIAA.

70. Ibid.

71. A Brief Overview of Recent Survey Findings on the Economic Image of America Abroad, November 1958, RG 306, Office of Research, Program and Media Studies, 1956–62, box 1, NA2.

72. Communist Propaganda and the Brussels Fair, 22 January 1958, RG 306, Office of Research, Production Division Research Reports, 1956–59, box 5, NA2.

## FURTHER READING

Costigliola, Frank. *Awkward Dominion: American Political, Economic, and Cultural Relations with Europe, 1919–1933*. Ithaca: Cornell University Press, 1984.

Friedman, Thomas. *The Lexus and the Olive Tree*. New York: Farrar, Straus & Giroux, 2000.

Hixson, Walter. *Parting the Curtain: Propaganda, Culture, and the Cold War, 1945–1961*. New York: St. Martin's Press, 1997.

Hunt, Michael. *Ideology and U.S. Foreign Policy*. New Haven: Yale University Press, 1987.

Lucas, Scott. *Freedom's War: The American Crusade against the Soviet Union*. New York: New York University Press, 1999.

Nolan, Mary. *Visions of Modernity: American Business and the Modernization of Germany*. New York: Oxford University Press, 1994.

Pells, Richard. *Not Like U.S.: How Europeans Have Loved, Hated, and Transformed American Culture since World War II*. New York: Basic Books, 1997.

Rosenberg, Emily. *Spreading the American Dream: American Economic and Cultural Expansion, 1890–1945*. New York: Hill and Wang, 1982.

The musical is—
and always has been—
America's most political theater.

—John Lahr,
"The Lemon-Drop Kid," 1996

# MUSICALS AND MODERNIZATION: RODGERS AND HAMMERSTEIN'S *THE KING AND I*

CHRISTINA KLEIN

In the late 1950s and early 1960s Yul Brynner starred in two films that imagined the relationship between the United States and the developing world. In 1956 he played the King in *The King and I,* Rodgers and Hammerstein's musical about an English schoolteacher in the royal court of Siam. Four years later he appeared in *The Magnificent Seven,* John Sturges's western about a group of American gunfighters hired by beleaguered Mexican villagers to defend them from a local bandit. Both these films, although set in the nineteenth century, are imbued with what Michael Latham has called the postwar ideology of modernization. Together they suggest the extent to which the conceptual framework of modernization theory, so beloved by postwar social scientists and foreign policymakers, extended beyond the realms of the political elite and suffused contemporary popular culture as well.

Richard Slotkin, in his magisterial three-volume study of the myth of the frontier in American culture, has shown how the western has long served as a bearer of ideology about U.S. expansion, national identity, and the idea of progress. *The Magnificent Seven,* he has argued, offers a fantasy of counterinsurgency modernization. Working within the well-established conventions of the western genre, it anticipates and models the logic of Kennedy's foreign policies in Vietnam: Brynner heads up a group of professional, Green Beret–like killers who cross the border into Mexico, defend a peasant village from the political tyranny of a local warlord, and in a spectacular act of violence—what Slotkin has described as a commando-style "surgical strike" on the village itself—kill the warlord and eliminate the threat to the peasants. Having restored peace, the gunfighters return back across the border, leaving behind a newly Americanized native leadership that will guide the village into the future.[1]

*The King and I* also engages directly with the issue of modernization. Brynner's character here is based on Siam's legendary King Mongkut who opened up his country to Western influence in the 1860s, and the film imagines with some nuance the advantages, as well as the costs, of Westernization. *The King and I* shares with *The Magnificent Seven* certain narrative similarities: although it replaces the band of male gunfighters with Anna Leonowens, a female schoolteacher, *The King and I* tells the story of an Americanized figure, hired because of her specialized skills, who defends a non-Western community from political tyranny and sets it on the road to progress and democracy under a newly Americanized native leadership. But whereas *The Magnificent Seven* employs the language of the western, *The King and I* views modernization through the sentimental lens of the musical. Here, "backward" Siam is transformed through love and friendship, and the premodern is swept away in a spectacular episode of song and dance.

A close reading of *The King and I* in relation to postwar modernization theory allows us to see the musical as an ideological genre on par with, but radically different from, the more familiarly ideological genre of the western. The film scholar Thomas Schatz has distinguished between westerns and musicals by classifying them, respectively, as genres of order and genres of integration. Westerns tend to feature individualized male heroes who embrace a masculine code of self-reliance; their dramatic conflicts are externalized as violence and resolved through the elimination of the threat to the social order. Musicals, in turn, tend to feature a collective hero, usually a couple or a community, in which feminine and familial values dominate. Dramatic conflicts in a musical are expressed as emotion and resolved by the integration of antagonistic characters into a harmonious community, usually through the mechanism of romance. Social readings of these two genres proceed from their respective emphases on the elimination or incorporation of antagonistic forces. The western's ideological power derives largely from the way it imagines violence: who can legitimately use it, against whom, and in the defense of what. The musical's ideological power, in turn, resides in the way it imagines community: the differences among people that can be transcended, the kinds of bonds that can be forged, and the nature of communities that can be created. If the western translates ideology into ritualized forms of action, the musical translates it into structures of feeling: what the western imagines as a deadly gunfight, the musical imagines as a romantic dance. The musical also opens up its ideological workings to include the viewer in ways that the western never does. According to the Broadway lyricist E. Y. (Yip) Harburg, the musical's ideological force arose from two sources: its ability to translate controversial ideas into easily absorbed emotions and the inescapability of song in the age of mass culture. A listener, surrounded by a musical's songs as they circulate on recordings, radio, TV, and film, can easily become caught up in its vision of the world. The particularly infectious quality of the Rodgers and Hammerstein songs opened up them up to widespread participation: designed to be sung by as many people as possible, they invited listeners to sing along with their catchy tunes and rhyming lyrics. This singability allowed audience members to step out of their role as passive observers and temporarily join in the process of community formation that was taking place on stage or on screen.[2]

Given these generic differences, the western and the musical were ideally suited to express two alternative strains of Cold War ideology: the logic of containing communism and the logic of international integration. Diplomatic historians have long recognized containment and integration as dual impulses driving postwar foreign policy, although they have differed in the importance they assign to them. Realists, who emphasize strategic and balance-of-power issues, have generally seen the containment of the Soviet Union as the fundamental principle motivating U.S. foreign policy. Revisionists, in turn, have argued that

Washington was driven by the need to integrate the capitalist nations into a U.S.-dominated international economic order, which would in turn be sustained by the political and military integration of the "free world." Cultural historians of the Cold War, extending the realists' vision of a bipolar and hostile world organized around the principle of difference, have often seen postwar America as dominated by a "containment culture" that policed the boundaries of social, political, and sexual difference. Westerns, with their emphasis on the frontier as a border between civilization and savagery and their resolution of conflict through violence, tend to fit comfortably within this category of containment culture.[3]

I want to suggest that we extend the insights of revisionist diplomatic historians and think about postwar America in terms of a culture of integration instead. No less ideological than containment culture, the culture of integration worked with an alternative set of terms. Integration replaced containment's negative logic of opposition with a more positive vision of alliance. Instead of focusing on a world split in half between enemies, it offered a weblike model of international relations in which the nations of the "free world"—North and South, East and West, developed and developing—were knit together through a network of political and military treaties, trade deals, and flows of foreign aid. As a cultural logic, integration sidestepped containment's metaphors of impermeable barriers—such as the iron and bamboo curtains—and imagined the possibility of forging bonds across the boundaries of differences instead. *The King and I* is an exemplary instance of this postwar culture of integration: it imagines that differences could be transcended rather than policed, and Others could be transformed through an intimate embrace rather than exterminated through violence.

## A NARRATIVE OF MODERNIZATION

*The King and I* was one of the most popular representations of Southeast Asia produced in the 1950s. The second in Rodgers and Hammerstein's trilogy of Asia-Pacific musicals (along with *South Pacific* and *Flower Drum Song*), it opened on Broadway in 1951 with Gertrude Lawrence as Anna and Yul Brynner as the King. The show ran in New York for three years, toured nationally for a year and a half, and played in London for two and a half years. In 1956, 20th Century-Fox faithfully translated the show into a film version, this time pairing Yul Brynner with Deborah Kerr; it won six Academy Awards and its soundtrack remained on the charts for 274 weeks.[4]

*The King and I* had its roots in European imperial and American missionary history. The real Anna Leonowens was an Englishwoman born and raised in colonial India. She worked as a teacher in the royal court of Siam from 1862 to 1867 and wrote two fictionalized accounts of her experiences, *The English Governess at the Siamese Court* (1870) and *The Romance of the Harem* (1873). Margaret Landon, an American, rediscovered Leonowens and her narratives during a decade spent in Siam with her husband, an educational missionary who later went on to work on the Far Eastern staff of the State Department. Landon combined Leonowens's accounts with her own archival research to produce *Anna and the King of Siam,* a fictionalized biography that became a best-seller in 1944. In 1946 20th Century-Fox turned Landon's novel into a nonmusical film of the same name. Rodgers and Hammerstein's version of Anna's story must thus be understood not as an exclusively postwar text, but as part of a narrative tradition that stretches back to the late nineteenth century.[5]

The story of Anna Leonowens and the King of Siam has served since the nineteenth century as America's favorite narrative about Thailand. In writing his libretto, Oscar Hammerstein II retained many of the fundamental pieces of the story that Leonowens, Landon, and the Hollywood screenwriters in 1946 developed. In all the versions, King Mongkut of Siam, seeking a Western education for the royal family, hires the young English widow as a teacher for his large brood of children. Although an Englishwoman, Anna is an Americanized figure who uses the politics and culture of the Civil War—Lincoln's struggle to free the slaves, Harriet Beecher Stowe's *Uncle Tom's Cabin*—as her frame of reference. The King stands on the cusp of a new era: a traditional ruler, he realizes that he must bring Siam into closer conformity with modern Western intellectual and social currents in order to protect the independence of his country and his people. Anna becomes the King's partner in his project, and over the course of her tenure in Siam she educates the King's wives and children in Western habits of behavior and thought. She teaches them Western science and geography, Western social rituals and table manners, Western forms of dress, and Western political ideals. The King's awkward position between tradition and modernity often leads to tensions with Anna, and their relationship is marked by conflicts and disagreements. Eventually, however, the King comes to trust her judgment, and he promotes her from tutor to secretary to political adviser. When the King dies, his son and Anna's most avid student, Prince Chulalongkorn, takes over the throne and expresses his commitment to furthering his father's program of bringing Siam into closer harmony with the West.

Hammerstein's libretto, which he based on Landon's novel and the 1946 screenplay, modified the narrative in several ways. In keeping with his own liberal racial politics, Hammerstein excised much of Leonowens's and Landon's ethnocentric and racist language and bypassed the yellow-peril characterizations of the 1946 film. He downplayed the notion of unbreachable cultural differences and heightened the message of tolerance and mutual understanding. He also turned Leonowens's protofeminist tale of female bonding across the racial divide into a heterosexual romance of unconsummated transracial love. Only in Hammerstein's version does the friendship and mere hint of an attraction between Anna and the King—presented for the first time as an attractive, eroticized man—turn into love. Hammerstein also heightened Anna's Americanness by giving *Uncle Tom's Cabin* a more central role in the narrative. In all its versions, however, the story of Anna and the King is a story of how a Western woman promotes the modernization and democratization of a small Southeast Asian nation: Anna Leonowens is an agent of the West who remakes Siam along Western lines. The repetition of this narrative, from Leonowens's nineteenth-century accounts to Hammerstein's postwar version and into the 1999 Jodie Foster–Chow Yun-fat version, attests to the appeal, for Americans at least, of this model of U.S.-Asian relations.

The twentieth-century popularity of Anna Leonowens's story coincided with the increased geopolitical importance of Thailand to the United States. Although Japanese-occupied Thailand was officially part of the Axis during World War II, when Landon published her novel, the Thai people remained strongly pro-Western and their underground resistance movement welcomed American OSS agents. In the decade between 1946 (when the first film version of *Anna and the King of Siam* was released) and 1956 (when the film version of Rodgers and Hammerstein's *The King and I* was released), Thailand became one of

America's strongest allies on the Asian mainland. After the "loss" of China to communism in 1949, U.S. policymakers increasingly saw the countries of Southeast Asia, in the words of Secretary of State John Foster Dulles, as "the forward positions against which the waves of Communism are beating and where the issues of war and peace, of freedom and captivity, hang in precarious balance." Within this increasingly volatile region, Americans saw Thailand as a unique island of stability. Alone among its neighbors, Thailand had remained free from European colonial domination, which meant the Thai people did not harbor the anti-Western sentiments that hampered U.S. dealings with other nations in the region. It was also the only Southeast Asian nation not wracked by nationalist and Communist-supported revolutions, and was thus seen by Washington as a dike against the surrounding "waves" of destabilization. When Thailand's rulers made clear their pro-Western and anti-Communist orientation, the United States responded with generous financial support. In 1950 the Truman administration pledged $10 million in military, economic, and technical aid to Thailand, and over the course of the 1950s the Eisenhower administration poured in hundreds of millions of dollars more.[6]

Although most of this money went to the Thai police and military forces, who turned Thailand into a repressive police state, the official goal of this aid was to help Thailand modernize and Westernize. The United States began funding cultural and scientific programs in Thailand with its first infusion of aid in 1950. Washington brought in technical experts to help improve Thailand's agriculture, irrigation, transportation, communications, harbor facilities, commerce, and public health. It also funded educational advisers and established an American-supervised language center for teaching English. These programs established a tutelary relationship between the two nations, with the United States assuming the position of teacher and guide to modernization, and Thailand the position of eager student.[7]

U.S. officials in these years grounded their policies toward Thailand in the principles of modernization theory, which beginning in the late 1940s and 1950s became a primary conceptual framework for thinking about U.S. relations with the developing world. The U.S.-assisted modernization of Asia did not begin in the postwar period, of course: Japanese modernizers had sought U.S. assistance after the Meiji restoration of 1868, as had Thai reformers after 1900 and Chinese reformers following the collapse of the Qing dynasty in 1911. But it was not until the Cold War that modernization theory fully developed in the United States as both an academic field and a political project. Universities and think tanks gave it an institutional foundation, government officials translated it into foreign policy, and W. W. Rostow popularized it in his "Non-Communist Manifesto," *The Stages of Economic Growth* (1960). Rostow and his colleagues at the Center for International Studies at MIT were universalists: they posited that all societies existed on a singular continuum between "tradition" and "modernity" and that each one must inevitably progress from one condition to the other through a clearly marked set of stages. As policy advisers they aimed to intervene in the process in order to accelerate it and direct it in ways compatible with U.S. interests. Modernization theory thus intersected neatly with the larger Cold War goals of integration and containment: by helping "backward" nations become "modern," Americans hoped to alleviate the conditions that made communism an attractive option and thus secure these nations' participation in the "free world" alliance. For these theorists, modernization looked very much like Americanization: taking the United States as the epitome of the modern state, they held it up as a model for developing nations to emulate, and they formulated policies designed to reproduce American social, political, and economic structures in developing nations. According to Rostow, U.S. history offered a "blueprint" that the developing world must inevitably follow.[8]

Modernization theory, far from being a postwar invention, belonged rather to a long tradition within U.S. foreign policy discourse. As part of a continuing effort to deny its own imperialism, the United States has regularly explained its overseas expansion in terms of progress and modernization. In contrast to European imperialism, which many Americans saw as based on naked exploitation and self-interest, U.S. expansion was seen as fostering economic development, infrastructure modernization, political liberalization, and the promotion of free trade. In reality, however, modernization theory continued many of the precepts of the "civilizing mission" which had underwritten Western colonialism. It assumed that the nonwhite portions of the world were backward, that they needed to be educated and uplifted by the West, and that they would need long periods of supervision before they would be ready for complete self-government. Modernization theory thus recycled many of colonialism's legitimating ideas: it saw the developing world as trapped in a timeless past, unable to help itself, and bound to follow Western models. In contrast to nineteenth-century imperial ideology, however, modernization theory eschewed an explicit ideology of racial hierarchy in favor of a more social scientific ideology of Western developmental superiority. Not coincidentally, modernization theory emerged simultaneously with decolonization. It offered a means to continue Western access and authority, and third world dependency, in the absence of formal colonial ties.[9]

Culture played an important role in postwar modernization projects. Academic and policy experts sought to create not only new social, political, and economic systems in the developing world, but also new men and women. As part of their effort to achieve this goal, U.S. officials launched a broad range of cultural diplomacy initiatives, from the Fulbright educational exchange program to the United States Information Agency–sponsored tour of the Family of Man photography exhibition. Programs such as these aimed to eliminate doubts about America's global intentions and deflect charges of imperialism by educating other nations' elite classes about American history, culture, and values. Through such educational and cultural exchanges, the United States tried to demonstrate that it shared a fundamental body of beliefs and aspirations with other countries, and that as a result these nations should not fear it as a coercive outside power, but rather accept it as the strongest member of an organic community. These initiatives aimed to create a sense of common ground between the United States and developing nations, which would in turn provide a field in which modernization programs could take root and grow. According to USIA director Theodore Streibert, the agency aimed to "emphasize the community of interest that exists among freedom-loving peoples and show how American objectives and policies advance the legitimate interests of such people." Cultural diplomacy programs also reinforced the universalizing assumptions of modernization theory, by offering proof that in spite of their differences, Americans and people in developing nations could learn to understand each other.[10]

Like modernization theory itself, these cultural programs trailed long roots into the history of U.S. global expansion. Since the turn of the century, U.S. officials had funded cultural and educational programs as part of their efforts to "modernize" Asia. After the Boxer Rebellion of 1900, Washington used the Chinese government's forced indemnity payments to set up scholarships for Chinese students studying at American institutions. And as part of its colonial policy in the Philippines, the United States established a comprehensive educational system based on the American public school system. By instructing Filipinos and Chinese in the English language and American culture, these programs sought to facilitate the achievement of U.S. interests in Asia through nonmilitary, nonpolitical means. While both the Philippine education system and the Boxer scholarships were held up as proof of American benevolence and commitment to modernization, they also served as cultural instruments for pursuing U.S. economic and political interests abroad.

*The King and I* tells a classic story of sentimental modernization, in which a white woman guides the Westernization of a small Asian country. According to Vicente Rafael, the political discourse of sentimental modernization stretches at least as far back as the conquest of the Philippines. It represents colonialism as a feminized project of modernizing backward peoples by inculcating in them a set of habits and a consciousness associated with middle-class domesticity. Instead of exterminating backward peoples through savage war, as imagined by the frontier discourse of continental expansion, sentimental modernization called for their incorporation through a process of nurturance and education. As a sentimental modernizer, Anna Leonowens wields her influence in Siam not through violence or force or political coercion, but through the power of love and the tools of culture.[11]

In keeping with the logic of sentimental modernization, Anna employs the ideology of middle-class domesticity as a progressive force, a body of values whose acceptance will facilitate Siam's transition into modernity. Much of Anna and the King's relationship revolves around a quarrel over whether she will live in a separate house, as originally promised, or within the palace—that is, in the harem. This argument serves as a device through which the multiple differences between Anna and the King can be animated—differences of sex, gender, culture, religion, and status. The debate over competing models of sexuality and domestic life serves primarily, however, as a vehicle for their larger argument over traditional vs. modern political authority. Although the King seeks to modernize his country, he expects to continue exercising power as an authoritarian ruler. The harem serves as the concrete manifestation of his traditional authority: he rules absolutely over a household of hundreds of women and children who must do his bidding unquestioned, who can never oppose him, and who show their submission by prostrating themselves in his presence. Anna, in turn, champions Western liberal political ideology, whose abstractions she communicates via the terms of middle-class domesticity and sexuality: she uses romantic love, monogamy, the nuclear family, and the private home as her examples for explaining the rights of the individual and of the rule of law. Anna's critique of the harem in favor of monogamous romantic love, therefore, becomes the core of her challenge to the King's premodern political authority.

With *The King and I,* what Mary Louise Pratt has called the American "narrative of anti-conquest" reached its apex. Far from being an imperialist, Anna helps preserve Siam's independence by deflecting the unwanted attentions of a colonial power. Like the modernization theorists, Rodgers and Hammerstein found receptive audiences among postwar Americans because they told a familiar story that tapped into a long-standing American and Western tradition of imagining overseas expansion as the liberalization of oppressive societies. Rodgers and Hammerstein's Anna, like MIT's Walt Rostow, was only the latest in a long line of Europeans and Americans who claimed to be modernizing the East by educating it in the ways of the West.[12]

## MUSICAL NUMBERS AS SPECTACLES OF MODERNIZATION

Anna Leonowens is an explicitly feminized modernizer whose power derives from her access to the sphere of culture. She is a teacher, and she transforms Siam by bringing in new ideas. Margaret Landon, in her novelized biography of Leonowens, gave Anna an internal monologue in which she voiced her goal of transforming the East through Western education. In it, Anna imagined herself teaching not just a few children but the whole nation: she dreamed of "shaping" the "child mind" of a "future king" and thus enabling him to lead "a new and better world." Burning with a secular sense of "mission," she imagines herself a "liberator" who will "fight with knowledge" rather than guns to instill a respect for "human freedom" and "human dignity" in her charges. Rodgers and Hammerstein's Anna extends this characterization. In her hands, modernization becomes a maternal task of shaping the consciousness of children and students by introducing them to Western, and specifically American, culture.[13]

As a musical, *The King and I* communicates much of its meaning through its deployment of song and dance. Its musical numbers serve as spectacles of education and cultural transformation, reworking the ideology of modernization into utopian moments of community formation. I want to consider three numbers and read them as successive steps in the process of modernization: the first, an appeal to the West for education by the Siamese; the second, the process of education itself; and the third, the results of that education displayed.

"The March of the Royal Siamese Children" takes place early in the narrative. Soon after arriving in Siam Anna threatens to leave because the King has broken his promise of a separate house; in this number the King entices Anna to stay by showing off his large and charming brood of children. The number shows that Anna does not impose modernization on the Siamese against their will, but rather that they request it. An orchestral number with no singing or dialogue, it opens with Anna and the King alone together and progresses as the King directs a small throng of his children, her future pupils, to greet Anna. The children enter the room one by one, quiet, stately, and lavishly dressed; they salute Anna with a bow, touch their heads to her hands in a sign of respect, then back away from her and sit down a few feet away, at no time turning their backs to her. As the number ritualistically proceeds, Anna's changing expression reveals her emotional response: the children's quiet charm and beauty win her heart, she falls in love with them, and she agrees to remain. Even as it bathes the scene in a warm glow of feeling, the number establishes a hierarchical relation of teacher and student between Anna and the Siamese. The Siamese children, although charming and appealing, are mute; they seek enlightenment and guidance from the representative of the West, who alone possesses knowledge. Employing a standard trope of colonial discourse, the number displays the Siamese invitation to the West to intervene.

"Getting to Know You," which follows soon after, takes place in the palace schoolroom as Anna teaches a group of children and wives a geography lesson. This number displays the process of education that the children have requested and figures it in terms of cultural exchange and transformation. With this song Anna inculcates a liberal internationalist perspective in her students as she introduces them to Western knowledge: while she sings of her pleasure in "getting to know" and "like" the people of Thailand, she teaches the children Western social rituals so that they may behave as Westerners. The number, and the educational process itself, work through mimicry: first Anna sings and shows them how to shake hands and curtsey, then the children reproduce her words and her movements. After Anna teaches them her dance, the children, with the aid of a dancer, teach her a Siamese fan dance, thereby enacting a process of cultural exchange in which the West and the East learn to understand each other's culture. The equality of the exchange, however, is deceptive: although Anna learns a new dance, the goal of the scene is to change the Siamese, not her. The use of sound effects in the original stage version marks the profound nature of their transformation: up to this point, the women and children's voices have been represented by orchestral sounds, and it is only as they learn English in this scene that they begin to speak lines of intelligible dialogue. On the one hand this can be seen as an attempt at cultural verisimilitude, an effort to avoid misrepresenting the Siamese as already speaking English. On the other hand, however, it suggests that only through Westernization do the Siamese acquire the markers of full humanity, the ability to speak and to represent themselves.[14]

"Getting to Know You" presents education as a process of East-West community formation. Anna uses song and dance to transform the children into an intellectual community, a Westernized native elite that can articulate Western ideas in a Western language. Emotional as well as intellectual ties forge the bonds of this community, and sentiment and pleasure work as the mechanisms of the children's transformation. The number presents teaching as an act and expression of love and as a process of creating emotional bonds. Anna does not drill the children mercilessly; rather, she plays with them, expresses her fondness for them, and at the end of the number, sweeps several of them up in her arms to hug them. The children are willing to change because Anna makes their transformation a pleasurably emotional experience.

The number also makes clear the profound transformation in consciousness that this education ushers in. In the geography lesson that precedes the singing and dancing, Anna compares two maps of the world. The first map depicts Siam as large and central, surrounded by an unfamiliar outline of other nations and accompanied by a drawing of the King (Figure 1); Lady Thiang, the King's head wife, explains that it shows the superior wealth and power of Siam in relation to its poorer neighbor, Burma. As Anna tells the children that this map is over twenty-five years old and thus hopelessly outdated, she pulls down a second map, "just arrived from England," which the viewer instantly recognizes as an "accurate" map of the world (Figure 2). When Anna points out Siam on this new map, now small and marginal, the children cry out in protest, but after she shows them that England is smaller yet, they acquiesce. The number proper then begins, with the singing and dancing taking place against the backdrop of the new map. With this new map, Anna replaces the children's distorted local knowledge with a more accurate global perspective that will form the basis of their new East-West community. The maps, like the song that follows, show Anna replacing the children's parochial national consciousness with a more cosmopolitan global one—her education situates the children in relation to the world at large and not just in relation to the nation.

*The King and I* has as its showpiece number "The Small House of Uncle Thomas," in which the Siamese display the effects of their Western education. Two main themes converge in this number: the idea of modernization as cultural transformation and the idea of domesticity as democratic political ideology. The King has approached Anna for advice about a developing crisis: British imperialists are threatening to make Siam a "protectorate" of the crown, using its supposed lack of civilization as a pretext. Anna, outraged, advises the King to outwit the British by inviting them to see a display of how civilized Siam has already become. This display takes the form of a twenty-minute musical number, a show-within-a-show Siamese version of Harriet Beecher Stowe's *Uncle Tom's Cabin*. Performed before an audience that includes Anna, the King, and the British officials, the number condenses Stowe's novel into a single episode in which the slave Eliza and her baby escape from Simon Legree by running across the frozen Ohio River to join her husband George.

This number marks one of Hammerstein's greatest departures from the previous versions of Anna Leonowens's story. Leonowens had used

Figures 1 and 2. Modernization as a process of cultural education: Anna replaces the local Siamese knowledge of the world . . . with a global perspective that will form the basis of their new East-West community. (Top: Museum of Modern Art/Film Stills Archive; bottom: Photofest)

Stowe's sentimental abolitionism as the intellectual foundation for her own condemnation of Thai slavery and the harem, and she modeled some of her characters and episodes on those in Stowe's novel; Landon, in her 1944 novelized biography, played up the references to Stowe. The 1946 film version introduced the idea of Anna as an anti-imperialist figure who helps the King ward off European imperialism by staging a show, but in that version the show is a display of Siamese history and is only referred to rather than presented visually. Hammerstein expanded on these references to Stowe's novel and turned the staged performance of *Uncle Tom's Cabin* into the heart of his own show.

Within the plot of the musical, this number exerts incredible political power. At one level, it preserves Siam's independence. The British, convinced that Siam is indeed on the road to Westernization, withdraw their threat of colonization and depart, leaving Siam the independent country that U.S. and Thai Cold Warriors would later hail as the "land of the free." At another level, it creates a public forum for the only direct opposition to the King's authoritarian rule. The performance is written and narrated by the Burmese concubine Tuptim, an early convert to Anna's domestic ideology; she is in love with a young countryman and wants to escape the King's sexual slavery to form a monogamous relationship. Anna had earlier given Tuptim a copy of Stowe's novel as a way to comfort her and reinforce her aversion to slavery, and from it Tuptim selected the scene of escape and marital reunification that forms the basis of the show. Tuptim uses the stage performance as an opportunity to denounce the King and make a public appeal for her freedom: after joyfully announcing the death of "King" Simon Legree in the icy waters of the Ohio River, Tuptim breaks out of character as the narrator and declaims to the King and assembled guests, "I too am glad for the death of King. Of any King who pursues slave who is unhappy and tries to join her lover!" At the end of the number, Tuptim puts her beliefs into action and runs away with her lover. This act of political protest, like the defeat of the British imperialists, results from Anna's education. In giving Tuptim a copy of Stowe's novel, Anna has given her a model for political rebellion, a manual for opposing her own slavery and claiming her individual right to marriage. Anna's teaching results in the discourse of romantic love functioning as the only effective way to articulate opposition to the

King's authoritarian rule. Tuptim, by insisting on her right to monogamous sexuality, becomes the first member of the royal household to fully embrace modernity.

What is it about this number that makes it such a powerful political—specifically anti-imperialist and anti-authoritarian—weapon? First, the number proves that Siam is becoming like the West by offering a spectacle of the integration of Western and "Siamese" cultural forms. While the narrative of escaping from slavery and all the characters are recognizably American, the music, costumes, and style of dance and acting are all "traditional" Siamese (by way of Broadway): Eliza wears a saffron-colored costume and golden pagoda headdress, Uncle Tom sports a carved mask, and his cabin has the turned-up wings of traditional Thai architecture. A group of the King's wives perform the number's music on Thai instruments, and Tuptim narrates in a slightly awkward English that rephrases "Uncle Tom's Cabin" as "The Small House of Uncle Thomas." The number brings to fruition the lessons in Westernization that began in the classroom scene of "Getting to Know You": putting their education on display, the characters emphasize the role of snow and ice—the point of Anna's geography lesson—in helping Eliza escape across the Ohio River. The number is a spectacular melding of American and Siamese cultural forms, both for the internal audience of British colonialists and for the viewer. It develops the idea of a U.S.-Asian intellectual community from "Getting to Know You" and presents Siam as sharing a cultural common ground with the United States.

In doing so, the number translates some of the assumptions of modernization theory into a spectacle of song and dance. As the culmination of the show's process of national transformation via education and cultural exchange, the number shares a certain logic with Cold War cultural diplomacy programs. Both embrace the idea of culture as a medium of political communication and revolve around the idea that the United States does not force its influence on other nations, but rather engages in a mutual exchange of ideas. More pointedly, Anna offers American history and culture as a universal blueprint which the more backward Siamese can follow in order to progress up the ladder of modernity. By giving the Siamese American culture, Anna gives them a vehicle with which to express their political desire for independence from colonial domination. She gives them a fictional incarnation of American political history—the abolitionist movement—onto which they can graft their own political dilemmas. She seems to suggest that only by using the language and forms of American culture can the Siamese effectively speak their anticolonial and democratic desires. That Siam retains its political independence as a result of this indigenous retelling of an American story suggests that the United States offers a model of progress that the decolonizing world can and should follow.

What is one to make of Hammerstein's decision to give the show's most prominent number over to an abolitionist drama and to link it to the cause of anti-imperialism? What might it have meant to invoke the history of American slavery, set within a Southeast Asian context, in 1951? Actually, this invocation of abolitionism in the 1950s is not quite so odd as it first appears: by the late 1940s the whole idea of slavery had already been resurrected and put into the service of the Cold War as a familiar framework through which to comprehend the unfamiliar situations that the Cold War gave rise to. From the earliest days of the Cold War, Truman had made "slavery" one of his key synonyms for Soviet communism, and since then it had become entrenched in the American political vocabulary. NSC 68, one of the basic statements of Cold War foreign policy, invoked slavery to mark the distinction between Communist and non-Communist nations—"There is a basic conflict between the idea of freedom under a government of laws, and the idea of slavery under the grim oligarchy of the Kremlin"—and presidential candidate John F. Kennedy, like Anna Leonowens, compared himself to Lincoln as he conflated nineteenth-century slavery with twentieth-century communism: "In the election of 1860 Abraham Lincoln said the question was whether this nation could exist half-slave or half-free. In the election of 1960, and with the world around us, the question is whether the world will exist half-slave or half-free."[15]

As a metaphor for communism, "slavery" became linked in Cold War rhetoric with both "imperialism" and the "Oriental." In an attempt to discredit communism and link it with the collapsing European empires, American political leaders regularly described Soviet domination in Eastern Europe and Soviet aspirations in the developing world as "imperialistic" and affiliated communism with the "Oriental" qualities of Soviet secretiveness and conspiracy. At the same time, these invocations of slavery served as an inspiring history lesson. Like the many cultural diplomacy efforts that addressed the question of American racism, they were part of an effort to acknowledge and lay to rest a dark period in the American past by suggesting that the worst wrongs of racial oppression had been resolved a hundred years ago. These references to slavery suggested that America was best represented by its traditions of antiracist activism rather than by its racist, slaveholding history and its lingering consequences. This rhetorical strategy of defining the United States in opposition to slavery was part of the larger effort to identify it as a revolutionary force in the world, rather than ceding that status to the Soviet Union.[16]

The theme of Western education unfolds through these three numbers, from an appeal for education by the Siamese in "The March of the Royal Siamese Children," through its enactment in "Getting to Know You," to its fruition on stage before British imperialists in "The Small House of Uncle Thomas." Throughout, this process of education has been figured in cultural—as opposed to military or conventionally political—terms: the embrace of Western, specifically American, cultural forms marks the successful modernization of the country. Because Anna works in the realm of culture, she remains untainted by charges of "imperialism"; in fact, the cultural transformations she initiates protect Siam from imperialism. Feelings are what her cultural education produces: feelings of friendship for her as a figure of the West, feelings of romantic love that undercut the King's authority. This collaboration of culture and sentiment, linked as it is with the overall feminization of the idea of progress, serves to legitimate the principles of modernization by stripping them of any imperialist overtones of force, coercion, and exploitation. Anna's explicit anti-imperialism—an invention of the postwar versions of the story—and its expression through the deployment of American culture serve to establish American-oriented modernization as a clear alternative to imperialism and as an agent of political independence. But while *The King and I* rejects imperialism's methods of outright domination and rule, it does not reject the principle of wholesale transformation under and according to Western standards. Rather, the entire narrative revolves around achieving some of the ends of imperialism through nonimperial means.

Anna's effort to bring Siam into harmony with the West culminates in the number "Shall We Dance?", in which she teaches the King to polka in celebration of their success at fending off the British. The scene serves as the culmination of the sexual tension that has been building up between them and, like that sexual tension, is another of Hammerstein's inventions. The scene opens by reiterating the equation between Western gender roles and Western respect for individual rights that Anna has been insisting on all along. Anna and the King, seated in an empty ballroom, debate the relations between men and women: the King argues for the harem, a hierarchical relation of male dominance, while Anna argues for monogamous marriage, a more egalitarian relation between the sexes.

As part of her argument in favor of marriage, Anna introduces the polka as a ritual of Western courtship, an initiation into the Western sexual, and by implication political, order. She begins to dance by herself and the King, transfixed, looks at her with desire and joins in as she sings about dancing with a lover. He demands to learn this dance and Anna complies, teaching him the polka's "1-2-3-and" rhythm; after some humorous interplay, he catches on and they dance together, only to stop abruptly when the King declares that they are not dancing the way he saw the "Europeans" dance that evening. In the film, a long pause follows as the music stops and the camera frames the two in a close shot: Anna slowly admits the King's point, and the King, looking her straight in the eye and with his hand rigidly outstretched in an unmistakably phallic gesture, takes her in a firm, close embrace around the waist; they look at each other intently, their breasts heave, and when the music erupts they begin to dance and whirl around the room (Figure 3). The number is intensely erotic: Anna wears a low-cut gown that, for the first time, displays her in a sexual manner, while the King wears a loose costume that exposes his hairless chest and bare feet; their dancing brings their bodies into close and active contact. The dance enacts the key moment of couple formation: in their first and only musical number together—and the last number of the show—Anna and the King finally surmount the barriers of race, sex, and culture that have kept them at odds for so long.

This number works as a spectacular moment of East-West integration, as the Western woman and the Asian King coordinate themselves with each other through the shared effort of the dance. Their voices and their movements bind them together into a harmonious unit, their

Figure 3. Anna initiates the King into the Western sexual, and by implication political, order with a polka. (Museum of Modern Art/Film Stills Archive)

synchronized bodies offering a physical manifestation of a joint effort undertaken to express a common sentiment. Their exaggerated costumes express their absolute difference from each other as Victorian lady and Oriental despot, yet at the same time each one's opulence complements the other visually. It is a moment of perfect understanding between East and West, as Anna teaches, the King learns, and they communicate their feelings for each other through words and music, looks and touches.

This number brings to a climax the processes of cultural transformation initiated in "Getting to Know You." It is structured as an educational moment: Anna teaches the King how to polka, showing him the steps, the beat, and teaching him the words to the song. Like the children earlier on, the King mimics Anna's words and movements, only this time he repeats romantic words about individuals falling in love. Anna sings the first chorus of the song alone; the second time around, the King, having learned the words, joins in, finishing in harmony with Anna the lines that she had begun alone. As in "Getting to Know You," sentiment works here as the medium of education: the King wants to learn the polka because the respect and friendship he feels for Anna are turning into love. However, the veneer of cultural exchange has dropped away, and the King demands to dance just like the Europeans do.

Extending the dynamic of "The Small House of Uncle Thomas," "Shall We Dance?" offers a final spectacle of Siam's Westernization. As Anna converts the King to her domestic ideology of romantic love, she converts him also to her political ideology of respect for individual rights. When he demands that Anna teach him how to dance, the King demands that she teach him how to express with his body the very ideology that he rejects with his mind, and as he learns the form of this Western ritual, he imbibes its underlying content as well. The King performs his love for Anna in Western liberal and romantic rather than Oriental despotic form. The dance expresses Anna's liberal belief in individual rights and equality: unlike the relations between men and women of the harem, in which the women must prostrate themselves before the King, here the man and the woman stand and face each other as partners. The very song they sing—"Shall We Dance?"—takes the form of a request that may be accepted or rejected rather than the King's characteristic commands to "Eat, eat, eat," "Sit, sit, sit," or "Teach, teach, teach." The scene represents a moment of delicate balance between Anna and the King—he still has the power to command her, but he commands her to teach him the objective correlative of Western liberal ideology, the same ideology that enabled Tuptim to defy his authority publicly.

The ideological power of this number, and of the musical as a genre, derives from its ability to invite the viewers to participate in the events taking place on screen. Just as the King is drawn in to Anna's liberal political ideology by joining in her song and dance, so the viewer is led to embrace the ideals of international integration and third world modernization by our own sense of participation. We are first drawn in by the physicality of the number. As the dancers whirl around the room, the camera moves with them and seems to move us, too, so that we share in their sense of motion and exhilaration. Their obvious pleasure in dancing together is infectious—it spills out into the audience and makes us want to dance, too. The billowing fabric of Anna's dress has an almost tactile quality that, when combined with the dancers' exposed bodies, offers an unexpected sense of physical intimacy. The educational quality of the number also invites us in. As the King learns the words to the song and the steps to the dance, so do we, and we can not help but at least mentally sing along. The number gives us the sense that we are participating—joyfully—in the King's political transformation and that we, too, can join the mixed-race, multinational community that is being forged on screen.

"Shall We Dance?" marks the turning point in Siam's modernization. The number comes to a crashing halt when the King's aides drag in Tuptim, whom they caught trying to run away with her lover, and hold her spread-eagle and face down on the floor (Figure 4). The King pushes Anna away and, furious at Tuptim's challenge to his sexual and political authority, seizes a whip. As he raises it to strike Tuptim, Anna cries angrily, "You've never loved anyone . . . You *are* a barbarian." Anna accuses the King of acting not out of love but out of brute power; he wants to whip Tuptim not because she has made him jealous, but because she has defied his absolute authority. Anna condemns him as a barbarian for his failure—inseparable in Anna's mind—to love in the Western fashion and to recognize Tuptim's rights as an individual.[17]

Anna's accusation traps the King by demanding that he finally choose between modernization and tradition. Desirous of Westernization yet hesitant to renounce the sexual and authoritarian underpinnings of his rule, the King snaps: he throws the whip to the ground and runs from the room, clutching his heart. He cannot bring himself to trample on Tuptim's right as an individual to love whomever she chooses. He realizes that the modernization he has set in motion has destroyed his ability to rule in his traditional manner, that the force of Westernization has proved more powerful than himself. Recognizing Anna's responsibility for the King's collapse, the Prime Minister shouts at her, "You have destroyed King . . . He cannot be anything

Figure 4. The King choosing between tradition and modernity. (Courtesy The Rodgers and Hammerstein Organization)

that he was before. You have taken all this away from him." In Anna's hands the romantic musical number becomes a political tool, a weapon capable of toppling a head of state—her polka kills the King.[18]

The musical concludes a few minutes later, as the King lies on his deathbed and his more democratically inclined son—and Anna's protégé—takes over the throne. In his first proclamation as ruler of Siam, Prince Chulalongkorn declares that henceforth Siam will be governed with greater respect for the individual and that no longer will the Siamese have to prostrate themselves before the king. He proscribes the physical manifestation of his father's authoritarian rule—"No bowing like toad. No crouching. No crawling"—and replaces it with the physical expression of respect between individuals that "Shall We Dance?" introduced: "You will stand with shoulders square back, and chin high . . . face king with proud expression . . . looking in each other's faces with kindness of spirit, with eyes meeting eyes in equal gaze, with bodies upright." In calling for individuals to stand upright and face each other with mutual respect, he repudiates his father's authoritarian rule, embodied in the image of Tuptim held prostrate on the floor awaiting her whipping, and institutionalizes the politically liberal image of Anna and the King dancing together. By making his first political act in effect an emancipation proclamation, Chulalongkorn suggests that Siam has learned the lessons of *Uncle Tom's Cabin* and will henceforth follow the blueprint of American history.[19]

Chulalongkorn stands as a model of the enlightened, democratically inclined leadership that Washington hoped would be produced by its modernizing mission. The Prince, as the dying King acknowledges with ambivalent pride, has been "trained for Royal government" by a Westerner. Chulalongkorn meets the requirements that U.S. policymakers developed for the nationalist leaders they cultivated in Southeast Asia throughout the 1950s: like Phibun in Thailand, Magsaysay in the Philippines, and Diem in Vietnam, Chulalongkorn is an indigenous leader sympathetic to the West, imbued with the ideals of individualism and individual rights, yet thoroughly native even down to his dress, and youthful enough to lead his nation into the future. These pro-U.S. leaders were crucial not only for supporting U.S. policies in the region but also for helping to shield the United States from accusations of imperialism: as one key policy memo explained in 1949, "The long colonial tradition in Asia has left the peoples of that area suspicious of Western influence. We must approach the problem [of communism in Asia] from the Asiatic point of view in so far as possible and refrain from taking the lead in movements which must of necessity be of Asian origin. It will therefore be to our interest wherever possible to encourage the peoples of India, Pakistan, the Philippines and other Asian states to take the leadership in meeting the common problems of the area."[20]

With the leadership of the fictional Siam now in the hands of a mere boy, Anna survives at the end of the musical as the last adult authority figure. Acceding to a young princess's plea that she not let them "fall down in darkness," Anna decides to stay on as caretaker to oversee Siam's transition to modernity. As a maternal figure and teacher, Anna becomes the ideal representative of the United States as a modernizing force in Asia. Her goal has been to reproduce herself in the children, to mold them in her own image, so that their ideas and values echo hers: her job has been to produce a new nation by producing children who possess a new consciousness. Anna's mothering and teaching work as forces of what Richard Brodhead has called "disciplinary intimacy." As forms of loving education, they establish an exemplary hegemonic relationship: they achieve their goals through sentiment rather than through physical force and by inculcating a desire on the part of their objects to behave in a certain way. They suggest power exercised not through direct political or military control, but through relations of exchange and influence. Anna's influence, like American-guided modernization, results in local leaders governing themselves but always according to Anna's precepts. In the Cold War battle for men's minds, parental love and a teacher's dedication become the most appropriate forms of power. Mothers and teachers are the representatives of the West presented as best suited to the task of nurturing, guiding, and shaping a new international consciousness.

## RECEPTION

*The King and I,* according to this close reading, was clearly imbued with the geopolitical ideals of modernization and integration. But such a textual analysis often raises questions about authorial intention and audience reception. Did Rodgers and Hammerstein really intend their musical to resonate with contemporary political affairs? Did audiences actually read it in relation to the Cold War? While I have not found any smoking-gun document in which either Rodgers or Hammerstein lays out the show's ideological agenda—and would have no reason to accept it as the definitive word on the show even if I did—there is plenty of evidence that Hammerstein engaged himself with contemporary world politics. Hammerstein was a staunch supporter of world federalism, which during the 1950s marked the left-most boundary of acceptable political discourse. He joined the world government movement in 1947, the year that the Truman Doctrine established containment as one of the twin poles of postwar foreign policy, and he actively promoted its goals until his death in 1960. He used his celebrity to educate the public about international issues and to advocate for a global political system that would bind Americans more tightly to other nations around the world. He served as vice-president of the United World Federalists, delivered public speeches on world government, and wrote articles for the *Saturday Review* and the *Congressional Digest.* Norman Cousins, the *Saturday Review* editor who, as president of the United World Federalists, worked with Hammerstein, identified him as "one of the first starry-eyed and divinely discontented astronomers to bring the Federalist concept to our attention" and praised his ability to bring out the "human" dimensions of internationalism. While this is not evidence of any intentionality on Hammerstein's part to infuse the musical with political ideologies, it does suggest that he had a well-developed political consciousness and more than a passing interest in Cold War geopolitics. Richard Rodgers, for his part, gestured toward a political reading when asked to explain his and Hammerstein's decision to do the show: they were drawn, he said, by "the theme of democratic teachings triumphing over autocratic rule."[21]

As for contemporary audiences, one can imagine many reasons why they enjoyed *The King and I:* its romantic narrative, memorable songs, talented actors, and beautiful costumes and set design. Unfortunately, there exists no documentation that records the views of the millions of people who saw the show or the movie or who listened to its songs. Those responses that were recorded, however, suggest that some audience members did connect *The King and I* to the contemporary political world, despite its nineteenth-century setting. Some reviewers praised the musical for its "social commentary" and its willingness to engage with "serious" issues, while others condemned it as a "sermon" and complained that its songs tended to dissolve in a "paroxysm of social commentary." A number of reviewers saw *The King and I* as grappling with the same issues that policymakers did when they looked out at Asia: the "conflict between East and West," the need to protect "individual . . . rights," and the need for "social reforms" in non-Western countries. Some saw the King as a "dictator" and Anna as an instructor in the ways of "democracy." Others read it as a parable of modernization and either approved of Anna as a bearer of "progress" to a "backward country" or questioned the validity of her nineteenth-century vision of the West as "the giver of light and knowledge" to the East. At least one reviewer connected the show to decolonization, by noting the show's relevance at a time when "Eastern lands have impinged themselves" on the American consciousness through the "widening independence movement" and the "fight against what they regard as Western imperialism and domination."[22]

Newsmagazines often used the familiar story of Anna and the King to introduce their readers to Thailand as an important U.S. ally. They frequently identified the current king of Thailand as the great-grandson of Anna's employer and the grandson of her protégé. In 1954, *Newsweek* invoked the show to teach its readers about the long history of friendship between the United States and Thailand and to justify the latest increases in economic and military aid. Foreign affairs journalists looked to *The King and I* as a conceptual bridge between Americans and their increasingly valuable ally in Southeast Asia; they used it to teach readers about complex issues in international relations and to remind them of what they already knew about Thai history.[23]

Popular magazines also connected *The King and I* to Thailand's economic development. When costume designer Irene Sharaff dressed the cast of the show in a distinctive silk weave from Thailand, she boosted the business of the Thai Silk Company, a Bangkok corporation owned by Jim Thompson, an American. Thompson, a former OSS agent, had returned to Thailand after the war and single-handedly reinvigorated the local silk industry. Within a few years it employed thousands of workers in dozens of companies, and Thai silk became the nation's fastest-growing export. Dozens of publications told Thompson's story, and he became a symbol of the benefits that America could bring to the developing world. The conservative *Reader's Digest,* which regularly promoted private capitalist investment in the developing world as an alternative to taxpayer-funded foreign aid, trumpeted the story of Thai silk as a model of how U.S.-Asian economic relations should be structured. In 1959 it published an article that hailed the convergence of Thompson's Thai Silk Company and *The King and I* as "an example of 'foreign aid' at its best." It reported that Thompson paid his workers well, giving them a share of the profits and a bonus of three months' wages every year, and that soon they were able to buy American-produced household goods, luxuries, even automobiles. When the principles of the free market were adhered to, it suggested, both nations' economies would benefit. The liberal *Saturday Review* also publicized Thompson's capitalist model of economic development. It reported that, in the aftermath of *The*

*King and I,* Thompson's company was earning almost $1 million a year and his weavers were "buying television sets and sending their sons off to U.S. colleges." Both *Reader's Digest* and the *Saturday Review* suggested that private capital investment, aided by American popular culture, could help modernize Thailand by elevating living standards, consumption patterns, and even education levels to those approaching Americans'.[24]

Even before Rodgers and Hammerstein produced their musical version, popular nonfiction writers used Anna Leonowens's story as a template for narrating America's democratizing influence in Asia. In January 1948, *Reader's Digest* published "Elizabeth and the Crown Prince of Japan," a condensed article about Elizabeth Gray Vining, an American Quaker who was hired by the emperor of Japan to tutor the crown prince. The article, which echoed the themes as well as the title of Margaret Landon's *Anna and the King of Siam,* detailed how an American woman integrated herself into the Japanese imperial family in the years after World War II and helped transform a former enemy into an ally. Continuing the discursive tradition of sentimental modernization, it presented Vining as a feminized emblem for the entire U.S. occupation and reformation of Japan: "the work of one American woman," it suggested, "may have untold influence on the future of 78,000,000 Japanese." Several years later *Reader's Digest* published another article that drew on Anna Leonowens's story, this time filtered through the musical version, to explain the modernization of Nepal. In February 1957, it published "Erika and the King of Nepal," a first-person account about a German masseuse who became incorporated into Nepal's royal family as a bearer of Western knowledge and who taught the king how to dance the foxtrot. When the king confided to her that he was trapped between an impending attack by Communist China and an authoritarian prime minister who had seized control of the government, Erika served as a go-between to sympathetic forces in India. Her efforts succeeded, and the king, now safe from both communism and authoritarianism, set Nepal on the road to modernization.[25]

A number of political actors and observers saw the liberal internationalist sentiments of "Getting to Know You" as capturing Eisenhower's ideal of personal diplomacy. Organizers of the People-to-People program, a quasi-governmental program that sponsored exchanges between Americans and private citizens around the world, selected "Getting to Know You" as the program's theme for 1958. The song also served as the motto for *Project Hope,* a People-to-People hospital ship that traveled throughout Southeast Asia in the late 1950s dispensing medical services. For Eisenhower's critics, "Getting to Know You" came to summarize all that they disliked in his foreign policies. The writer Christopher Isherwood lambasted the musical for its implicit geopolitics—"I *hate* Anna, that sweetly smiling, gently snooty apostle of democracy and 'our' way of doing things"—and described "Getting to Know You" as containing some of the "vilest" lyrics that Hammerstein had ever written. George Kennan, head of the State Department's policy planning section under Truman and originator of the containment doctrine, expressed his skepticism toward what he saw as Eisenhower's amateurization of diplomacy by pointedly noting that U.S. relations with Asia could not be effectively handled, "as many Americans like to believe, merely by thrusting ordinary people together and 'letting them get to know each other.' "[26]

Rodgers and Hammerstein's King of Siam held a powerful appeal for postwar Americans: Yul Brynner spent the rest of his life playing the leader of a developing nation who welcomes the West into his country and willingly dies rather than impede the process of modernization. *The King and I* made the transition to modernity seem painless, as long as political elites followed the West's instructions and knew when to step aside. But nine years after first playing the King of Siam, he starred in *The Magnificent Seven,* in which he played an American who must force modernization and freedom on a developing people almost against their will. These two roles suggest a fundamental ambivalence that always existed at the heart of modernization theory: while the peaceful transformation of the developing world was most desirable, it would be achieved through violence if necessary. Walt Rostow, like Yul Brynner, expresses this ambivalence in his own career: the academic planner of third world development was also a hawk on Vietnam. This ambivalence allows us to see how the ideals of integration and containment, community formation and violence, polkas and gunfights always existed side by side in both the politics and the culture of the Cold War. By thinking about *The King and I* and *The Magnificent Seven* together, we can see how both sides of this ambivalence circulated through American culture.

The relationship between *The King and I* and modernization theory is not a direct one, and neither one is a cause of or a response to the other. Rather, both Rodgers and Hammerstein's musical and the social scientific/foreign policy project grew out of a common political and cultural tradition of imagining relations between the United States and the non-Western world. *The King and I* and modernization theory were both powerfully appealing to their contemporaries precisely because they had strong roots in well-established political and cultural traditions. We can read *The King and I* as a Cold War text, insofar as it grappled with contemporary geopolitical issues: it imagined the integration of the United States and Asia as a sentimental project of forging emotional bonds and instilling domestic and democratic values. But we should also see it as a specifically Eisenhower-era text. By 1960—the year Kennedy was elected president, the year *The Magnificent Seven* was released—the terms of imagining that integration were beginning to change. While the militarization of foreign policy had begun already in 1950, with the writing of NSC 68 and the outbreak of the Korean War, that militarization increased significantly under Kennedy. *The Magnificent Seven* expressed that emerging focus on the military approach to modernization in a way that *The King and I* never did.

## NOTES

This essay is adapted from a chapter in my book, *Cold War Orientalism: Asia in the Middlebrow Imagination, 1945–1961* (Berkeley: University of California Press, forthcoming). Excerpts from *The King and I* used by permission of The Rodgers and Hammerstein Organization. 

1. Richard Slotkin, *Regeneration through Violence: The Mythology of the Frontier* (Middletown, Conn.: Wesleyan University Press, 1973); *The Fatal Environment: The Myth of the Frontier in the Age of Industrialization, 1800–1890* (New York: Atheneum, 1985); *Gunfighter Nation: The Myth of the Frontier in Twentieth-Century America* (New York: Atheneum, 1992), 441–86.
2. Thomas Schatz, *Hollywood Genres: Formulas, Filmmaking, and the Studio*

*System* (New York: McGraw Hill, 1981), 34–35; Rick Altman, *The American Film Musical* (1987; Bloomington: Indiana University Press, 1989); Harburg quoted in John Lahr, "The Lemon-Drop Kid," *New Yorker,* 30 September 1996: 74.

3. John Lewis Gaddis, *Strategies of Containment* (New York: Oxford University Press, 1982); Thomas J. McCormick, *America's Half-Century: United States Foreign Policy in the Cold War and After* (1989; Baltimore: Johns Hopkins University Press, 1995); Melvyn P. Leffler, *A Preponderance of Power: National Security, the Truman Administration, and the Cold War* (Stanford: Stanford University Press, 1992); Elaine Tyler May, *Homeward Bound: American Families in the Cold War Era* (New York: Basic Books, 1988); Alan Nadel, *Containment Culture: American Narratives, Postmodernism and the Atomic Age* (Durham: Duke University Press, 1995).

4. Stanley Green, *Rodgers and Hammerstein Fact Book* (New York: Lynn Farnol Group, 1980) 579–97. David Foil, liner notes, Broadway Classics recording of *The King and I.*

5. Susan Morgan, "Introduction," *The Romance of the Harem* by Anna Leonowens (Charlottesville: University Press of Virginia, 1991). For discussions of factual inaccuracies in Leonowens's books, see: A. B. Griswold, *King Mongkut of Siam* (New York: Asia Society, 1961), W. S. Bristowe, *Louis and the King of Siam* (New York: Thai-American Publishers, 1976), and William Warren, "Anna and the King: A Case of Libel," *Asia,* March/April 1980: 42–45.

6. Frank Darling, *Thailand and the United States* (Washington: Public Affairs Press, 1965), Dulles quoted 133.

7. Ibid., 79–80.

8. Michael E. Latham, *Modernization as Ideology: American Social Science and "Nation Building" in the Kennedy Era* (Chapel Hill: University of North Carolina Press, 2000); Frederick Cooper and Randall Packard, eds., *International Development and the Social Sciences* (Berkeley: University of California Press, 1997); W. W. Rostow, *The Stages of Economic Growth: A Non-Communist Manifesto* (Cambridge: Cambridge University Press, 1960).

9. Michael Hunt, *Ideology and U.S. Foreign Policy* (New Haven: Yale University Press, 1987), 160; Emily Rosenberg, *Spreading the American Dream: American Economic and Cultural Expansion, 1890–1945* (New York: Hill and Wang, 1982), 46.

10. Walter L. Hixson, *Parting the Curtain: Propaganda, Culture, and the Cold War, 1945–1961* (New York: St. Martin's Press, 1997); Streibert quoted in John W. Henderson, *The United States Information Agency* (New York: Praeger, 1969), 65.

11. Vicente L. Rafael, "Colonial Domesticity: White Women and United States Rule in the Philippines," *American Literature* 67 (1995): 639–66.

12. Mary Louise Pratt, *Imperial Eyes: Travel Writing and Transculturation* (New York: Routledge, 1992), 39.

13. Margaret Landon, *Anna and the King of Siam* (New York: John Day, 1944), 86–87.

14. Richard Rodgers and Oscar Hammerstein II, *6 Plays by Rodgers and Hammerstein* (New York: Random House, 1955), 374.

15. Ernest R. May, ed., *American Cold War Strategy: Interpreting NSC 68* (Boston: Bedford Books, 1993), 27; Kennedy quoted in Garry Wills, "Introduction," *Scoundrel Time* by Lillian Hellman (1976; New York: Bantam, 1977), 18.

16. Harry Truman, "Communist Attack on North Korea a Violation of UN Charter," *Vital Speeches,* 1 August 1950: 612; Hixson, *Parting the Curtain,* 14; George Kennan, "Long Telegram," in Thomas H. Etzold and John Lewis Gaddis, eds., *Containment: Documents on American Policy and Strategy, 1945–1950* (New York: Columbia University Press, 1978), 55.

17. Rodgers and Hammerstein, *6 Plays,* 439.

18. Ibid., 440.

19. Ibid., 449.

20. Ibid., 448; United States Department of Defense, *United States–Vietnam Relations, 1945–1967, Book 8* (Washington: Government Printing Office, 1971), 249.

21. Hugh Fordin, *Getting to Know Him: A Biography of Oscar Hammerstein II* (New York: Random House, 1977), 283–84; Oscar Hammerstein II, "Getting Off the Pyramid," *Saturday Review,* 23 December 1950: 22–23; Oscar Hammerstein II, "Should the U.S. Support a Federal Union of All Nations?" *Congressional Digest* 31 (August-September 1952): 212, 214; Oscar Hammerstein II, "Inertia . . . ," address in Boston, 29 April 1959, New York Public Library Theater Collection; Cousins quoted in Green, *Rodgers and Hammerstein Fact Book,* 737; Richard Rodgers, *Musical Stages: An Autobiography* (1975; New York: Da Capo Press, 1995), 270–71.

22. Rudolph Elie, "King and I—But Who Is the King in This?" (no source); Elliot Norton, "King and I Triumphant New Musical Play," *Boston Sunday Post,* 11 March 1951; "After Hours," *Harper's,* September 1951; Norton, "King and I Triumphant"; Brooks Atkinson, New York *Times,* 8 April 1951: II:1:1; *Punch,* 14 October 1953; Ed Baker, "Rodgers, Hammerstein Score Again with King and I," *Seattle Times,* 17 August 1954; Robert Coleman, "King and I Has Heart, Comedy, Lyrics," *New York Daily Mirror,* 30 March 1951; Brooks Atkinson, "Theatre: London Trio," *New York Times* 17 May 1955: 33:4; Thomas R. Dash, review, *Women's Wear Daily,* 19 April 1956. (All of the above are from New York Public Library Theatre Collection clipping files.)

23. "Do the Reds Stop Here?" *Newsweek,* 26 July 1954: 30.

24. William Warren, *Jim Thompson: The Legendary American of Thailand* (1970; Bangkok: Asia Books, 1979), 70–71; Francis and Katherine Drake, "Jim Thompson and the Busy Weavers of Bangkok," *Reader's Digest,* October 1959: 231–36; Horace Sutton, "Jet Trails around the World—8: Babes in Thailand," *Saturday Review,* 11 April 1959: 29.

25. Lee Hills, "Elizabeth and the Crown Prince of Japan," *Reader's Digest,* Jan-

uary 1948: 129–31; Erika Leuchtag, "Erika and the King of Nepal," *Reader's Digest,* February 1957: 94–97.

26. "Getting to Know You," *Reader's Digest,* March 1958: inside front cover; Project Hope pamphlet, no date, Eisenhower Library; Christopher Isherwood, *Diaries, Volume I: 1939–1960* (London: Methuen, 1996), 624; Kennan quoted in Priscilla Clapp and Morton Halperin, "U.S. Elite Images of Japan: The Postwar Period," in Akira Iriye, ed., *Mutual Images: Essays in American-Japanese Relations* (Cambridge: Harvard University Press, 1975), 213.

## FURTHER READING

Altman, Rick. *The American Film Musical.* Bloomington: Indiana University Press, 1989.

Kaplan, Amy, and Donald E. Pease, eds. *Culture of United States Imperialism.* Durham: Duke University Press, 1993.

Latham, Michael E. *Modernization as Ideology: American Social Science and "Nation Building" in the Kennedy Era.* Chapel Hill: University of North Carolina Press, 2000.

Leffler, Melvyn P. *A Preponderance of Power: National Security, the Truman Administration, and the Cold War.* Stanford: Stanford University Press, 1992.

McCormick, Thomas J. *America's Half-Century: United States Foreign Policy in the Cold War and After.* Baltimore: Johns Hopkins University Press, 1995.

Rafael, Vicente L. "Colonial Domesticity: Engendering Race at the Edge of Empire, 1899–1912." In Rafael, *White Love and Other Events in Filipino History.* Durham: Duke University Press, 2000.

Schatz, Thomas. *Hollywood Genres: Formulas, Filmmaking, and the Studio System.* New York: McGraw Hill, 1981.

Slotkin, Richard. *Gunfighter Nation: The Myth of the Frontier in Twentieth-Century America.* New York: Atheneum, 1992.

# PART III

# CONTESTING MODERNIZATION AROUND THE WORLD

# *ESTADO NOVO,* *HOMEM NOVO* (NEW STATE, NEW MAN): COLONIAL AND ANTI-COLONIAL DEVELOPMENT IDEOLOGIES IN MOZAMBIQUE, 1930–1977

MICHAEL MAHONEY

Modernization theory was not limited to the liberal Western bloc during the Cold War. The other contributors to this collection have shown how, during the 1950s, a coterie of American academics—most notably Walt W. Rostow—articulated a theory of modernization in opposition to Marxist theories of social development. Modernization theory spread into every nook and cranny of American postwar culture, from academic social science (especially area studies) to foreign policy, from the media landscape of middle-class America to the versions of Americana imported overseas. Moreover, for all the claims about the distinctiveness of modernization theory, its similarities to Soviet development theory were more important than its differences. The political scientist James Scott has referred to both the American and the Soviet versions as "high modernism": the state-centered rationalization of society and nature, devoted to mechanizing and homogenizing the real world, opposed to the messy, organic diversity of the local.[1] Given the strength of American and Soviet global hegemony at the time, it is perhaps not surprising to find that high modernism was distributed widely in the Cold War world. And yet, just as it would be wrong to see all Cold War–era conflicts merely as proxy wars between the Soviets and Americans, it would also be wrong to note the global prevalence of high modernism and leave it at that. The more ideas, practices, and symbols spread all over the world, the more they acquire diverse, even divergent, meanings. On closer examination, globalization almost always involves diversification, not homogenization.

Take, for example, the African country of Mozambique and its war for independence from Portugal, fought from 1964 to 1974. At first glance, this was a classic "proxy war," with the NATO member Portugal on the one side and the Marxist-Leninist liberation movement FRELIMO[2] on the other. Not surprisingly, high modernism figured in the ideology of both sides. Still, to identify this as a case of globalization is to raise questions instead of answering them. The Portuguese government from about 1930 to 1974 was a conservative, quasi-fascist dictatorship that called itself the *Estado Novo*, or "New State." FRELIMO was as much an African nationalist movement as it was Marxist-Leninist. In other words, Portugal was not the United States, and FRELIMO was not the Communist Party of the Soviet Union. How were ideas of high modernism translated into these particular local contexts? What were the causes and consequences of this translation?

The turn to high modernist ideology was not inevitable for either the Portuguese government or FRELIMO. Instead, in both cases we see a transition from particularism (cultural nationalism) to universalism (high modernism). In fact, both groups started out by favoring a blend of cultural nationalism and traditionalism that was at best ambivalent toward modernity. During the 1930s the New State adopted the ideology of lusotropicalism (the prefix "luso-" meaning Portuguese), which countered accusations of backwardness with the claim that Portuguese colonialism offered the world a model of racial democracy instead of segregation and white supremacy, of high Christian ideals instead of base materialism. As for FRELIMO, from its inception in 1962 party leaders urged the rejection of Western culture and the defense of what they called African tradition. By 1969, however, both the Portuguese and FRELIMO were no longer glorifying their particular cultures, but rather competing with each other to see who was more modern. For both sides the turn to universalism and high modernism was the result of similar factors: geopolitical considerations certainly, but also the particular logic of the war between Portuguese colonialists and African nationalists, as well as the internal development of the parties concerned. Perhaps this unanimity regarding high modernism goes some way toward explaining why the development policies of both sides burdened Mozambicans instead of benefiting them, leaving the country one of the poorest in the world.

## THE PORTUGUESE CIVILIZING MISSION IN THE 1930S

The Portuguese, like other European colonialists before World War II, referred to their colonial ideology as their "civilizing mission" (*missão civilisadora* in Portuguese). But whereas the British and French civilizing missions had more universalistic pretensions, the Portuguese positively reveled in the uniqueness—the particularism—of their contribution. They had little choice: by the standards of the British and French, the Portuguese utterly failed to develop their colonies, prompting some prominent Europeans to call for the transfer of those colonies to British or French control. The Portuguese response was to argue that what their colonies lacked in order, efficiency, and material wealth they more than made up for in spirituality and racial equality.

Portugal's African empire, and Mozambique in particular, could hardly be considered a colonial success story in the 1930s. The Portuguese had more difficulty than did any other European colonizers in "pacifying" their colonies during the "Scramble for Africa" that began in the 1880s. African resistance in Mozambique was so tenacious that it could be overcome only with large amounts of money and military brutality, and the process still had not been completed in some parts of the country as late as 1935. The cash-strapped Portuguese delegated the colonization of Mozambique to various chartered companies dominated by British capital, and much of the colony's income came from taxing the remittances of migrant workers who had gone to the gold mines in neighboring South Africa. Colonial authority in Portuguese Mozambique was weak, and the Portuguese were dependent on British and South African money to maintain what authority they did have.[3]

The chartered companies hardly had any more resources at their disposal than did the Portuguese colonial administration in Mozambique, so both cut corners by relying heavily on force. The government and the companies charged taxes payable in cash, in kind (mainly in cotton and sugar), and in labor. Instead of enforcing payment by means of an extensive and expensive apparatus of police, courts, and prisons, the government and the companies relied on what colonial theorists called "exemplary violence" and "collective punishment." In other words, small military detachments went out on short but devastating punitive expeditions, wreaking violence indiscriminately on large groups of people who often had only the remotest connections with the original "crime." Corporal punishment by means of whips and paddles was also generously applied. Even by the standards of colonial Africa, the Mozambican colonialists were poor in both material and manpower resources, and their use of violence was therefore excessive. It was these factors that prompted one historian to characterize Portuguese rule in Mozambique as "weak but brutal."[4]

Perhaps the worst aspect of the whole system was the forced labor regime. As noted above, many Mozambican Africans—especially young men—were charged taxes payable not in cash or in kind, but in labor. In other words, they owed the state a certain number of days of labor each year at wages below the already-meager going market rate. The state and private employers paid low-level European officials and local African notables a commission for every worker turned out. Burdensome enough in theory, forced labor was even worse in practice, for there was little to prevent these agents turning out people who had already fulfilled their obligations. Moreover, forced labor was also a standard punishment for a whole catalog of offenses, and officials had every incentive to find the accused guilty, for otherwise the officials would lose out on their commissions.

Forced labor gave colonialists from other countries a reason to call for the transfer of Portugal's colonies to British or French possession. In the 1890s such arguments had been made on the grounds that these colonies would be wasted on the Portuguese, who lacked the resources to properly develop them, in terms both of "civilizing" the indigenous population and of providing economic benefits for the mother country. After a few decades of dormancy, the old arguments reemerged, but with the added force of moral indignation. During the 1920s the League of Nations conducted investigations into accusations that Portugal's compulsory labor policy in Africa amounted to slavery. An American academic, Edward A. Ross, was sent to Mozambique and asked to report on his findings.[5] Ross's 1925 report fueled foreign criticism of the Portuguese for decades. Ironically, many of the critics were French or British, and both those governments had their own—albeit marginally less burdensome—systems of compulsory labor in Africa. And, of course, the chartered companies who operated the system in much of Mozambique had mainly British stockholders.[6]

So for a time in the 1920s it seemed as though Portugal was in jeopardy of having its African colonies taken away. But Portugal faced an even greater problem at the same time: the republic that had replaced the Portuguese monarchy in 1910 was, by the mid-1920s, paralyzed by parliamentary gridlock and financial insolvency. A right-wing military coup in 1926 failed in the short run to produce either an effective, unified government or a way out of the government's fiscal problems. In 1928, the ruling junta appointed an economist, University of Coimbra professor Antonio Salazar, to the position of finance minister. By 1932, Salazar had become prime minister and, in effect, dictator of Portugal, and his regime had become known as the *Estado Novo*, or "New State."

Though the New State was a contemporary of—and in many ways similar to—the fascist regimes in Mussolini's Italy and Hitler's Germany, it was not itself, strictly speaking, fascist. It would be more accurate to call Salazar an antimodern traditionalist. In Portugal, at least, the New State avoided repressive violence: it never issued the death penalty, and allowed greater personal freedom than was the case under Mussolini or Hitler. While the Fascisti and Nazis aimed to mobilize the entire population, either through their parties or parallel organizations, the New State preferred to demobilize the masses. In dramatic contrast to Mussolini and Hitler, the uncharismatic Salazar did not encourage the emergence of a cult of personality. Fascists elsewhere were either overtly hostile to Christianity or, at best, ambivalent, but in Portugal the New State was aggressively and unambiguously Catholic. Both Mussolini and Hitler claimed to be socialists, but their economic policies were more Keynesian, favoring deficit spending to encourage both production *and* consumption. Salazar's economics were pre-liberal, even mercantile, with an overriding emphasis on "fiscal discipline."[7] For all their appeals to nostalgia, Mussolini and Hitler were also genuine revolutionaries who reveled in technological marvels and (a certain kind of) modern architecture. Salazar, on the other hand, valued stasis and stability above all, and was deeply suspicious of urbanization, industrialization, and their consequences.

The significance of the New State's ideology was perhaps nowhere more apparent than in Portuguese colonial theory under Salazar. Salazar's brand of Portuguese nationalism was premised on colonialism to a greater degree than was the case with, say, British or French nationalism of the same period. Consider, for example, the Colonial Act of 1930, which contained the most important and frequently repeated statement of Salazar's official colonial policy: "It is the essential attribute of the Portuguese nation to fulfill the historic function of possessing and colonising overseas dominions and civilising the native populations inhabiting them, as also that of exercising the moral influence ascribed to it."[8] This statement would be reproduced verbatim in article 133 of Portugal's 1933 constitution and in Mozambique's colonial charter of the same year. The wording of the statement demonstrates two things. First, colonialism was not just something that the Portuguese nation happened to engage in, but was "essential" to its very nationhood, suggesting that without colonialism there could be no Portugal. Second, Salazar and his supporters believed that colonialism was not just good for the Portuguese, but also for the people the Portuguese had conquered. In fact, like British and French colonialism, Portuguese colonialism had a "civilizing mission." The difference was that Christianization—the "moral influence" to which Salazar referred—was far more integral to Portuguese colonial theory than to the British or French civilizing missions.

In defending the Portuguese government against criticism of its labor policies in Mozambique and elsewhere, the New State's spokespersons repeatedly emphasized the centrality of Christianity in Portugal's civilizing mission. For example, one Portugal colonialist ideologue took foreign critics to task for their "exclusively materialist preoccupations."[9] Another said, "For us Portuguese, the Negro is hardly an abstract unit of labor,"[10] implying that the Portuguese, unlike the British or French, appreciated the humanity of their colonial subjects. A third writer identified three elements in Portuguese colonialism: the material element certainly, but also the geographic element—that is, imperial expansiveness for its own sake—and the heroic element, which was his name for evangelization. This last writer found the Portuguese civilizing mission to be civilizing precisely because it was evangelizing, "for civilization always has, above all, a spiritual aspect. The Portuguese, like nobody else, have undertaken, through their enterprise of exploration and conquest, a transcendent crusade, a sharing of moral riches."[11] These statements were all published in Portuguese, suggesting that it was not only foreign critics who needed convincing. Indeed, many scholars have pointed out that while Portugal could have survived without the colonies, the New State could not: Salazar's regime derived its very legitimacy from colonialism.[12]

Another source of ideological support for Portuguese colonialism under Salazar was the new work of the Brazilian sociologist Gilberto Freyre. During the 1930s, Freyre articulated a theory of what he referred to as "lusotropicalism" or "lusotropicology." According to this theory, Portugal's greater proximity to Africa and Asia, and long history of intimate interactions with Africans and Asians, made Portuguese colonialism more interactive and democratic. Like the other colonialists, Freyre argued, the Portuguese spread the benefits of European culture and the Christian religion to the more benighted parts of the world. But whereas the French and British stood aloof from Africans and Asians and from African and Asian culture, the Portuguese encouraged the "marriage" of both cultures and individuals. The result was that Portuguese culture all over the world—in Brazil, in Africa, and in Asia—was more "mixed," and so too were the Portuguese people: all "mixed" in a racial sense. Portuguese colonialism thus supposedly had all kinds of advantages over the British or French variety. The Portuguese were more open to adopting whatever was good from African and Asian culture, and this openness made the Africans and Asians more willing to adopt the best of European culture. Miscegenation produced what Freyre called "racial democracy." With no clear lines between white and black, Freyre argued, there could be no segregation or white supremacy. While the governments of Portugal and Brazil eagerly promoted these ideas for obvious reasons, more than sixty years' worth of scholarship has shown that Portuguese "racial democracy" was a complete myth.[13]

After 1928, Salazar and his colleagues moved to eliminate the more overtly racist aspects of Portuguese policy in Africa. At the turn of the century, Portuguese officials in Mozambique such as Antonio Enes and Mouzinho de Albuquerque opposed liberals who favored some steps toward racial integration and racial equality. Instead, Enes and Mouzinho supported Portuguese Social Darwinists like Oliveira Martins, who argued in 1893:

> It is as utopian to transform blacks into citizens and equals of the whites, as it is to encourage Portuguese emigrants to go work with the hoe in Africa in competition with the blacks. Whites and blacks have different roles, indicated by nature and the facts of life, which cannot be altered. . . . The poetic plan for educating the blacks attracts to-day those enthusiastic souls who, unable to put up with the old religions, seek to found new philanthropic cults. Out of the vast number of naive superstitions of our time, this is neither the least widespread nor the least conspicuous. . . . the philanthropists persist in hoping that the Bible, translated into Bundu or Bantu, will convert the savages, and that the schoolmaster's rod will turn them into men like ourselves. From the mystic alliance of the Testament and cotton-goods will emerge what the bells and crucifixes, the music and incense of Catholicism, have failed to accomplish, whether in America or Africa.[14]

Thus turn-of-the-century Portuguese colonialists found even the "civilizing mission" too liberal and favored unmitigated, permanent white supremacy instead. In 1929, however, Salazar introduced a new "Political, Civil, and Criminal Statute for Natives." According to this statute, all *indígenas,* or "natives," would be subject to "customary law" and forced labor. If, however, the Africans learned to speak Portuguese, converted to Christianity, and met certain income and property qualifications, then they could become *civilisados,* or "civilized persons," with all the rights of any other Portuguese citizen, including exemption from forced labor.[15]

However, the New State devoted few resources to the pursuit of its "civilizing mission," so few Africans ever enjoyed the privileges of becoming "civilized." The New State left the business of both Christianization and education in Africa to the Christian missions, but did little to support them materially. On the ground the Christian missionary presence in Portuguese Africa was thin, especially in Mozambique. It is therefore not surprising that, as late as 1960, only 10 percent of African Mozambicans were Christian, or that only 9 percent of Mozambican school-age children attended school in 1936, a figure that had risen to only 24 percent by 1960. If education was difficult to acquire, property or a well-paying job was even more elusive. Finally, Portuguese colonial officials were often very stingy when it came to approving African applications for "civilized" status. As a result, by 1950 only 5,000 Mozambican Africans out of a population of a few million had become *civilisados*.[16]

Salazar's economic policies produced economic dependence and stagnation in Mozambique and Portugal's other African colonies. As an "economic nationalist," Salazar worked to minimize imports and foreign investments from outside the Portuguese Empire. By the 1940s this policy had led to the elimination of the British-dominated chartered companies and their concessions in Mozambique. However, economic nationalism also limited the amount of money available for investment in the colonies, and its high tariffs made imports from neighboring South Africa and other countries more expensive than imports from distant Portugal. Price controls on cotton and sugar meant that the Mozambican economy benefited little from its exports to Portugal. To preserve markets for surplus Portuguese manufactures, Salazar relied not only on tariffs for non-Portuguese manufactures, but also on government-imposed limits on industrialization in the colonies. It was only in 1936 that he allowed even the most rudimentary industrialization in Mozambique. Mozambique's first development plan came in 1937, but it focused on agriculture and the transportation infrastructure, and no loans or grants-in-aid were used to pay for Mozambican development plans, such as they were, until after World War II. Mozambique's development had to pay for itself. In 1928, Salazar passed laws mandating that compulsory labor be paid, and prohibiting the contracting out of government laborers to private employers, but the laws were full of loopholes and lacked adequate provisions for enforcement. Worst of all, forced cultivation of cotton and sugar was extended, so while it was easier for Mozambican peasants to stay on their own farms, the state still told them what to grow on those farms. The result of all this was little economic growth in Portugal and even less in Mozambique.[17] In the 1930s, Salazar himself identified economic austerity and cultural assimilation as the main planks of his colonial policy: "[W]e must revise and put into execution plans for public works that are indispensable within the moderate financial resources available and have a guarantee of an effective return; and, before everything, as the highest and noblest work of all, we must organise on the best possible lines measures for safeguarding the interests of those inferior races whose inclusion under the influence of Christianity is one of the greatest achievements of Portuguese colonisation."[18]

## PORTUGAL'S TURN TO MODERNIZATION THEORY, 1945–1974

In the 1950s and 1960s, various economic and political changes prompted the New State to turn away from a "civilizing mission" that was very suspicious of modernity, instead embracing the "modernization theory" that was emerging in academic and policy circles in the liberal West. Much of the rhetoric of Portuguese colonialists after 1945 was, as with their predecessors during the 1930s, devoted to defending Portuguese colonialism from foreign criticism. Now, however, they focused more on economics and technology rather than on Christianity and Portuguese culture. Moreover, within Portugal this new generation of colonialists clearly aimed to convince advocates of fiscal austerity that social, economic, and infrastructure investments would be repaid many times over.

All of these changes were connected, in one way or another, with World War II. Like the United States, Portugal benefited from increased demands for its exports, but was sheltered from wartime destruction (Portugal was neutral during the war). The war initiated a period of more than thirty years of economic growth for Portugal, during which the country made the transition from an agrarian economy to an industrialized economy. The war destroyed fascist hegemony on the European continent and replaced it with NATO hegemony in the West and the Warsaw Pact in the East. Though still a right-wing dictatorship, Portugal joined NATO in its fight against the Communist menace. The war also fatally wounded the British and French colonial empires, which had largely conceded independence to their African and Asian colonies by the early 1960s. Then, in 1961, African nationalists in Portuguese Angola launched an armed struggle for independence, which forced Salazar to accept deficit spending and increased foreign investment in Portugal and the colonies.[19]

These changes were a boon to technocrats in the New State. In the 1920s colonial officials like Norton de Matos in Angola and Brito Camacho in Mozambique had called for massive state intervention in developing the colonies, including improvements in education and public health. For both officials, social services made Africans both more productive and more loyal. Norton de Matos suggested that these proposals might be implemented through what he called "lay civilizing missions," indicating his feeling that the Portuguese state should take over many of the functions previously reserved for Christian missions. Salazar's avid Catholicism and fiscal austerity ensured a minimal role for secular developmentalism from about 1928 to 1945.[20] After World War II, however, university-educated "experts" began to replace traditional bureaucrats and military officials in the upper echelons of the New State. For these men, Christianity and spirituality were not nearly so important as science, technology, and economic growth.

Perhaps the most notable postwar New State technocrat was Marcelo Caetano. A former law professor, Caetano was a high-ranking official in Salazar's government from 1940 to 1958, whose career included stints as overseas (colonial) minister (1947–50) and director of economic planning for both Portugal and its colonies (1955–58). Caetano maintained that colonial initiatives in transportation, communications, public health, and education improved African standards of living, but also enabled the more rational exploitation of Africa's natural resources.[21] Meanwhile, it was a lack of such achievement—measured in economic and technological terms—that had left Africans unfit to govern themselves: "The blacks in Africa must be directed and molded by Europeans. . . . The Africans by themselves did not account for a single useful invention nor any usable technical discovery, no conquest that counts in the evolution of humanity, nothing that can compare to the accomplishments in the areas of culture and technology by Europeans or even by Asians."[22] Such statements showed that much had changed since the 1930s, when the Portuguese criticized other colonial powers for their "exclusively materialist preoccupations." With their colonial experience and their faith in bureaucratic rationalism, technology, and the interventionist state, technocrats like Caetano could not help but transform Portuguese colonial ideology.

In the early 1960s, Adriano Moreira—Caetano's successor as overseas minister—translated the old Portuguese "civilizing mission" into technocratic, modernizing language. First, for Moreira it was vital that university-educated experts be recruited into service in Africa and that, once there, they should not have their expertise subordinated to the whims of career civil servants.[23] Perhaps more important, Moreira tried to show that Freyre's theories were modern and scientific: The validity of lusotropicalism had been proven, Moreira claimed, by modern social science research. Moreover, lusotropicalism was supposedly a better model for economic and technological development in the tropics than was anything emanating from the Western or Soviet blocs. Lusotropicalism had developed over centuries for the very purpose of ensuring the successful translation of European techniques into tropical settings, while Western and Soviet techniques had been developed in decidedly nontropical settings. Moreira quoted Freyre himself approvingly to this effect:

> The Portuguese tropical interpretation is one which is implemented in practice in a way that without being exaggerated may be regarded as triumphant. It may come to be useful in time to the Anglo-Americans and the Soviet Russians themselves when they will need to reinterpret their systems of relationship with the areas presently considered backward; two systems presently animated by a zeal for increasing economic productivity, particularly in industry, by mechanical means valid in colder regions, but whose validity for the development of human civilization in general and, in particular, for that of the non-colonial civilizations in the tropics, some of the very apologists for these systems have begun to doubt.[24]

Here Moreira anticipated the rhetoric of "appropriate technologies" and "bottom-up development" used by populist, left-wing development experts in the 1970s, but he employed that rhetoric to legitimate the quasi-fascist New State's continued hold on its African territories.

In 1967, Franco Nogueira, then foreign minister, took Moreira's arguments one step further and made the breathtaking claim that the New State, and not its critics, was anticolonial and antiracist. Nogueira maintained that what passed for "anticolonialism," whether of the pro-Western or pro-Soviet variety, was actually the most pernicious colonialism of all. Those countries that had recently obtained, or were about to obtain, independence were ill prepared for anything more than independence in name only. Such countries would inevitably fall into a state of neocolonial dependence, this time on either the Western or the Soviet bloc. The Portuguese solution, Nogueira argued, was far better. The 1930 Colonial Act, the 1933 Constitution, and a whole host of administrative reforms since then had established that Portugal's colonies were not colonies at all, but "overseas provinces" equal in every respect to the provinces of European Portugal. The inhabitants of these "overseas provinces" were Portuguese citizens, with all the rights of Portuguese citizens in Europe. Nogueira also maintained that Portugal opposed both white racism and what he called black racism. The latter consisted of the attitudes of black African nationalists who, he alleged, wanted to replace white supremacy with black supremacy and push whites into the sea. At the same time, Nogueira was also critical of white racism as practiced in South Africa or Rhodesia. With some justification, he pointed out that in Portuguese territories miscegenation was legal, segregation was illegal, and people of all races enjoyed equality before the law (whatever that meant under a dictatorship).[25]

The claims that Portugal's colonies were not really colonies, and that racism did not exist in Portuguese territories, were nothing new. Nogueira's innovation, like Moreira's, was to couch this nonracialism in a modernizing idiom. Thus, Nogueira was at pains to argue that the economic and technological development of what he called the "Third World" could come about only after a long period of tutelage under a more advanced nation. Moreover, Nogueira maintained, Portugal was eminently qualified to provide that tutelage:

> The Third World countries have suddenly become aware of the potentialities offered by science and technology and are eager to bring material progress within reach of the masses. They believe that, from the human standpoint, it is not necessary to pass through intermediate stages of development, training, and adaptation. . . . When we [the Portuguese] are told that we have no technicians, nor means, nor capital, nor instruments of progress, we reply that our African provinces are more devel-

> oped, more progressive in every respect than any recently independent territory in Africa south of the Sahara, without exception.[26]

Here again we see how in the 1960s apologists for Portuguese colonial policy emphasized Portugal's modernity, in stark contrast to their predecessors in the 1930s who emphasized Portugal's cultural heritage and spirituality.

The Portuguese government tried to back up these claims with concrete development efforts and reforms. These included the First Six-Year Plan (1953–58), the Second Six-Year Plan (1959–64), the Interim Plan (1965–67), and the Third Six-Year Plan (1968–73). During this twenty-year period, the New State gradually shed its reluctance to spend money on the colonies. In examining these plans, one can see the New State's gradual abandonment of various principles. For example, the £20 million apportioned to Mozambique for the First Plan was already far greater than any previous development expenditure. But the country received £41 million in the Second Plan and a share of £180 million total in the Interim Plan earmarked for all five of Portugal's African colonies. More important, the Mozambican government and the other "provincial" governments had to come up with less and less of this money on their own: Mozambique itself paid for 42 percent of the First Plan, but only 10 percent of the Third Plan, the rest of the money coming from loans and grants-in-aid from Portugal and, amazingly, foreign countries. This last was quite a turnaround from Salazar's decades-long refusal to allow extensive overseas investment in Portugal and its territories, lest Portugal lose its economic independence. Finally, spending for education and social services steadily increased, from 0 percent of the First Plan's budget, to 14 percent in the Second Plan, and even more thereafter. Throw in the fact that Salazar began to lift restrictions on colonial industrialization as early as the 1950s and it becomes clear that Portugal's colonial development policies had changed dramatically. No wonder it was often said that Portugal did more to develop its "overseas provinces" in the last thirteen years of the colonial era than in the previous five hundred.[27]

At the same time, the New State did more to make Mozambique and the other overseas provinces Portuguese, but this only highlighted the ambiguities of Portuguese development theory. For example, in distinct contrast to the Americas, white immigration to Angola and Mozambique was extremely limited. On the eve of World War II there were still fewer than 20,000 whites in Mozambique, compared with a few million blacks. Part of the postwar development kitty was devoted to encouraging further white immigration to Africa, so that by 1974, on the eve of independence, there were more than 200,000 whites in Mozambique, or 2 percent of the population. As for the blacks, the official name for *civilisados* (civilized persons) became *assimilados* (assimilated persons) after the war, and in 1961 reforms made this status much easier to acquire: supposedly, all one had to do was declare oneself an *assimilado* and one automatically received official recognition as such. Compulsory labor was also finally abolished. Still, legal racial equality with whites and full citizenship rights continued to mean little under a New State dictatorship lacking democratic elections and full civil rights for anybody, regardless of race.[28]

The pace of Portuguese development and reform intensified after 1968 owing to several factors. First, Salazar had a stroke and was replaced as prime minister by Marcelo Caetano, who was much more inclined toward reform and aggressive government spending. Second, the liberation movement in Mozambique was making serious gains, increasingly putting the Portuguese on the defensive. New State officials now admitted publicly that the war could not be won by military means alone, but only with a concerted development effort. Before this, Portuguese both inside and outside of the Salazar regime had privately referred to much of development and reform as being "for the English to see." Now the expressed purpose became, and had to be, "to win the hearts and minds" of Africans, with the Portuguese borrowing both the rhetoric and the policies that their American allies had used in Vietnam.

The last six years of the war (1968–74) coincided with the Third Development Plan, the most ambitious Portuguese colonial development plan yet, especially in Mozambique. The plan had two main projects. First, in 1968, in one of his last acts before his stroke, Salazar gave the go-ahead for the massive Cabora Bassa hydroelectric project, at the time the fifth-largest dam in the world, on the Zambezi River in Mozambique. As the centerpiece of a massive scheme involving agricultural and mining development, Cabora Bassa was intended to facilitate the further industrialization and rural electrification of Mozambique and serve as a spur to massively intensified economic growth. But Cabora Bassa was also a several-hundred-million-dollar instrument of propaganda. It was intended as a defiant assertion—in the face of international challenges—of Portugal's intentions to remain in Africa for "another 500 years." Moreover, Cabora Bassa was supposed to decisively refute any suggestion that Portuguese colonialism, in particular, was "stagnant."[29] The New State's intentions were clear in the statements of prominent officials. At the ceremony marking the beginning of construction on 16 September 1969, the new overseas minister, Joaquim da Silva Cunha, identified Cabora Bassa as "a symbol of moral, social, and economic progress . . . undeniable proof of confidence in the destinies of Portuguese Africa."[30] As Cunha said on another occasion, the project would give "the progress of the whole area a rapid, dynamic impulse."[31]

The other plank of Portugal's Third Development Plan in Mozambique was a program of *aldeamento,* a Portuguese word best translated as "villagization." According to this policy, peasants in many parts of Mozambique, but especially in the areas surrounding Cabora Bassa, were to be relocated and concentrated in government-built villages. The perimeters of the villages would be placed under surveillance and patrolled by the military, ostensibly to protect the inhabitants from anticolonial guerrillas. Within the villages the new inhabitants would find improved facilities for health care and education, as well as infrastructural developments in the areas of water provision, agriculture, and the like. As in the Cold War–era counterinsurgency strategies of Portugal's NATO allies, *aldeamento* in Mozambique served a military purpose by cutting guerrilla rebels off from their bases of support among the peasantry. But, as was also the case elsewhere, *aldeamento* was further intended quite explicitly to "win the hearts and minds" of Africans through modernizing development. On the other hand, regime spokespersons publicly denied any similarities with villagization programs elsewhere. As the New State's foremost African apologist in Mozambique, Miguel Murupa, put it: "The 'aldeamentos,' however, are not 'concentration camps,' nor are they anything similar or near to 'new villages' or 'strategic hamlets.' The aldeamentos are only and solely a means of bringing rapid evolution, progress, and welfare to populations otherwise scattered in small, unproductive tribal nuclei, living under primitive and backward conditions. For this reason it would be much fairer to call them strategic development hamlets."[32] Nevertheless, even taking representatives of the New State at their word, the Portuguese government had by this point conceded a whole lot. On the one hand, villagization and mammoth development projects like Cabora Bassa showed that the Portuguese could modernize just like anybody else. On the other hand, as a result it became more and more difficult to maintain that Portugal had anything special to contribute to Mozambique at all.

The relationship between development and decolonization in the Portuguese case followed patterns already established by Portugal's NATO allies France and Great Britain. Colonialism and modernization theory would have been mutually exclusive if, as Michael Adas claims, "modernization as it has been understood since World War II" had actually been "inconceivable in the colonial context."[33] Yet, as Frederick Cooper has shown for the British and French empires in Africa, "modernization" in Africa originated very much as a colonialist initiative. British and French colonizers developed a variety of modernization theory after World War II, during what has become known as the era of welfare colonialism. Colonial modernization was intended to serve two purposes. First, it was to increase colonial production for the benefit of both the colonies and their mother countries, which were recovering from the devastation of the war. Second, colonial modernization was supposed to provide ideological legitimation for continued colonial rule, especially in the face of growing attacks from the burgeoning labor and nationalist movements in Africa. Ultimately, the Portuguese learned the same lesson in the 1970s that the British and French had learned in the 1960s: colonial modernization had the potential to render colonizers superfluous, for trained Africans could lead the modernization effort just as well as Europeans could.[34]

As it happened, military setbacks and the emphasis on development created a crisis of confidence within the Portuguese ranks. "Community development" programs were initiated in the 1960s with the dual mandate of combating "subversion" and promoting "modernization." Perhaps inevitably, by the early 1970s some community development officers were publicly expressing their disillusionment with the privileging, in practice, of counterinsurgency over development.[35] Around the same time, the army tried to dissuade young men from draft-dodging and desertion with the slogan "The army is not only an instrument of war, it is essential in the development of society."[36] The army's fears were real, but its strategies were not effective. During the early 1970s there emerged the MFA (Armed Forces Movement), a secret movement of disaffected Portuguese soldiers from all sectors of the political spectrum. In 1974 the MFA staged a successful coup d'état in Portugal, overthrowing Caetano, conceding independence to Portugal's African colonies, and paving the way for free, multiparty elections in Portugal the following year.[37]

## THE IDEOLOGICAL EVOLUTION OF FRELIMO

For its part, FRELIMO's development ideology followed a path similar to that of the New State: from cultural particularism (Portuguese under Salazar, African in the case of FRELIMO) to universalism (right-wing modernization for Portugal, Marxist modernization for FRELIMO).

FRELIMO only came into existence in 1962, the same year that the French joined the British in conceding independence in principle to the last of their African colonies. The emergence of nationalist political parties in Africa depended on three key factors: relatively high levels of education, especially at the secondary level and beyond; the emergence of an urban proletariat; and official tolerance of organized African political parties, especially in the initial stages. All three conditions were particularly unfavorable in Mozambique. As late as 1972 there were still only 44,368 secondary school students in Mozambique out of a total population of 9 million,[38] a very low level even by the standards of colonial Africa. Levels of urbanization were also extremely low, and far more Mozambicans performed wage labor outside of Mozambique—mainly in South Africa and Rhodesia (present-day Zimbabwe)—than within it. Finally, the New State's prohibition of political parties made it difficult for all but the most "loyal" African political organizations to survive. There was still pervasive anticolonial protest—whether violent or nonviolent—but the leadership necessary to channel that protest was all too easily eliminated or co-opted by the state. Given the unfavorable conditions within Mozambique, and the presence of large numbers of emigrant migrant laborers outside of it, it is not surprising that the largest Mozambican political parties of the postwar era were founded in exile. By 1961 these included

UDENAMO (founded in Zimbabwe), MANU (founded in Kenya), and UNAMI (founded in Malawi). All three organizations consisted almost entirely of migrant laborers—overwhelmingly young and male—with leadership devolving to the handful with a secondary education and to the even smaller minority with university degrees. In Dar es Salaam, Tanzania, in 1962, UDENAMO, MANU, and UNAMI coalesced to form FRELIMO,

At first FRELIMO was attracted to the popular doctrine of "African socialism," which derived its principles not from Marx's "scientific" universalism, but from the particularly "communalistic" nature of African culture. FRELIMO thus rejected the African right wing—such as the ruling parties in Kenya and Côte d'Ivoire—which favored free markets and a pro-Western orientation. But FRELIMO also rejected the radical African left—such as the ruling parties in Mali, Guinea, Algeria, and Somalia—which was more adversarial toward the former colonizers and made steps in the direction of government control of the means of production. Instead, FRELIMO aligned itself with the majority of ruling parties in newly independent African states that claimed an independent socialist orientation and tended to support the nonaligned "third world" movement of India's Nehru and Indonesia's Sukarno. Indeed, "African socialism" became something of a cliché in African politics during the 1960s and 1970s. African socialism was usually socialist only insofar as it involved the creation of a rudimentary social democratic "safety net" on the model of the Western welfare states. The African socialist states were far more nationalist than they were socialist. This nationalism was above all economic, involving import-substitute industrialization, nationalization of basic industries, currency controls, limits on foreign ownership and investment, and high tariffs. In principle, the nationalism was also cultural, and this was what distinguished mainstream African socialism from the more Marxist varieties. Whereas African Marxists derived their socialism from Soviet, Chinese, and Cuban models, mainstream African socialists derived their socialism from "traditional" African communalism.

FRELIMO elected Eduardo Mondlane to be its general secretary. Mondlane was one of the lucky educated few. He was able to obtain a secondary education, and the authorities responded to his political activism in high school by exiling him to Lisbon. While there, however, he began his university studies and met Portuguese Marxists and African nationalists, including the future leaders of the independence movements in Angola and Guinea-Bissau. Government harassment then prompted Mondlane to leave Portugal and attend college in the United States. There he received a Ph.D. in anthropology and sociology at Northwestern University and became a professor at Syracuse University. A special UN passport gave him immunity that allowed him to visit Mozambique in the early 1960s on fact-finding missions. As the first and, up to that point, only black Mozambican to have received a Ph.D., and as the most prominent Mozambican nationalist activist on the international stage, Mondlane was the logical choice to lead FRELIMO.

Despite his Western education, and despite the fact that his wife Janet was a white American, Mondlane did not reject African culture. Instead, he maintained that, before colonization, Africa was more developed than Europe was at the time, and he measured this development in scientific and technological terms: "While Europeans were still living in primitive tribal societies isolated in the Northern forest belt, North Africans were learning to control their environment, developing technology and science and forming a complex, settled society. . . . It was this society that absorbed the first primitive Moslem invaders and by a cultural fusion created the advanced Islamic culture of Africa, from which Europe gained many of the scientific ideas that made the Renaissance possible."[39] Mondlane did not dismiss Western culture out of hand, but rather felt that a delicate balance had to be maintained. "We can learn from other cultures, including the European," he wrote, "but we cannot graft them directly on to our own. It is for this reason that a certain understanding of our own cultures and our own past is essential."[40] Not surprisingly, when Mondlane was assassinated in 1969, FRELIMO eulogized him "as the Inheritor of the traditional African culture; the man who fought against the cultural alienation of our country."[41]

Between 1969 and 1971 there was a dramatic turnabout in FRELIMO's development ideology. In 1969 cultural nationalism—the promotion of one's own "national" culture and its defense against encroachment from "foreign" cultures—was expressed in even stronger terms by FRELIMO as a party than it was by Mondlane as an individual. FRELIMO's position at the time of Mondlane's death was that the party was on the side of African culture against Western culture: "Colonial domination has been imposed through the disruption of traditional ways of living and thinking, and the correlative introduction of alien ideas and values, since the essential feature of the colonization of a people is the systematic destruction of their identity."[42] Just two years later, in 1971, FRELIMO was expressing precisely the opposite attitude toward African tradition:

> In the areas still under enemy control, as in any country before a revolution, there are two main forms of cultural oppression: colonial-capitalist oppression and traditional and feudal oppression. Traditional and feudal culture is based essentially on a metaphysical rationale, where man is seen as subject to hostile nature from which he can gain favors only through the mediation of the spirits of God. Once it questions the very foundations of this rationale, science is shunned as heresy. This is a tribal culture which underestimates, negates, or is even hostile to other so-called foreign cultures. Women and the youth are oppressed. This culture therefore destroys the initiative of the masses and, in a world in constant evolution, it seeks to remain like an island, isolated, frozen, unchanging. Today we are building a new culture, a national culture which is negating both the tribal micro-culture and the colonial anti-culture.[43]

Something had changed in the two intervening years. What exactly had happened?

FRELIMO's shift from cultural nationalism to antitraditionalism reflected the party's decisive turn in the direction of Marxism from about 1969, which in turn resulted from the victory of a quasi-Marxist faction in an internal power struggle that began in 1968. There were three axes of conflict in FRELIMO during the 1960s: between northerners and southerners, between those who favored and those who opposed white participation in the struggle, and between Marxists and African cultural nationalists. Mondlane seems to have seen his main task as maintaining the unity of the movement and keeping these disparate factions together. By 1968, however, this was becoming impossible. That year a conflict erupted at FRELIMO's school, the Mozambique Institute, in Tanzania. An African Catholic priest who taught there and several students launched a bitter protest against the presence of white teachers at the school, and against the participation of whites in

FRELIMO in general. At the same time, FRELIMO Central Committee member Lazaro Nkavandame, a northerner, was coming under criticism for his conduct in those "liberated zones" of Mozambique which he was in charge of. Specifically, Nkavandame, who had been a businessman before the war, was trying to reestablish his business enterprises in the liberated zones, something that the Marxists strenuously opposed. Mondlane, who was a southerner and had a white wife, sided with the Marxists, standing firm against the students at the Mozambique Institute, and ultimately purging Nkavandame from FRELIMO in January 1969. Mondlane was assassinated in Tanzania the following month when he opened a mail bomb; the plot to kill him apparently involved Nkavandame, other FRELIMO defectors, and the Portuguese secret police. By May 1970 one of the other members of the Central Committee, Samora Machel, became sole leader of FRELIMO. Crucially, the former medical orderly Machel was also a southerner, a devout Marxist, and a leading officer in FRELIMO's army.[44]

This account reveals *how* the Marxists within FRELIMO managed to dominate the party, but it does not tell us *why* this particular ideology managed to spread so widely and become so attractive to so many party members. One answer could be that the turn to Marxism was strictly pragmatic. Certainly, Portugal's membership in NATO prevented the U.S. government from openly and generously supporting FRELIMO, while the Communist bloc had no such qualms. But this would be an oversimplification. FRELIMO also received aid from the Organization for African Unity and other African countries, most notably Tanzania, not to mention from the Arab bloc, from nongovernmental organizations throughout the West, from Scandinavian governments, and even, early on, from the CIA.[45] Moreover, FRELIMO's acceptance of Communist bloc aid and its own growing Marxist orientation did not prevent it from pursuing a rather independent line diplomatically, refusing to take sides in the various conflicts among Communist nations, such as that between the Soviet Union and China. Instead, FRELIMO did what it could to maximize the number of countries willing to give it aid.[46]

If FRELIMO's turn to Marxism was not simply a matter of geopolitical calculations, what was it? Some scholars have argued that Marxism offered what liberal modernization theory could not: a radical model for ending both colonialism and underdevelopment. Marxism, especially of the Leninist variety, also offered a proven plan for the creation of a revolutionary party, its seizure of power, and its later institutionalization. Perhaps most important, the "practical" Marxist theory of Lenin, Mao, and other revolutionary leaders showed how the masses could be mobilized in support of the party. If FRELIMO modeled itself on numerous other Marxist and non-Marxist revolutionary movements, then it is not surprising that—like those other movements—FRELIMO became radicalized over the course of its own "revolution."[47] Other scholars emphasize more affective factors. Colonialism was a deeply humiliating experience for the colonized, not least because it left them with a troubling dilemma. On the one hand, they could accept the colonial culture and "assimilate," but in so doing they would be accepting colonial notions of African inferiority and sentencing themselves to a life of permanent cultural alienation. On the other hand, African culture was not much of an alternative because it had been so thoroughly compromised by colonial conquest and cooptation. Besides, Africa had to "catch up" with the rest of the world, and it was difficult to find in African culture a blueprint for doing so. Marxism rejected both "colonialism" and "tradition." Even though it was in many ways a product of the West, just like colonialism, Marxism was supposedly scientific, and therefore universal. Marxism was premised on the notion of a dictatorship of the proletariat; it was not a tradition inherited from the past, but rather a future to be worked toward, through struggle and the mangle of "practice." [48]

While all these explanations have an element of truth in them, it is also important to emphasize the dialogic, interactive nature of FRELIMO's ideological evolution. For a dozen years FRELIMO and the New State were chained together in a long dance, with each side evolving in part in response to the other. It is no coincidence that FRELIMO's purging of its cultural nationalists in 1969 coincided with the initiation of the Cabora Bassa hydroelectric project and the quickening of the *aldeamento* strategy. The onset, in the early 1960s, of the armed struggles for African independence forced the Portuguese to accelerate development and "sell" their African subjects on Portuguese rule by means of tangible quality-of-life improvements. The 1960s were also the heyday of the space race, when "modernity" became a locus of ideological competition between the superpowers. This was no less true for the protagonists in the Mozambican struggle. If Portugal was no longer emphasizing its "civilizing mission" and the value of assimilating to Portuguese culture, but rather cast itself as an arch modernizer, then FRELIMO's championing of "traditional African culture" threatened to become irrelevant, even counterproductive.

In short, in a context in which "modernity" was such a widely shared value, FRELIMO and the New State had to compete to become, so to speak, "more modern than thou." This competitive modernity is particularly apparent in the events surrounding Salazar's first airplane flight, in 1966 at the age of seventy-seven. FRELIMO mocked Salazar in language that parodied European descriptions of African primitivism: "Can we conclude from this fact that Salazar is undergoing evolution? It is true that to fly today is an extremely unusual thing even for the average man of the 20th century. But we must understand that Salazar does not belong to our time. We have to understand the natural reluctance of the Portuguese head of state to use any mode of transportation other than wagons pulled by donkeys, and his atavistic suspicion of anything which smells 'modern.' "[49] FRELIMO could have chosen to invert the terms of debate, criticizing modernity and promoting the African traditions that so many Europeans disparaged. And the organization did do this often, as late as 1969. However, it is significant that it increasingly chose instead to accept the terms of the debate and compete with the Portuguese government for modernity.

If the Portuguese government's modernity was implicit in the regime's name for itself, *Estado Novo* (New State), then FRELIMO's modernity was encapsulated in its notion of *Homem Novo* (New Man), which became a recurring theme in FRELIMO rhetoric from 1969 onward. The notion of the "New Man" was borrowed from the revolutionary theories of Mao Zedong and Frantz Fanon, both of whom argued that the revolution had to transform not only the state and society, but individuals as well. This transformation was supposed to occur through struggle, even violence.[50] FRELIMO's "New Man" was above all scientific, rejecting the past and looking toward the future. As early as 1969 FRELIMO identified the creation of this scientific and modern sort of "New Man" as the objective of education: "FRELIMO's purpose in establishing a new system of education is part of the general goal of building a new man, able to transform nature to the benefit of his society, able to cure the ancient man from colonial forms of alienation, able to give an effective contribution to the total liberation of man."[51] FRELIMO rearticulated this principle in 1977, three years after the end of the war. That year the organization held its third congress, the first since Mozambique had received its independence, and at that congress the party declared its commitment to "scientific socialism" and the "scientific ideology of the proletariat." Not surprisingly, the "New Man" figured prominently in FRELIMO's plans. As the report of the Central Committee put it, "We have taken to a more advanced phase the struggle provoked during the revolutionary armed struggle for the creation of the New Man, free forever from ignorance, obscurantism, superstition, preconceptions, conscious of the obligations of solidarity and cooperation."[52] Far from bringing the modernizing struggle to an end, Mozambican independence actually marked the intensification of that struggle.

It is very important to note that Mozambique is today one of the poorest countries in the world, and many scholars have held FRELIMO's modernizing development policies responsible for this state of affairs. There have certainly been a whole host of other factors at work: Portugal ruled the territory for more than 450 years, with important consequences for both Mozambique's domestic economy and Mozambique's place in the world economy. Portugal's hold on Mozambique was shaken off only after a ten-year war of independence. Finally, between 1977 and 1992 there was a civil war between FRELIMO and RENAMO, a right-wing African nationalist organization that received material support from white-ruled Rhodesia and South Africa as well as from the United States. The fact that Mozambique remains today, more than ten years after the end of the last war, one of the most heavily land-mined countries in the world is only the most vivid and tragic indication of how the past acts upon the present. Still, even scholars who acknowledge these factors also trace many of the difficulties to the nature of FRELIMO's own development policies. In particular, those scholars argue that development under FRELIMO was premised on an elitism that imposed policies on peasants with little input from the peasants themselves, and on an urban bias that allowed city folk to eat cheaply at the peasantry's expense. (Of course, these were biases that FRELIMO's development theory shared with both Soviet development theory and Western modernization theory.) As a result, since independence the Mozambican state has weighed heavily on the Mozambican masses, and Mozambican peasants in particular, impoverishing them and limiting their freedom at the same time. In this sense, even left-wing opponents of RENAMO argue that RENAMO and the civil war were as much the creation of FRELIMO as of foreign right-wing regimes, for many ordinary Mozambicans responded to FRELIMO's oppressiveness by supporting RENAMO.[53] Those who are critical of FRELIMO's elitist, urban-biased, and state-centered development theory are only part of a larger scholarly tendency. More and more scholars are taking states to task for imposing heavy-handed development schemes on the poorest of the poor, and sometimes even blaming "modernity" for providing the ideological and institutional conditions for such state interventionism to exist.[54]

It is true that FRELIMO's development policies emphasized the state, "modernity," and the big development project. The Soviet Union, FRELIMO's main source of aid for economic development, encouraged mechanized state-sector projects, and much of its aid to Mozambique came in the form of machines that would allow such projects to be undertaken.[55] And such policies were not simply imposed on FRELIMO, they were embraced by FRELIMO. For Samora Machel, the very purpose of *both* the state *and* Marxism was "development projects." Note the similarity of the following two pronouncements, both made by Machel in 1980:

> The State cannot continue to be involved in hundreds of people's shops. The State cannot manage small businesses. The State must devote itself to directing the economy and carrying out major development projects.[56]

> Marxism-Leninism does not concern itself with garages, it does not concern itself with selling eggs in the market. . . . Marxism-Leninism concerns itself with major economic development projects.[57]

Machel and FRELIMO were clearly enamored of high modernism.

And yet it is important to point out that Machel—as FRELIMO's leader and most prominent theorist—was also aware of the potential pitfalls of state-centered, modernizing development. Indeed, his own speeches and writings contain precisely the same arguments that later critics of high modernism would make. The following close examination of Machel's thought suggests that the problems with FRELIMO's development policies stemmed more from the practical implementation of those policies than from ideology or general principles. For example, Machel realized that scientific and technical knowledge should be valued not for its own sake, but only insofar as it improved the lives of the masses. He said in a speech: "If someone learns a lot and never goes to the masses, is never involved in practice, he will remain a dead compendium, a mere recorder who is able to quote by heart passages from scientific works, from revolutionary works, but who will live his whole life without writing a single new page, a single new line. His intelligence will remain sterile, like those seeds locked in the drawer."[58] Machel was even more troubled by the possibility that those who had acquired scientific and technical knowledge would try to form themselves into a new elite: "There are those who consider themselves irreplaceable. Full of arrogance, they refuse to learn from others, they monopolize knowledge, they delight in the failures of their comrades. Acting this way, they try to establish themselves as a privileged class, exploiting the masses, lording it over their petty, miserable estates. Individualism, egoism, ambition, and arrogance are microbes transmitting division; they are incubators of outmoded and exploitative ideas of society."[59] Machel hardly had some sort of unmitigated faith in a technocratic elite.

Neither did he simply hold the masses in contempt. Again, for Machel scientific knowledge acquired value only once it had been placed at the disposal of the masses. "It is because the masses see science in action," he wrote, "because the masses verify the results of science, because we continually explain to the infirm and the masses the causes of and means of combating disease, that the hospital is able to become a solid base in the fight against obscurantism."[60] But he went further than this. He also argued for expanding the definition of "scientific knowledge" to include all valid knowledge verified through practice. In this respect, even ordinary people became scientists:

> Without ever having been to school, our illiterate peasants know more about cassava, cotton, groundnuts, and many other things than the honorable capitalist gentleman who has never touched a hoe. Without knowing how to read, it is clear that our mechanics know more about car engines, how to assemble and repair them and how to mend broken

> parts, than the honorable capitalist gentleman who has never wished to soil his hands with motor oil. We see our "ignorant" masons, our "stupid" carpenters and laborers, so despised by the capitalist gentleman, making beautiful houses, beautiful furniture which the honorable capitalist gentleman appreciates immensely and which he has no idea how to make. This clearly shows that we learn through production.[61]

Far from fetishizing scientific and technical knowledge, on one occasion, in a clever turn of phrase, Machel even likened such knowledge to manure: "Soil without manure produces weak plants, but manure without soil burns the seeds and also produces nothing. Our intelligence, our knowledge, are like that manure. Manure must be mixed with soil, intelligence with practice."[62] Machel may have called for the creation of a "New Man" who rejected tradition and embraced modernity, but he also called for vigilance against allowing the possession of scientific knowledge to serve as the basis for new forms of oppression.

Much as I have done here, the scholars Ashis Nandy and James Scott—among many others—have noted how high modernist development ideology was shared by governments that were otherwise very much opposed to one another, whether they were Marxist or pro-Western, colonial or anticolonial. However, Nandy and Scott also go further and maintain that the violence and failures of twentieth-century development can be directly traced to very nature of this high modernist development ideology.[63] For my part, I hope to have shown that for all the similarities between colonial and anticolonial development ideologies in Mozambique, there were some important differences. FRELIMO and the New State both formulated their development ideologies in response to the other, and in a global context of consensus about the positive values of modernization and state-centered development. Both groups initially felt excluded from modernity—as Africans and as Portuguese, respectively—and initially appealed to their own cultural particularism. As their struggle intensified and economic development became a major element of regime justification, both FRELIMO and the New State changed and came to call for development that valued being modern and scientific above all else, with the state as the main agent of transformation. Ultimately, however,

FRELIMO could call for democratic, "people-centered" development in a way that the Portuguese New State simply could not. That FRELIMO's development policies failed anyway would seem to support the arguments of those who criticize "modernity" and state-centered development. Still, FRELIMO presented a theory of development that, in principle at least, actually accords well with the "popular empowerment" favored by such critics. Therefore, against Nandy and Scott, I would argue that the reasons for the failure of state-centered development must be sought in something more particular than the regime's basic ideological orientation.

## NOTES

1. James Scott, *Seeing Like a State: How Certain Schemes to Improve the Human Condition Have Failed* (New Haven: Yale University Press, 1998).

2. In Portuguese, FRELIMO is an acronym for *A Frente da Liberação de Moçambique*, or "The Front for the Liberation of Mozambique."

3. Allen Isaacman and Barbara Isaacman, *The Tradition of Resistance in Mozambique: The Zambezi Valley, 1850–1921* (Berkeley: University of California Press, 1976); Leroy Vail and Landeg White, *Capitalism and Colonialism in Mozambique: A Study of Quelimane District* (Minneapolis: University of Minnesota Press, 1980).

4. Allen Isaacman, *Cotton Is the Mother of Poverty: Peasants, Work, and Rural Struggle in Colonial Mozambique, 1938–1961* (Portsmouth, England: Heinemann, 1996), 9.

5. Edward A. Ross, *Report on Compulsory Labor in Portuguese Africa* (New York: n.p., 1925).

6. A. T. Nzula et al., *Forced Labour in Colonial Africa* (London: Zed Press, 1979).

7. Manuel de Lucena, "The Evolution of Portuguese Corporatism under Salazar and Caetano," in Lawrence Graham and Harry Makler, eds., *Contemporary Portugal: The Revolution and Its Antecedents* (Austin: University of Texas Press, 1979), 49–71.

8. Quoted in Malyn Newitt, *A History of Mozambique* (Bloomington: Indiana University Press, 1995), 446.

9. Alves de Azevedo, "O sentido espiritual da colonização portuguesa," *O Mundo Português: Revista de Cultura e Propaganda, de Arte e Literatura Coloniais* 6, no. 61 (1939): 29. In this essay, all translations from Portuguese originals are my own.

10. Morais Cabral, "A vitória do nosso espirito colonizador," *O Mundo Português* 6 (1939): 216.

11. João Ameal, "Mostruário do Império: A propósito da exposição colonial do Porto," *O Mundo Português* 1, part 1 (1934): 98.

12. Gervase Clarence-Smith, *The Third Portuguese Empire, 1825–1975: A Study in Economic Imperialism* (Manchester: Manchester University Press, 1985), 193; Keith Middlemas, *Cabora Bassa: Engineering and Politics in Southern Africa* (London: Weidenfeld and Nicolson, 1975), 26–27, 74–76, 316.

13. For Freyre's contributions to "lusotropicology" in Africa, see Ronald Chilcote, *Portuguese Africa* (Englewood Cliffs, N.J.: Prentice-Hall, 1967), 47–48, and Russell G. Hamilton, *Voices from an Empire: A History of Afro-Portuguese Literature* (Minneapolis: University of Minnesota Press, 1975), 10–11. For criticisms of Freyre's theories within the Brazilian context, see Thomas E. Skidmore, "Gilberto Freyre and the Early Brazilian Republic: Some Notes on Methodology," *Comparative Studies of Society and History* 6, no. 4 (1964): 490–505; Luiz A. de Castro Santos, "A casa-grande e o sobrado na obra de Gilberto Freyre," *Anuário Antropológico*, no. 83 (1985): 73–102; and Anthony Marx, *Making Race and Nation: A Comparison of South Africa, the United States, and Brazil* (Cambridge: Cambridge University Press, 1998), passim.

14. Quoted in Richard Hammond, "Race Attitudes and Policies in Portuguese Africa in the Nineteenth and Twentieth Centuries," *Race* 9, no. 2 (October 1967): 208.

15. Malyn Newitt, *Portugal in Africa: The Last Hundred Years* (London: C. Hurst, 1981), 100–101.

16. Ibid., 124, 138–40.

17. Clarence-Smith, *The Third Portuguese Empire*, chap. 6.

18. Quoted in Barry Munslow, *Mozambique: The Revolution and Its Origins* (London: Longmans, 1983), 7.

19. Richard Robinson, *Contemporary Portugal: A History* (London: George Allen & Unwin, 1979), chaps. 3–4.

20. Valentim Alexandre, "The Colonial Empire," in António Costa Pinto, ed., *Modern Portugal* (Palo Alto: The Society for the Promotion of Science and Scholarship, 1998), 45–46.

21. Marcelo Caetano, *Colonizing Traditions, Principles, and Methods of the Portuguese* (Lisbon: Agência-Geral do Ultramar, 1951), 52.

22. Marcelo Caetano, *Os Nativos na Economia Africana* (Coimbra, 1954), 16, quoted in Allen Isaacman and Barbara Isaacman, *Mozambique: From Colonialism to Revolution, 1900–1982* (Boulder: Westview Press, 1982), 27.

23. Adriano Moreira, *Portugal's Stand in Africa* (New York: University Publishers, 1962), 75. See also D. M. Abshire and M. A. Samuels, *Portuguese Africa: An Introduction* (London: Pall Mall, 1969), 148.

24. Quoted in Moreira, *Portugal's Stand in Africa*, 154.

25. Franco Nogueira, *The Third World* (London: Johnson, 1967).

26. Ibid., 34.

27. Newitt, *Portugal in Africa*, 195–97, 220–21, 237–38.

28. Clarence-Smith, *The Third Portuguese Empire*, 178–80, 213–15.

29. Middlemas, *Cabora Bassa.* After Mozambique achieved independence in 1975, the dam's official name was changed to "Cahora Bassa."

30. Joaquim da Silva Cunha, *Cabora-Bassa: The Signing of the Cabora Bassa Agreement on the 19th September 1969* (Lisbon: Agência-Geral do Ultramar, 1970), 9–10.

31. Joaquim da Silva Cunha, *Cabora Bassa—Who Will Benefit By It?* (Lisbon: Agência-Geral do Ultramar, 1970), 7.

32. Miguel Murupa, *Portuguese Africa in Perspective: The Making of a Multi-Racial Nation* (n.p.: Anuário, 1973), 35.

33. Michael Adas, *Machines as the Measure of Men: Science, Technology, and Ideologies of Western Dominance* (Ithaca: Cornell University Press, 1989), 413.

34. Frederick Cooper, *Decolonization and African Society: The Labor Question in French and British Africa* (Cambridge: Cambridge University Press, 1996).

35. Alexandre Cancelas, *Contributo para uma política social moçambicana* (Braga: Editora Pax, 1972).

36. Middlemas, *Cabora Bassa,* 173.

37. Kenneth Maxwell, *The Making of Portuguese Democracy* (Cambridge: Cambridge University Press, 1995).

38. Newitt, *Portugal in Africa,* 239.

39. Eduardo Mondlane, *The Struggle for Mozambique* (London: Penguin, 1969), 58–59.

40. Ibid., 177.

41. *Mozambique Revolution*, no. 38 (March-April 1969): 6.

42. *Mozambique Revolution*, no. 37 (January-February 1969): 23.

43. *Mozambique Revolution*, no. 49 (October-December 1971): 10.

44. Edward Alpers, "The Struggle for Socialism in Mozambique, 1960–1972," in Carl Rosberg and Thomas Callaghy, eds., *Socialism in Sub-Saharan Africa: A New Assessment* (Berkeley, Calif.: Institute of International Studies, 1979), 267–95. A similar dispute between cultural nationalists and modernizers, a dispute with significant repercussions for development policy, took place in India during the late colonial and early postcolonial periods. The cultural nationalists were represented by Gandhi and the modernizers by Nehru. See Sugata Bose, "Instruments and Idioms of Colonial and National Development: India's Historical Experience in Comparative Perspective," in Frederick Cooper and Randall Packard, eds., *International Development and the Social Sciences* (Berkeley: University of California Press, 1997), 45–63.

45. Thomas Henriksen, *Revolution and Counterrevolution: Mozambique's War of Independence, 1964–1974* (Westport, Conn.: Greenwood Press, 1983), 182–92.

46. Thomas Henriksen, "Angola, Mozambique, and the Soviet Union: Libera-

tion and the Quest for Influence," in Warren Weinstein and Thomas Henriksen, eds., *Soviet and Chinese Aid to African Nations* (New York: Praeger, 1980), 56–71.

47. Henriksen, *Revolution and Counterrevolution*, 212–16.

48. Margaret Hall and Tom Young, *Confronting Leviathan: Mozambique since Independence* (Athens: Ohio University Press, 1997), 61–68, 85–86.

49. *Mozambique Revolution*, no. 25 (June-July 1966): 14.

50. Henriksen, *Revolution and Counterrevolution*, 216; Hall and Young, *Confronting Leviathan*, 61, 68, 93; Tom Young, "The Politics of Development in Angola and Mozambique," *African Affairs* 87, no. 347 (April 1988): 169.

51. *Mozambique Revolution*, no. 40 (25 September 1969): 38.

52. FRELIMO, *Relatório do Comité Central ao 30 Congresso* ([Maputo?]: Departamento do Trabalho Ideológico da FRELIMO, [1977?]), 74.

53. Hall and Young, *Confronting Leviathan;* Joseph Hanlon, *Mozambique: The Revolution under Fire* (London: Zed Books, 1984).

54. For examples of this tendency, see Ashis Nandy, "Introduction," in Nandy, ed., *Science, Hegemony, and Violence: A Requiem for Modernity* (New Delhi: Oxford University Press, 1988), 1–23, and Scott, *Seeing Like a State.*

55. Roger Kanet and Boris Ipatov, "Soviet Aid and Trade in Africa," in Weinstein and Henriksen, eds., *Soviet and Chinese Aid to African Nations,* 19, 22.

56. Quoted in Thomas Henriksen, "Communism, Communist States, and Africa: Opportunities and Challenges," in Henriksen, ed., *Communist Powers and Sub-Saharan Africa* (Stanford: Hoover Institution Press, 1981), 122.

57. Quoted in Hall and Young, *Confronting Leviathan,* 95.

58. Samora Machel, *The Tasks Ahead: Selected Speeches of Samora Moises Machel* (New York: Afro American Information Service, 1975), 38.

59. Samora Machel, *No trabalho sanitário materializemos o princípio de que a revolução liberta o povo* (Lisbon: Publicações Nova Aurora, 1973), 16.

60. Ibid.

61. Machel, *The Tasks Ahead,* 37.

62. Ibid., 40–41.

63. See note 54.

## FURTHER READING

Hall, Margaret, and Tom Young. *Confronting Leviathan: Mozambique since Independence.* Athens: Ohio University Press, 1997.

Hanlon, Joseph. *Mozambique: The Revolution under Fire.* London: Zed Books, 1984.

Isaacman, Allen, and Chris Sneddon. "Toward a Social and Environmental History of the Building of Cahora Bassa Dam." *Journal of Southern African Studies* 26, no. 4 (December 2000): 597–632.

Middlemas, Keith. *Cabora Bassa: Engineering and Politics in Southern Africa*. London: Weidenfeld and Nicolson, 1975.

# WEST MEETS EAST: THE CENTER FOR INTERNATIONAL STUDIES AND INDIAN ECONOMIC DEVELOPMENT

DAVID C. ENGERMAN

The history of American economic aid to India in the 1950s and 1960s was shaped, more than anything, by a case of mistaken directions. American and Indian policymakers alike wanted to see India move toward the West—but they nevertheless had different destinations in mind. To Americans promoting aid to India, the West was defined politically; it described the American camp in the Cold War, as against the Eastern (i.e., Soviet) bloc. Walt Rostow, the impresario of modernization theory, for instance, saw economic development in terms of Soviet-American confrontation. Speaking before a group of scholars, diplomats, and foundation officials in 1956, he claimed that the goals of economic development were "psychological and political."[1] The Center for International Studies (CENIS) at MIT, Rostow's institutional home in the 1950s, had this goal as a founding principle. The center would, according to an early mission statement, apply "basic social science research to problems of U.S. policy in the current world struggle."[2] Its program on economic development, in other words, was initiated with the Cold War very much in mind.

To many leading Indians, in contrast, East and West were economic categories. Jawaharlal Nehru, India's first prime minister and a force behind the country's economic modernization in the 1950s, provides an excellent example here. His enthusiastic endorsement of India's rapid industrialization came out of a desire to see India learn from the West—which he defined in terms of economic development, not political allegiance. The Cold War conflict between American and Soviet camps mattered less to him than the differences between those nations that had achieved a significant degree of industrialization—which he called Western—and those that had not. Nehru did not equate American and Soviet models of development, but he insisted that despite their conflicts the United States and the USSR were "branches of the same tree."[3] While he recognized the vociferousness of the conflict between them, then, Nehru stressed economic similarities as well as political differences.

Indian and American debates about economic development offer numerous insights into the Cold War. First, the debates reveal the enthusiasm held outside the United States for visions of industrial modernity. Indian leaders sought rapid industrialization through central planning as the fast track for reaching economic independence. Indo-American relations suggest, second, the degree to which many American policymakers and scholars defended economic development as a weapon in the Cold War. While Indian leaders strove to enter the economic West, American policymakers and the "action intellectuals" advising them fought to put India in the political West. This uncomfortable relationship between politics and economics unraveled in the Indian case, at least so far as MIT was concerned, in late 1964. Conflicts over Indian economic priorities combined with accusations that CENIS was an arm of the American government—run through the CIA, no less—and led to divisive scandals that eventually doomed the center's work in India.

## THE POLITICS OF ECONOMIC DEVELOPMENT IN THE UNITED STATES

Only months after India attained its independence from Britain in August 1947, American diplomats discussed the geopolitical value of economic assistance to the new nation. Such aid, wrote the first American ambassador to postcolonial India, "is the most effective channel for keeping India on our side and under our influence." Four years later, after the emergence of the People's Republic of China, the next American ambassador expanded on this argument, this time invoking the threat that the economic growth of Communist China would soon surpass India's. The fate of the Indian economy, Chester Bowles wrote, would be a "decisive factor in determining whether or not Communism takes over this part of the world." While most congressional leaders agreed that Indian development was a Cold War concern, many in the Republican majority saw few reasons to deal with nations, like India, which refused to join the Western camp in the Cold War.[4]

CENIS scholars sided with those seeking to expand American aid to India and other developing nations. Many factors were at play here: an earnest desire to help the former colonies get to their own economic feet; an interest in applying their social-scientific training to real-world tasks; and an aspiration to improve their nation's international position. Especially in public forums, though, these factors received less attention than the refrain that economic development was a political necessity in the Cold War. From the first years of its operation, CENIS had undertaken research on economic and political development so that (in the words of one early proposal), it could "project alternative future paths of development and . . . identify possible courses of action, particularly for the United States."[5] From its origins in 1951, the center maintained close contacts with government agencies, including Director Max Millikan's former employer, the CIA. Early CENIS projects focused on pressing foreign policy concerns like a summary of the scholarly literature on the USSR and China (funded by the CIA).[6]

Rostow's own concerns about the political implications of economic growth predate his arrival at MIT in 1950. He asserted that the topic of his doctoral dissertation—industrialization in nineteenth-century Britain—was "a matter of wide and not wholly academic concern" which would shed light on "aspects of contemporary foreign policy." Rostow's broader work on *The Process of Economic Growth* used these historical insights to describe the interconnections between social (especially technological) factors and economic growth. It defined the crucial stage of "take-off," after which point an economy could expand rapidly. To get to the take-off, however, required significant capital investments. Technological innovation might help provide this capital, but it was most likely to result from increased sales of raw materials, especially agricultural products. Without a healthy agricultural sector, he argued, achieving a boost in investment rates would require a drastic decline in standards of living.[7] The need for agriculture pointed to a fundamental flaw in Communist strategies of industrialization, Rostow argued in an article called "Marx Was a City Boy." Soviet and Chinese plans for rapid industrialization could succeed only by makjing the countryside economically and politically subservient. He even praised India by exaggerating its focus on agriculture; he misleadingly claimed that India in the early 1950s was "plowing its scarce capital . . . primarily into agriculture."[8]

Rostow's determination to apply his economic arguments grew as the Soviet Union expanded its international aid program in the early 1950s. He saw American development aid as an indispensable weapon in fighting this front of the Cold War. Believing that Communists saw the economy purely as "an instrument for increasing the effective authority of Communism, at home and abroad," Rostow astutely recognized the centrality of economic development to former colonies in Asia and Africa. Because Rostow defined communism in political terms, he saw Soviet and Chinese offers of economic aid—to India or elsewhere—as methods designed to lure unsuspecting nations into a political alliance. American economic aid was the only appropriate response to this aspect of the Communist threat, Rostow concluded. Max Millikan made a similar claim about the politics of economic development, for instance in a paper presented to the State Department's Foreign Service Institute titled "Economic Policy as an Instrument of Political and Psychological Policy."[9]

Millikan and his staff worked hard in the mid-1950s to bring long-term development aid into the American policy mix. The boldest policy statement by CENIS officials about development aid came in 1956 and 1957, with the distribution (first private, then public) of a case statement for aid, *A Proposal*. Determined to overcome the reluctance of the U.S. Congress to fund long-term aid projects overseas, coauthors Millikan and Rostow made the case for development aid as the "key to an effective foreign policy." They attacked the State Department's reliance on "pacts, treaties, negotiation, and international diplomacy," arguing instead that it should be working to "develop viable, energetic and confident democratic societies throughout the

Free World." American development aid, considered over a suitably long time frame, could counteract potential Soviet expansion in the third world. Such aid was necessary, Millikan and Rostow insisted, to keep third world nations on the right economic track—which would, in turn, ensure their political reliability.[10] Staff members established close contacts with Senator John F. Kennedy and his senior aides; they were also in frequent correspondence with other foreign policy organizations.[11]

Most of the center's development staff saw Indian growth as a linchpin for keeping the Communist strategy of development aid at bay.[12] India's size (a population of over 400 million), location, and economic profile made it a natural counterexample to the Soviet-style rapid industrialization then under way in China. CENIS conceptualized a broad role for itself in development policy in general and American-Indian relations in particular. Its work brought together academic research, behind-the-scenes lobbying, publicity, and training in order to shape the course of American foreign policy toward India as well as Indian economic development.[13] In 1955 it established a center in New Delhi, staffed by three American economists under the leadership of Wilfred Malenbaum. By 1957 CENIS officials were meeting with leading Indian economists and policymakers, offering their own independent analyses of India's economic strengths and weaknesses while seeking to shape policy. As their mission demanded, CENIS economists also publicized the political stakes of Indian development. Malenbaum wrote for other scholars about the political significance of Indian development. In more urgent tones, he also addressed policy audiences, warning that if India chose a Communist path, "it would be as decisive a victory for [the USSR] as can be visualized in any war, however hot."[14] Especially in their public pronouncements, CENIS scholars located India's determination to modernize within the geopolitical framework of the Cold War. But Indian interest in development planning—including its work with the center—had far different grounds.

## INDIAN PLANNING: USING ECONOMICS TO EVADE POLITICS

The intellectual and institutional backdrop for Indian planning in the 1950s dates back before independence, to Soviet planning in the 1930s. Indian planners in general, and Prime Minister Nehru in particular, looked to the Soviet experience as they began their own planning process. They were hardly alone in studying central planning in the USSR. The first Soviet five-year plan (1928–32) attracted widespread attention and enthusiasm both within and outside the USSR. The prospect of turning an agricultural nation into an industrial powerhouse—"a country of metal, a country of automobiles, a country of tractors," in Stalin's phrase—in less than a generation appealed not only to Communists in the Soviet Union, but also to workers hoping to live in better conditions and engineers whose own technocratic vision intersected with the plans.[15] Outside Soviet territory, where enthusiasts did not have to suffer the immense dislocations and severe shortages resulting from the drive for industrialization, leftists and technocrats alike cheered the five-year plans. Many foreign observers recognized the high costs involved, but regretted them as unfortunate by-products of an inevitable and desirable process; the American economist Stuart Chase put it most bluntly: "A better economic order is worth a little bloodshed."[16] Even a famine which devastated rural areas, especially in Ukraine, could be understood in terms of the plan's aspirations—as Russia's attempt to "starve itself great." Such utterances were not the monopoly of leftists; anti-Soviet economists and journalists also employed similar images, down to the exact wording.[17]

Nehru's excitement about the USSR in the late 1920s and early 1930s emerged in this context of widespread excitement over Soviet planning. For Nehru interest in the Soviet Union was the product of a technocratic worldview as well aspirations for economic and political independence; it was not an indicator of political affiliation. The parallels he saw with his own nation, then still under British rule, heightened his ardor for Soviet economic policy. Both Russia and India, Nehru wrote after a trip to Moscow in 1927, were agricultural nations with vast problems of poverty and illiteracy; "if Russia finds a satisfactory solution for these," Nehru hoped, "our work in India is made easier."[18] The Soviet example, he wrote later, "shows how a people can revitalize itself, become youthful again, if it is prepared to pay the price for it." He was clear about the costs involved in the Soviet experience—Soviet citizens had "tightened their belts and starved and deprived themselves," he wrote—but nevertheless endorsed the efforts at rapid industrialization through central planning.[19] Hardly swayed by Marxism or communism, Nehru saw the Soviet Union as an economic model worthy of emulation.[20] And his writings about the American economy at this time suggest that his focus was on economics rather than politics. In spite of his criticisms of American foreign policy and American culture in general, Nehru offered a strong endorsement of the New Deal, especially to the extent that it introduced "state control over industry."[21]

Nehru brought this appreciation of economic planning to his work in India.[22] He served as the first chair of the National Planning Committee of the Indian National Congress, created in 1938. The committee included among its principal operating assumptions the notion that India's major concerns of poverty, unemployment, national defense, and economic expansion "cannot by solved without industrialization." And rapid industrialization required central planning: only with a staff of economists directing public investment, regulating prices, and setting production goals, Nehru believed, could India's economy expand rapidly.[23] Planning held one other crucial advantage for Nehru—it sought to solve economic problems through technical rather than political means. Recalling (from the vantage point of 1946) the earliest years of the National Planning Committee, Nehru waxed nostalgic about the absence of political disputation and the tendency to treat all problems as admitting of technical solutions: "As each particular problem was viewed in its larger context, it led us inevitably in a particular direction. To me the spirit of co-operation of the members of the Planning Committee was particularly soothing and gratifying, for I found it a pleasant contrast to the squabbles and conflicts of politics." The technical solutions presumed a consensus about the need for rapid and centrally planned industrialization—"only thus could we solve our problems of poverty and unemployment."[24] Following from this overarching goal, the planning process soon came to center around a single measure of progress: increased production.[25]

While the arrest of many members of the National Planning Committee—including Nehru—slowed its work considerably during World War II, the desire for centralized planning was hardly squelched. The postindependence successor to the National Planning Committee, the Planning Commission, began its work in 1950. It quickly generated the first Indian five-year plan, scheduled to start in 1951. With such a short lead time, this first plan built on historical precedents rather than outlining a new approach to economic development; in the words of one recent analyst, it was "little more than a collection of public projects that had been under consideration during the last years of the British Raj."[26] The planning documents pulled together proposals for irrigation and agricultural development, for transportation and communications improvements, and for social services. Industry, the plan's first historian concluded, "came in a very bad fourth" in priorities.[27]

Even without radical new policies, though, the Planning Commission employed new practices. It lauded the application of technical expertise in developing and implementing the plans. In its first official documents about the inaugural five-year plan, the commission noted essential conditions for success. First was general agreement about the goals of planning—an agreement which, by implication, had already been reached. The remaining goals emphasized the technocratic elements of India's economic apparatus. Success depended on gathering "effective power . . . in the hands of the state" as well as on the "earnest and determined exercise of that power," and finally, on an able and efficient administration.[28] The planning document, therefore, began with the assumption of a national consensus around the goal of rapid economic development. The job of planners was to use state power in order to achieve that development. Planning was ultimately a set of technical executive decisions designed to further economic growth in this new political entity, the Indian nation.

As the first five-year plan unfolded, though, a more concerted effort at central planning and rapid industrialization was in the works. Under the leadership of Prasanta Mahalanobis, a physicist who had become India's chief planner, a group of Indian economists tried to mobilize the government's economic organs for a plan more closely resembling Soviet plans of the 1930s. Indian plans under Mahalanobis paralleled the Soviet experience in three aspects: they shared similar models, priorities, and methods.

Mahalanobis developed a theory of economic growth without direct reference to European or American scholarship on the topic.[29] He divided the economy into two hypothetical sectors—one producing consumer goods, the other producing machinery—and worked out a variety of scenarios. His calculations suggested that this hypothetical economy would face a low ceiling of growth unless it emphasized the production of capital goods such as factory equipment.[30] Without producing this machinery, the model indicated, the economy would require imports, which would need to expand as the industrial sector grew. Mahalanobis's model is almost identical to one of the central models in the Soviet planning.[31] India's second five-year plan, based on Mahalanobis's model, thus shared much with the early five-year plans in the USSR in part because they were based on similar economic models.

Mahalanobis's plans for India also shared the Soviet emphasis, both financial and symbolic, on steel. The key to rapid industrialization, Mahalanobis claimed, was investment in heavy industry in general, and in steel in particular. While he had derived the need for heavy industry from his growth model, he chose steel after reflecting on Soviet economic history. It was steel, he claimed, which had catapulted underdeveloped Russia into the ranks of the industrial nations in fewer than four decades. The Indian emphasis on steel built on some foundations established in the early 1950s. Most significant among these was the design of a huge steel complex at Bhilai. This enormous public project seemed inspired by the Soviet complex at Magnitogorsk—which was in turn inspired by the U.S. Steel plant built in Gary, Indiana, at the turn of the century.[32] The Indian government first approached the World Bank (an institution dominated by the United States) to obtain financing for Bhilai, but was rebuffed since Bank policy forbade loans for publicly owned projects. Turning then to other sources, Indian officials signed an agreement with the USSR, which provided substantial credits as well as the services of over three hundred Soviet engineers.[33] The parallels between Indian economic goals and earlier Soviet plans were not lost on either nation's leaders. In an exchange of visits, Nehru and Soviet premier N. A. Bulganin celebrated the similarities between their respective economic plans. The Soviet leader nostalgically if condescendingly noted how the large Indian steel projects "reminded us of the atmosphere of our First Five-Year Plan, when we were building our first big enterprises."[34]

Finally, Indian plans paralleled earlier Soviet ones in methods of central planning. Mahalanobis was at least partially responsible for this vision of planning, though Nehru's earlier interest in Soviet plans also played a role. The Indian Statistical Institute, under Mahalanobis's leadership, hosted many prominent theorists and practitioners of Soviet-style economic planning. Fresh from his own tour of planned economies, Mahalanobis invited M. I. Rubinshtein from the Soviet planning agency as well as the distinguished Polish economist Oskar Lange. But not all institute visitors were from Soviet-bloc nations; well-known economists from Western Europe also traveled there, including Ragnar Frisch (Norway), Joan Robinson (U.K.), and Jan Tinbergen (the Netherlands). Harvard's John Kenneth Galbraith's encounter with Mahalanobis at a dinner party in Switzerland led to his visit to the institute. The Indian planner also consulted with at least one leading American student of Soviet planning. Indeed, many economists with the MIT project had close professional and personal ties at the institute.[35] Mahalanobis undertook such studies because he was convinced that India could make economic progress at an acceptable pace only with central planning to mobilize the necessary resources.[36] Mahalanobis's interests in planning, then, appear more as an economist's efforts to learn about theories and techniques than as a pledge to imitate Soviet-style planning.

The domestic significance of India's second five-year plan stood apart from its echoes of Soviet history. One prominent Indian economist called the plan, the result of detailed and sophisticated work by the domestic planning apparatus, "the single most significant document on Indian planning."[37] The most notable change between the first and second plans was the weight accorded industry, especially heavy industry. Public expenditures on industry and mineral sectors, which had been only 8 percent in the first plan, ballooned to 21 percent in the second. The shift in priorities came at the expense of agriculture and social services. While the first plan devoted 35 percent of public-sector outlays to agriculture and irrigation, its successor devoted only 21 percent to such projects. Similarly, social spending declined from 26 percent in the first plan to 21 percent.[38] The extent of government spending became the central indicator of planning priorities, as the planning operation turned increasingly toward state ownership of major industries—an essential aspect of building (as the plans often noted) "a socialist pattern of society."

For all these affinities with the Soviet Union and all the references to a socialist pattern, however, Nehru was far from a Communist or even a sympathizer. He invested a great deal of energy both domestically and internationally in maintaining India's autonomy vis-à-vis both the United States and the USSR. Upon ascending to the premiership in 1947, Nehru criticized both the Communist Party of India (CPI) and the Soviet Union for their political activities at the time of independence. His public and private statements alike emphasized India's distance from—and indeed displeasure with—both entities. When Soviet leaders called on the CPI to direct a rebellion against Nehru's government in 1947, the premier launched an all-out public campaign to discredit the party; he did so by castigating it for connections to the Soviet Union. He publicly condemned Soviet "aggression" and "expansionism" while accusing Indian Communists of "a complete lack of integrity and decency." They were not promoting a social theory, he fumed, but social chaos.[39]

Nehru also brought his aspirations for an India free from Soviet and American affiliations into the international arena, serving as a key spokesman for the Non-Aligned Movement. This movement sought to build links among the newly independent nations in Asia and (by the early 1960s) Africa. Originating in the Asian-African Conference held in Bandung, Indonesia, in 1955, the group of nonaligned states put nation-building and economic development ahead of political alliances. Nehru's leadership of this movement underscored his commitment to an independent foreign policy, and itself flowed from his determination, since the first days of Indian independence, to steer a path between the two superpowers. He wanted to work with both American and Soviet diplomats as need be—but with no intent of becoming a "camp follower."[40] In international relations, as in domestic politics, Nehru sought out an independent path, refusing to align with the East or West of the Cold War.

## INDIA AND THE UNITED STATES IN CONFLICT OVER ECONOMIC POLICY, 1957–1964

Nehru's activities with the Non-Aligned Movement as well as his longstanding and occasionally fierce battles with the Communist Party of India suggest that his commitment to creating a modern India far outweighed any desire to join the pro-Soviet camp in international politics, or to work with Communists at home. While Nehru gratefully accepted Soviet funds and technical assistance for Bhilai, he did so only after his request for a World Bank loan was rebuffed. Even more problematic than Bhilai for many American policymakers was Nehru's willingness to purchase military equipment from the Soviet Union. Yet this arrangement, too, came after rejection by the American officials—this time in the form of the Eisenhower administration's willingness to sell arms to Pakistan. As long as India and Pakistan contested territory in Kashmir—a conflict that has continued into the twenty-first century—one combatant's ability to purchase arms would leave the other at a significant military disadvantage. India's role as a recipient of Soviet economic aid and military equipment was explicable in terms of local factors—the desire for rapid economic development in the former case, and its ongoing dispute with Pakistan in the latter. Yet many American policymakers could view India only through Cold War lenses. On the heels of Bandung and Bhilai, the senior State Department official for Asian affairs insisted that India was about to join the Soviet camp, as demonstrated by "Mr. Nehru's consistent support of the Communist position and his opposition to U.S. policy."[41]

The Center for International Studies, however, was not ready to write off India. Rostow and Millikan aimed their modest *Proposal* precisely against arguments like this one. They saw the goals of long-term development aid in the same political framework as State Department officials, but insisted on a longer time frame. Economic aid would yield political dividends, they argued, but only after a decade or more. An aid policy "narrowly designed to win friends or promote military alliances," Millikan and Rostow stressed, "could easily backfire." What the United States needed—for its own national interest—was to prevent the instability "inherent in the awakening of formerly static peoples." In such instability, the Communist threat became all the more menacing.[42]

The center's battle to expand American development aid converged with India's development trajectory in 1957, creating a sense of urgency that gave both programs a boost. With the publication of *A Proposal* and the authors' testimony to congressional committees, CENIS was especially well poised to shape aid policy. That India would become the centerpiece of a new policy framework was overdetermined. Both senatorial sponsors of the aid bill, John F. Kennedy and John Sherman Cooper, had an interest in the country—Kennedy thanks to his close contacts with CENIS, and Cooper because of his prior appointment as ambassador to New Delhi.[43] Dramatic international events, furthermore, drew new attention to Asian economic development. The announcement of China's Great Leap Forward—further accelerating the pace of industrialization there—provided a direct point of comparison between Communist and non-Communist models of development. CENIS officials and a growing number of policymakers hoped to cast India in the latter role.

A burgeoning economic crisis in India further added to the urgency of American aid. The second five-year plan called for a stress on heavy industry at the expense of agricultural development. Both foreign exchange and agricultural problems plagued the plan, however, right from the start. Fully one-sixth of its budgeted expenditures would come from foreign aid, though prior aid had not come close to the amounts necessary. Aside from providing investment funds for the Indian government, the Planning Commission expected aid denominated in foreign currencies, thus facilitating imports of industrial equipment from Europe and the United States. Even if the anticipated foreign aid did materialize, there would still be a significant gap in revenues, "to be covered," in the plan's nebulous words, "by additional measures to raise domestic resources." These two unreliable categories, foreign exchange and unspecified domestic sources, accounted for fully one-quarter of the plan's expected revenues.[44] Agricultural production proved even more problematic, in part because the industrial sector's precedence left few resources for agriculture. The Planning Commission's goals for agriculture were derived from the needs of other sectors, not from any detailed analysis of the agricultural sector.[45] In order to achieve the desired rates of industrial expansion, one planner figured, agricultural production needed to increase by at least 35 percent—and without any significant investments in the sector. Planners raised this figure even higher soon after the second plan began.[46] The two problems also interacted, as foreign exchange shortages hindered efforts to purchase food abroad. The Indian economic crisis of 1957 also resulted from exogenous shocks. The American-Pakistani arms sales led to increased Indian defense spending, eating up scarce foreign exchange. And declining harvests added to the pressure for food imports. The situation worsened sufficiently for Nehru to overcome his reluctance and to make an explicit if indirect request for aid. As India's international position looked increasingly grim in late 1957, he expressed his interest—to a *New York Times* reporter—in obtaining an American loan on the order of $500 million.[47]

Kept well informed by its branch office in India, CENIS sounded the alarm in the United States even before Nehru's request. Rostow, by all reports, was among the most vocal in this regard, exclaiming at one point that the success or failure of Indian planning "will prove—one way or another—to be one of the decisive turning points of the twentieth century."[48] Even after dismissing Rostow for "exaggeration," Millikan expressed his concerns to a colleague: "I cannot escape the conclusion that the shape which development planning in India takes over the next few months may be as crucial a determinant of world history over the next decade as any other single factor."[49] Millikan led CENIS on multiple fronts; aside from his work on *A Proposal* and the Kennedy-Cooper bill, he also helped engineer news coverage favorable for the expansion of the aid program.[50] These efforts yielded the desired results, if not of the desired magnitude. In early 1958 administration officials declared that the U.S. government had assembled an aid package for India: $150 million in exchange credits from the Export-Import Bank and $75 million from the brand-new Development Loan Fund. This package was the centerpiece of a new development strategy for India. It was supplemented not only by food aid provided on generous terms (through a program predating Kennedy-Cooper) but also by American leadership in a World Bank consortium devoted to Indian development.[51]

CENIS sought to influence not only Washington but also New Delhi. Meeting with American and Indian government officials, center personnel sought to shape both American aid policy and Indian economic priorities.[52] By the mid-1950s the India project's initial contacts with the State Department had long since faded. The Ford Foundation provided a generous grant.[53] According to the terms of that grant, CENIS worked along three lines in India: (1) operational research to contribute to economic decision-making; (2) the expansion of economic research capacities at major Indian academic centers; and (3) the education of promising Indian economists at MIT. Yet conflicts soon emerged in the first two aspects of this work; the third was successful but small-scale.[54] The most significant issues arose when CENIS economists undertook research in support of Indian economic planning, in large part because they were caught in internal debates about the shape of the third five-year plan, then under consideration. Indian planners worked with CENIS economists Louis Lefeber and

Richard Eckaus to design computer models of the Indian economy. Mahalanobis's desire to outsource his computations no doubt grew after his entreaties that the United States provide the Indian Statistical Institute with a powerful computer were refused.[55]

But the results of these computations soon sparked divisive debates between CENIS economists and some Indian planners, as well as within the center itself. As the MIT model became increasingly sophisticated in the early 1960s, its authors' concerns about the direction of Indian planning multiplied.[56] By then, India was in the midst of its third five-year plan, and economists were working on the fourth. Computations based on the MIT model indicated that the third plan had overemphasized industry at the expense of agriculture; the model's authors worried that the fourth plan would continue to misallocate resources in a similar fashion. By early spring 1964 the MIT economists debated among themselves what to do about their conclusions. As one senior CENIS economist put it, they all agreed that "to prepare the Fourth Plan without using sophisticated economic models would be a great pity." The modelers themselves were soon separated by distance as well as desires: Louis Lefeber, one of the key members of the team, sat in New Delhi, convinced of the model's significance but wary of promoting the policy implications of the model. Citing the preliminary and technical nature of the conclusions, he wanted merely to encourage further research. Yet Lefeber was also determined that the model would "receive attention because of its profound implications for Indian planning"; to do otherwise, he insisted, would be to "play politics."[57]

The controversy soon left the realm of technical economics and entered Indian politics. Lefeber described the model's results—which cast doubt on the industry-heavy approach of the third plan, and by extension the fourth—to an interested group of Planning Commission economists. Meanwhile his co-worker Richard Eckaus joined Millikan in briefing less technically adept notables in Cambridge. Ambassador Bowles (on leave from his second term in New Delhi) expressed enthusiasm about the results, as did B. K. Nehru, India's ambassador-at-large for economic issues.[58] Some Indian policymakers outside the Planning Commission—most notably in the Ministries of Finance, Food, and Agriculture—endorsed the substance of the model's results. Not surprisingly, however, Planning Commission members who continued to promote heavy industry along the lines of Mahalanobis's early models disputed the conclusions of the MIT model; one such economist jokingly demanded that Lefeber be placed under house arrest. The situation was further complicated by resentments that the MIT group was given special access to economic data, thus giving its results extra weight. Finally, Nehru's death in May 1964 reduced the chance that this disagreement could remain a technical economic one. All these factors coincided to make economic planning an increasing political issue by 1964.[59]

In this charged and confused context, the revelation that CENIS maintained connections with the CIA was especially damaging. The news first received widespread attention in an American book with the lurid title *The Invisible Government*. In it, two journalists described Millikan's prior employment at the CIA as well as the agency's sponsorship of Rostow's *Dynamics of Soviet Society*.[60] Millikan's vague statements about the matter all but confirmed the CIA connection.[61] Such information, which earlier might merely have raised eyebrows in India as well as the United States, now fueled a fire. The book cast no aspersions on CENIS's India program, which had received the bulk of its support, publicly acknowledged, from the Ford Foundation. (The status of the India project's first contacts with the State Department—the terms of which included confidentiality—was not mentioned.)[62] One general-interest newsweekly in India, however, had no room for such distinctions; it called CENIS "an extended arm of the CIA research division, even if under a more respectable academic garb." Perhaps more damningly, it claimed that CENIS's India project was "a deliberate attempt . . . to sabotage the country's long-term development programme." How did CENIS allegedly sabotage the program? By calling into question "the major postulates of Indian planning, namely, the decision to develop a heavy industry base."[63] CENIS advice to Indian planners, offered as technical economic analysis, was received as the baldest form of political interference. As MIT economists came to realize that future CENIS advice would not be received in a strictly technical realm, they grew pessimistic about continuing their work in India.[64] CENIS quietly withdrew by spring 1965. And what of the hotly contested fourth five-year plan? After all that debate, it was never implemented. A severe economic crisis in 1965–66—resulting from poor harvests, armed conflict with Pakistan, and the suspension of American aid—led to a State of Emergency. From 1965 to 1970 India went planless. Subsequent economic plans, however, contained far more emphasis on agriculture.

The CENIS program's history indicated just how far apart American and Indian economists remained, and how difficult was the search for a common ground in terms of policy in development's early days. While Indian planners hoped that the planning process might reduce the intrusion of politics, the center's scholars sold their work publicly as a contribution to America's geopolitical interests. The research conducted by Lefeber and Eckaus was hardly political in intent—it was a contribution to evolving techniques of economic analysis—though the researchers recognized the political implications of their results. But the rhetoric of Cold War politics so often used by CENIS personnel in their policy-related encounters echoed far beyond meetings with Washington policy wonks.

The accusation that the center sought to limit Indian industry was, at best, a dramatic oversimplification, perhaps even a misrepresentation. Rostow had expressed his concern about Indian industrialization as early as 1954: "Underdeveloped countries . . . wanted prompt industrial progress but tended to identify such progress with steel mills rather than the well-balanced building of an industrial complex in close relation to available natural resources." Such desires, Rostow continued, were short-sighted if not catastrophic in both economic and political terms.[65] Yet even while he was at MIT, Rostow's involvement with the India project was limited to promotion and politicking. In any case, after Kennedy's ascension to the presidency, Rostow left MIT to promote his vision of economic development in Washington. Center personnel directly involved with the India project, furthermore, were far from unanimous about the feasibility of India's plans. Its staff included economists from England and Australia with very loose connections to MIT. While some of these economists criticized India's focus on heavy industry, others defended it. The four leading economists on the project even wrote an impassioned defense of India's desire for steel in *Fortune* magazine: "There may well be countries which . . . are misguided enough to promote steel for ideological reasons . . . [but] India is not one of them."[66] Even Eckaus and Lefeber, who feared that an overemphasis on industry could ruin the troubled agricultural sector, came to that conclusion tentatively and after years of work. But their agreement with Rostow's bold if unresearched claim did not help their case—especially when Indian proponents of steel rallied against them.

The demise of CENIS's India program, no matter how successful it was at modeling the Indian economy and at building up the Indian economics profession, is perhaps most noteworthy as a symbol of American development projects in the 1950s. Those hoping for a scandal about American sabotage must be sorely disappointed by the lack of evidence. In any case, the center's economists may have differed with Mahalanobis about how to best achieve economic growth in India, but they also disagreed among themselves. All of them, furthermore, were professionally and personally committed to Indian growth. Yet it is somehow fitting that a project using academic economics to fight a political battle (the Cold War) should come to an end with the realization that economics *was* politics. Economic knowledge was not simply a matter of technical expertise, but suggested certain solutions to the distribution of a society's resources. The end of CENIS's program had little to do with its computer model (which was refined for years after the withdrawal from India); it came about because decisions about resources are inherently political.

The CENIS program, furthermore, dramatizes many of the problems American foreign policymakers faced in the 1950s and 1960s. The optic of the Cold War—in which central planning meant communism meant dictatorship—had significant blind spots. For many nations in the world, centrally planned industrialization was a route to modernity, not to communism. And if the quickest route to economic modernity mimicked aspects of the Soviet experience—including continual problems in the agricultural sector—so be it. Economists in India and elsewhere staked their postcolonial identity on rapid industrialization; no computer printout, no matter how thick, could alter this decision. American and British economists recognized the desire for the substance and symbols of industrial modernity, but often treated it dismissively. As a result, America's poor diplomatic record contrasted sharply with its virtuoso economic performance in the postwar decades. The failure to recognize the sensitivity of both American academics and, especially, foreign leaders to CIA involvement, furthermore, was a harbinger of later disclosures of secret government involvement in Project Camelot and the Congress for Cultural

Freedom.[67] Finally, the political battles over economic development were frequently repeated through the 1950s and 1960s. Nehru saw Westernization in economic terms—as the process of modernization—while Rostow and many of his colleagues retained a political definition of the West as the American camp in the Cold War. The two destinations had the same name—the West—but they were in fact different places. Indian and American policymakers often differed, furthermore, over the pace of change. Though American economists could, at times, sensitively depict third world leaders' desire to take an express train to modernity, they ultimately called on them to take the local, stopping at each of Rostow's five stages. With different destinations and different speeds, it is hardly a surprise that CENIS's relations with India went off-track.

## NOTES

Thanks to Robert McMahon and my coeditors for their helpful comments on a draft of this essay, and to Abram Bergson, Richard Eckaus, Charles Kindleberger, Stephen Marglin, Lucian Pye, George Rosen, and W. W. Rostow for sharing their recollections. I am especially grateful to Donald Blackmer for so thoroughly undertaking both tasks. This essay was written while I was a fellow at the Charles Warren Center at Harvard University.

1. W. W. Rostow, Report on the Far East—Couchiching Conference (9 August 1956), Max F. Millikan Papers, MIT Archives, box 10, folder 308, 8.

2. "Origins and Objectives of the Center for International Studies" (April 1952), appendix to *The Center for International Studies: Past, Present, Future* (Cambridge, Mass.: CENIS, 1954), 18.

3. Jawaharlal Nehru, "Economic Democracy," speech in Parliament, 15 December 1952, in *Jawaharlal Nehru's Speeches*, 5 vols. (New Delhi: Government of India, 1957), 2:93.

4. Robert J. McMahon, *The Cold War on the Periphery: The United States, India, and Pakistan* (New York: Columbia University Press, 1994), quoted at 47, 112; Howard B. Schaffer, *Chester Bowles: New Dealer in the Cold War* (Cambridge: Harvard University Press, 1993), 53. See also Dennis Merrill, *Bread and the Ballot: The United States and Indian Economic Development, 1947–1963* (Chapel Hill: University of North Carolina Press, 1990), chaps. 1–3, and Andrew J. Rotter, *Comrades at Odds: The United States and India, 1947–1964* (Ithaca: Cornell University Press, 2000), chap. 4.

5. "Program of Research in Economic and Political Development" (February 1953), CENIS Papers, MIT Archives, box 2, folder 1, 14.

6. CENIS, *The Center for International Studies: A Description* (Cambridge, Mass.: CENIS, 1955). For more on the establishment and early operations of the Center for International Studies, see Donald M. Blackmer, *The MIT Center for International Studies: The Founding Years, 1951–1969* (Cambridge, Mass.: Center for International Studies, 2002). Professor Blackmer's well-researched and balanced account appeared while this essay was in the final stages of editing.

7. Rostow, *The British Economy in the Nineteenth Century* (Oxford: Clarendon, 1948), 127; Rostow, *The Process of Economic Growth* (New York: Norton, 1952), chap. 4; Rostow, "The First Take-Off: The British Industrial Revolution, 1783–1802," speech to the Economic Development Institute, 19 January 1956, Millikan Papers, box 10, folder 309, 21–23.

8. Rostow, "Marx Was a City Boy, or Why Communism May Fail," *Harper's* 210 (February 1955): 30. As noted below, agriculture accounted for only one-third of Indian public investment at that time.

9. See, for instance, W. W. Rostow, "Industrialization and Democracy" (n.d.), Millikan Papers, box 10, folder 317. Rostow with Arthur Levin, *The Dynamics of Soviet Society* (New York: Norton, 1952), chap. 4; Rostow et al., *The Prospects for Communist China* (Cambridge, Mass.: Technology Press, and New York: John Wiley, 1954); CENIS, *Some Aspects of United States Policy towards the Soviet Union and Its European Satellites* (Cambridge, Mass.: CENIS, 1953). Millikan's paper can be found in Millikan Papers, box 10, folder 302.

10. Millikan, Rostow, and others, *A Proposal: Key to an Effective Foreign Policy* (New York: Harper, 1957), 4, 1.

11. All senior staff at the center were involved in this lobbying effort. See, for instance, the correspondence in John F. Kennedy Pre-Presidential Papers, John F. Kennedy Library, Boston, box 573; also Rostow, *Eisenhower, Kennedy, and Foreign Aid* (Austin: University of Texas Press, 1985), chap. 8.

12. Rostow, "Take-Off into Self-Sustained Growth," *Economic Journal* 66 (March 1956): 37–38; Burton I. Kaufman, *Trade and Aid: Eisenhower's Foreign Economic Policy, 1953–1961* (Baltimore: Johns Hopkins University Press, 1982), 69–70.

13. "Proposal for the Completion of Economic and Political Development Research Program" (March 1954), CENIS Papers, box 2, folder 2, xi, 26.

14. Wilfred Malenbaum, "India and China: Development Contrasts," *Journal of Political Economy* 64, no. 1 (February 1956): 1–24; Malenbaum, "Some Political Aspects of Economic Development in India," *World Politics* 10, no. 3 (April 1958): 378–86; Malenbaum, *East and West in India's Development* (National Planning Association: Economics of Competitive Coexistence series, no. 5, 1959), 8.

15. Joseph Stalin, "The Year of the Great Break" (1929), in *Works*, 13 vols. (Moscow: Foreign Language Publishing House, 1955), 12:141. On one group of enthusiastic workers, see Lynne Viola, *Best Sons of the Fatherland: Workers in the Vanguard of Soviet Collectivization* (Oxford: Oxford University Press, 1987).

On engineers and industrial managers, see especially David R. Shearer, *Industry, State, and Society in Stalin's Russia, 1928–1934* (Ithaca: Cornell University Press, 1996).

16. Stuart Chase, *The New Deal* (New York: Macmillan, 1933), 156–57.

17. The phrase was widely applied in the early 1930s; for citations and context, see David C. Engerman, "Modernization from the Other Shore: American Observers and the Costs of Soviet Economic Development," *American Historical Review* 100, no. 2 (April 2000): 383–416.

18. Jawaharlal Nehru, "The Fascination of Russia" (1928), in *Selected Works of Jawaharlal Nehru*, 15 vols. (New Delhi: Orient Longman, 1972), 2:382.

19. Jawaharlal Nehru, *The Discovery of India* (New York: John Day, 1946), 44; also Nehru to Indira Gandhi, 9 July 1933, in *Glimpses of World History* (Delhi: Oxford University Press, 1990 [1935]), 855

20. Jawaharlal Nehru, "Russia and India" (1928), *Selected Works*, 2:451.

21. Nehru to Indira Gandhi, 4 August 1933, in *Glimpses*, 929. See also Kenton J. Clymer, "Jawaharlal Nehru and the United States: The Preindependence Years," *Diplomatic History* 14 (spring 1990): 151.

22. These paragraphs are informed by Partha Chatterjee's analyses of Indian state-building; see Chatterjee, *Nationalist Thought and the Colonial World: A Derivative Discourse?* (Minneapolis: University of Minnesota Press, 1986), chap. 5, and Chatterjee, "Development Planning and the Indian State," in Terence J. Byres, ed., *The State, Development Planning, and Liberalisation in India* (Delhi: Oxford University Press, 1997).

23. *Report [of the] National Planning Committee*, ed. K. T. Shah (Bombay: Vora, 1949), 5, 41; this book contains many documents dating back to the committee's founding.

24. Nehru, *Discovery*, 405.

25. Francine R. Frankel, *India's Political Economy, 1947–1977: The Gradual Revolution* (Princeton: Princeton University Press, 1978), 84–88.

26. Sugatha Bose, "Instruments and Idioms of Colonial and National Development: India's Historical Experience in Comparative Perspective," in Frederick Cooper and Randall Packard, eds., *International Development and the Social Sciences* (Berkeley: University of California Press, 1997), 53.

27. The plan is well summarized in A. H. Hanson, *The Process of Planning: A Study of India's Five-Year Plans, 1950–1964* (Oxford: Oxford University Press, 1966), chap. 4, quoted p. 96.

28. Planning Commission, *The First Five-Year Plan: A Draft Outline* (New Delhi: Government of India, 1951), 8.

29. Mahalanobis's key articles on the topic contain few explicit references to such scholarship, and he described his own research into these issues as "fragmentary": "National Income, Investment, and National Development," lecture

given at the National Institute of the Sciences of India, 4 October 1952, in P. C. Mahalanobis, *Papers on Planning,* ed. P. K. Bose and M. Mukherjee (Calcutta: Statistical Publishing Society, 1985), 4.

30. P. C. Mahalanobis, "Some Observations on the Process of Growth of National Income" (1953), in *Papers on Planning.*

31. The American economist Evsey Domar formalized and critiqued an important model behind the Soviet five-year plans, that developed by G. A. Fel'dman. Domar also noted the parallels with Mahalanobis's model. Evsey Domar, "A Soviet Model of Growth," in his *Essays in the Theory of Economic Growth* (Oxford: Oxford University Press, 1957); see also G. A. Fel'dman, "K teorii tempov narodnogo khoziaistva," *Planovoe khoziaistvo* 1928, no. 11, 146–70, continued in 1928, no. 12, 161–78. On the application of Fel'dman's model, see Alexander Erlich, *The Soviet Industrialization Debates, 1924–1928* (Cambridge: Harvard University Press, 1960), chaps. 7–8.

32. On the predecessors, see Stephen Kotkin, *Magnetic Mountain: Stalinism as a Civilization* (Berkeley: University of California Press, 1995), and Isaac James Quillen, *Industrial City: History of Gary, Indiana to 1929* (New York: Garland, 1986 [Diss., Yale University, 1942]), chap. 2.

33. Merrill, *Bread and the Ballot,* 118; William A. Johnson, *The Steel Industry of India* (Cambridge: Harvard University Press, 1966), 38.

34. Bulganin report, 29 December 1955, in K. Krishna Moorty, *The Road Begins at Bhilai* (Madras: Technology Books, 1987), 201.

35. Santosh Mehrotra, *India and the Soviet Union: Trade and Technology Transfer* (Cambridge: Cambridge University Press, 1990), 10–11; John Kenneth Galbraith, *Ambassador's Journal: A Personal Account of the Kennedy Years* (Boston: Houghton Mifflin, 1969), 73n; A. Mahalanobis, *Prasanta Chandra Mahalanobis* (New Delhi: National Book Trust, 1983), 57–58; Author interview with Abram Bergson, Cambridge, Mass., 7 December 1999.

36. See, for instance, "Recommendation for the Formulation of the Second Five-Year Plan" (3 November 1954); and "Approach to Planning in India" (11 September 1955), both in Mahalanobis, *Papers on Planning,* 24, 131.

37. Sukhamoy Chakravarty, *Development Planning: The Indian Experience* (Oxford: Clarendon Press, 1987), 3.

38. These data are derived from ibid., table 9.

39. Jawaharlal Nehru, "We Should Pull Together" (1949), in Nehru, *Independence and After* (New Delhi: Government of India, 1949), 181–83; see also Sarvepalli Gopal, *Jawaharlal Nehru: A Biography* (London: Jonathan Cape, 1975), 2:44–46, 63–64, 71.

40. Jawaharlal Nehru, "Asia and Africa Awaken," speech at the Asian-African Conference, 24 April 1955, *Speeches,* 3:291.

41. Walter Robertson, Assistant Secretary of State for Far Eastern Affairs, in Memorandum of Conversation, 18 November 1955, in *Foreign Relations of the*

*United States: 1955–57* (Washington: Government Printing Office, 1987), 8:296–98 (hereafter *FRUS*).

42. Millikan, Rostow, and others, *Proposal*, 6–7.

43. Rostow, *Eisenhower*, 5, 68–73.

44. Planning Commission, *The Second Five-Year Plan* (New Delhi: Government of India, 1956), 77–78. For Mahalanobis's initial targets, with even more funds to come from unspecified domestic sources, see P. C. Mahalanobis, "Draft Recommendations for the Formulation of the Second Five-Year Plan (1956–61)" (1955), in *Papers on Planning*, 46.

45. For instance, fewer than ten pages out of a 500-page report on the economics of the second five-year plan were devoted specifically to agriculture; see Planning Commission, Panel of Economists, *Papers Relating to the Formulation of the Second Five-Year Plan* (New Delhi: Government of India, 1955).

46. Frankel, *India's Political Economy*, 144–46.

47. Henry R. Lieberman, "India to Ask U.S. for Loan in Crisis," *New York Times*, 6 September 1957; Merrill, *Bread and the Ballot*, 142–44.

48. Rostow, "The Meaning of India" (n.d.), Millikan Papers, box 10, folder 325, 1.

49. Millikan to Trevor Swan, 5 March 1959, CENIS Papers, box 9, folder 10. Swan, an Australian economist, was then working for CENIS in India.

50. Millikan to A. M. ("Abe") Rosenthal, 25 November 1957, in CENIS Papers, box 9, folder 9; Millikan to Frederick Kuh, 18 January 1958, CENIS Papers, box 9, folder 15. Rosenthal was then a senior editor at the *New York Times*, Kuh an editor at the *Chicago Sun-Times*.

51. Merrill, *Bread and the Ballot*, 144–47. The food aid came through the 1954 Agricultural Trade Development and Assistance Act, commonly known as PL–480.

52. See, for instance, Paul Rosenstein-Rodan's memorandum, dated 4 March 1959, about the visit of B. K. Nehru, a senior Indian economic official, to Washington, in Kennedy Pre-Presidential Papers, box 573.

53. On the initial State Department activities, organized with the Technical Cooperation Administration, see Millikan to Haldone Hanson and Gustav Papanek, 17 June 1952, CENIS Papers, box 9, folder 17.

54. A total of twelve Indian scholars visited MIT under this program's auspices; see James Dorsey to Martha Sue McConnell, 16 June 1966, CENIS Papers, box 9, folder 22.

55. See, for instance, Ellsworth Bunker to Fred Bartlett, 27 June 1957, in *FRUS 1955–57*, 8:349; also Galbraith, *Ambassador's Journal*, 83.

56. The model is concisely specified in a piece co-written by one of its authors, Sukhamoy Chakravarty; see Jagdish A. Bhagwati and Sukhamoy Chakravarty, "Contributions to Indian Economic Analysis: A Survey," *American Economic Review* 59, no. 4 (September 1969): 12–20.

57. Paul Rosenstein-Rodan to Alan Manne, 22 April 1964, CENIS Papers, box

9, folder 22; Lefeber to Richard Eckaus, 11 October 152, CENIS Papers, box 10, folder 7.

58. Lefeber to Eckaus, 24 October 1964; Millikan to Stephen Marglin and Lefeber, 1 December 1964, both in CENIS Papers, box 10, folder 7. B. K. Nehru, *Nice Guys Finish Second* (New Delhi: Viking, 1997), 273.

59. This interpretation is consistent with participants' indispensable histories of the episode: George Rosen, *Western Economists and Eastern Societies: Agents of Change in South Asia, 1950–1970* (Baltimore: Johns Hopkins University Press, 1985), 130–37; and Blackmer, *MIT Center*, chaps. 4–5.

60. David Wise and Thomas B. Ross, *The Invisible Government* (New York: Random House, 1964), 243–44; Ben Bagdikian, "Working in Secret," *New York Times Book Review*, 28 June 1964.

61. John H. Fenton, "MIT Hints Unit Had Link to CIA," *New York Times*, 30 June 1964.

62. Jonathan Bingham to Max Milliken [*sic*], 11 April 1952, CENIS Papers, box 9, folder 17.

63. "Indian Plan, U.S. Model?" *Now*, 25 December 1964: 3–4.

64. The descent into external turmoil and internal dissension can be precisely tracked from the letters in CENIS Papers, box 10, folders 7–8.

65. Rostow, "Prospects for Economic Development" (1954?), Millikan Papers, box 11, folder 360, 4.

66. Ian Little, "Reflections on the Theory and Practice of Planning in India," CENIS Working Paper D/59–17, 1960; Eckaus, Lefeber, Millikan, and Rosenstein-Rodan, "India Article Criticized," *Fortune* 67 (August 1963): 94. See also Rosen, *Western Economists*, 110–19.

67. See Ellen Herman, "Project Camelot and the Career of Cold War Psychology," in Christopher Simpson, ed., *Universities and Empire: Money and Politics in the Social Sciences during the Cold War* (New York: New Press, 1998); and Frances Stonor Saunders, *The Cultural Cold War: The CIA and the World of Arts and Letters* (New York: New Press, 1999).

## FURTHER READING

Byres, Terence J., ed. *The State, Development Planning, and Liberalisation in India.* Delhi: Oxford University Press, 1997.

Chakravarty, Sukhamoy. *Development Planning: The Indian Experience.* Oxford: Clarendon Press, 1987.

Frankel, Francine R. *India's Political Economy, 1947–1977: The Gradual Revolution.* Princeton: Princeton University Press, 1978.

McMahon, Robert F. *The Cold War on the Periphery: The United States, India, and Pakistan.* New York: Columbia University Press, 1994.

Merrill, Dennis. *Bread and the Ballot: The United States and India's Economic Development, 1947–1963*. Chapel Hill: University of North Carolina Press, 1990.

Millikan, Max F., Walt W. Rostow, and others. *A Proposal: Key to an Effective Foreign Policy*. New York: Harper and Brothers, 1957.

Rosen, George. *Western Economists and Eastern Societies: Agents of Change in South Asia, 1950–1970*. Baltimore: Johns Hopkins University Press, 1985.

# MODERNIZATION AND DEMOCRATIC VALUES: THE "JAPANESE MODEL" IN THE 1960s

VICTOR KOSCHMANN

Until recently, Japan was an oddity in the geopolitics of development. In a world where modern clearly implied "Western" and white, the "modern" Japanese were Asian and nonwhite. Japan's anomalous status was, of course, frequently noted from the late nineteenth century on. Even in the wake of World War II, Japan's modernity remained a scandal; or it was belittled, as when the former Supreme Commander of Allied Forces during the Allied Occupation, General Douglas MacArthur, remarked of the Japanese before a joint session of Congress, "Measured by the standards of modern civilization, they would be like a boy of twelve as compared to our development of 45 years."[1] Indeed, postwar Japanese intellectuals themselves debated the question of whether it was possible for an Asian nation to become truly modern. Educated, liberal-minded Japanese were often more pessimistic than foreign observers about Japan's prospects. Post–World War II Japanese accounts of Japan's twentieth-century history and culture pointed to deep-seated "feudal" and "Asiatic" elements that had impeded liberal attitudes and behavior and fueled Japanese expansionism. Such pessimism remained latent among Japanese intellectuals well into the postwar period, even though by the late 1950s the Japanese economy had recovered from wartime devastation and was growing rapidly.

When American scholars brought modernization theory to Japan in the 1960s, therefore, their assessment of its relevance to Japan appears to have been threefold: First, they believed that Japanese scholars and other leaders should make a more systematic effort to study Japan's modernization experience "objectively," in a comparative framework. Second, they sought to convince Japanese scholars that by any objective measure Japan had already done very well, and therefore they should more self-confidently offer Japan's experience as a strategic model for the plethora of new countries that remained "underdeveloped." Finally, they hoped that Japanese scholars would recommend wise national policies to maintain a healthy growth rate while preserving stability within the free world orbit.

In retrospect, it is apparent that the Americans' objectives reflected Japan's anomalous geopolitical position. The first two represented the awareness, especially among scholars who studied Japan, of that country's growing economic strength and tangible value as a Cold War ally, not only militarily but ideologically. These objectives correlated with an elite American acceptance of the Japanese not, for the most part, as equals but at least as a nation potentially capable of acting at the same international level as the United States, its European allies, and their major Communist adversaries.[2] The third objective expressed the residual American fear that, like the "non-West" in general, Japan was especially susceptible to Communist ideological appeals (as well as subversion) and that therefore it was essential to convince educated Japanese that their postwar alignment with the "free world" and capitalism was the most advantageous road to follow.

The American initiative was controversial, and by no means entirely successful. At the same time, it seems in retrospect that there were few major differences between the views embraced by the Japanese scholars and those of their foreign guests. Modernization, whatever the nuances of how it was defined, was already firmly at the center of Japan's agenda and would have remained there even without scholarly blandishments from abroad. Moreover, the peculiarly American combination of "objective" social science and anti-Communist fervor encouraged the trend in Japan away from self-critical concern about peace and democracy toward a preoccupation with becoming a "great power" through economic prosperity.

## THE SETTING OF THE HAKONE CONFERENCE

No effort to assess the impact on Japan of American modernization theory can afford to ignore the 1960 Hakone conference. In the late 1950s a group of American historians and social scientists specializing on Japan received funding from the Ford Foundation for a series of six international meetings concerned with the modernization of Japan. Organized by University of Michigan historian John W. Hall and others as the "Conference on Modern Japan" under the aegis of the Association for Asian Studies, this group decided that a preliminary discussion among Japanese and foreign scholars should be held at Hakone, a hot-springs resort town beside Mount Fuji, from 29 August through 2 September 1960, and should be followed by five annual, week-long, summer seminars focused on different aspects of Japan's modernization. These aspects were to include attitudes and values, social change, entrepreneurship and technology, political ideas and institutions, and changing values in thought, literature, and the arts. At the time the conference was conceived, Ford Foundation representatives were in close contact with officials of various government agencies, including the Central Intelligence Agency, in a joint effort to develop area studies in American academic research centers.[3] The focal points of such efforts were, of course, the Soviet Union and China, but as Patricia Steinhoff has suggested, in the Cold War era Japan Studies often "rode the coattails" of China research when it came to government and foundation funding.[4] Whether that was the case here, or whether Ford and the government agencies behind the scenes actually took an independent, strategic interest in the modernization of Japan in the late 1950s, is still unclear. However, once the leading American expert on Japan, Edwin O. Reischauer of Harvard University, became active in Tokyo as the new ambassador, it became increasingly apparent that Japan would figure centrally in the emerging American ideology of modernization as a model of capitalist development.

Meanwhile, Hall and his American colleagues had invited a stellar lineup of Japanese scholars as their interlocutors at Hakone. Overwhelmingly from top-ranking national universities in Tokyo and Kyoto, they represented a broad spectrum of ideological persuasions and were all well-known leaders in their fields. Historians predominated, and they included the leading Marxist historian Toyama Shigeki as well as the more conservative political historian Inoki Masamichi. On the far right was the ultranationalist philosopher Kosaka Masaaki. Others included the intellectual historian and political scientist Maruyama Masao, French literature specialist Kato Shuichi, economists Horie Yasuzo and Ouchi Tsutomu, and sociologists Kawashima Takeyoshi and Nakano Takashi. Non-Japanese participants in the Hakone conference were mostly from the United States and included, in addition to Hall and Reischauer, historians Marius Jansen, Herschel Webb, and Roger Hackett, linguist and literary scholar Donald Shively, sociologists Marion J. Levy and Robert N. Bellah, economist Henry Rosovsky, and psychiatrist Robert J. Lifton. Others included sociologist Ronald P. Dore from England and economic historian E. S. Crawcour from Australia. Participants were, as might be expected, all male and were informed that if they wished to bring their wives to Hakone, they were obliged to pay their way. An administrative circular distributed in advance to participants noted, further, that arrangements had been made to "entertain" the wives while their husbands conferred, and that although wives would be invited to the social hour at the end of each day's discussion, they would have to take their meals separately from the conferees.

The American organizers also informed participants that conference discussions would be conducted primarily in the Japanese language, although non-Japanese participants could resort to English if they felt the need, and several bilingual individuals would be present to help out if necessary. This was an iconoclastic move that apparently affected the content and tenor of the conference.

Before we delve into the discussions, however, it is necessary to establish the historical context of the conference, which came directly in the wake of Japan's most serious postwar political crisis. The spring and summer of 1960 had been a veritable "season of protest" in defense of democracy. The occasion was created by Japanese and American efforts in the late 1950s to revise and reaffirm the security treaty between the two countries that had been in place since the end of the postwar Allied Occupation of Japan, which lasted from 1945 to 1952.

The Occupation had devoted itself diligently to democratic reforms until about 1948, going so far as to write a new constitution for Japan which, among other iconoclastic provisions, renounced resort to war and prohibited armed forces or other war potential. Then, from 1947–48 conservative elements in the Occupation gained increasing influence, and the early emphases on demilitarization and democratization were gradually replaced by a new set of priorities designed to rehabilitate Japan as a Cold War ally of the United States. Outbreak of the Korean War in June 1950 solidified the new direction and hastened negotiations leading to a peace treaty with Japan. As it turned out, on the same day that American and Japanese representatives signed the peace treaty in San Francisco, 8 September 1951, they also inked a bilateral security treaty. The security treaty committed the United States to maintain American forces in Japan to contribute to the security of Japan and "the Far East" and, if deemed necessary by the Japanese government, to "put down large-scale internal riots and disturbances." In effect, the treaty bound Japan to the U.S. side in the Cold War.

The treaty took effect, and Japan regained full independence, in April 1952. By the mid-1950s, however, it had become clear to both sides that some changes needed to be made. The 1951 treaty did not explicitly commit the United States to defend Japan; the provision for using American troops to quell internal disturbances seemed inconsistent with Japanese sovereignty; and the treaty contained no termination date. In July 1957, therefore, Japan's prime minister, Kishi Nobusuke—a wartime cabinet member whom the Americans had once indicted and imprisoned as a Class-A war criminal—traveled to Washington to initiate the process of revising the treaty. Kishi again visited Washington in January 1960 to initial a draft treaty that solved problems, and returned home to secure the pact's ratification in the Japanese Diet. So confident was he of success that he had invited American President Dwight D. Eisenhower to visit Japan immediately after the planned ratification.

In the meantime, countervailing forces were building in Japan, as opposition parties, unions, and other groups that opposed the pact as undemocratic and likely to embroil Japan again in war joined together in a national front against the treaty and began a series of strikes, demonstrations, and other actions. But the real crisis came in May and June. In order to ensure that the treaty was passed in time, Kishi sent in riot police to remove opposition legislators who were physically jamming the chamber and impeding deliberations. Widely seen as flagrantly undemocratic, Kishi's move seemed to symbolize his all-out assault on postwar peace and democracy, and brought hundreds of thousands more into the streets, focusing especially on the Diet building and its surroundings. On 15 June, when students attempted to force their way into the Diet compound itself, right-wing thugs as well as riot police attacked demonstrators, and many were injured. One, a female student leader from Tokyo University, was killed. Two days later the treaty went into effect, but Eisenhower's visit was canceled, and Kishi resigned on 23 June. Although the protests failed to prevent ratification of the treaty, they vividly crystallized the political struggle in postwar Japan between the forces for democracy that sought to defend and extend the postwar democratic reforms, and reactionary forces that were reviving prewar and wartime values and remilitarizing the nation. Democracy, however that was defined, had clearly become the critical political issue in Japan.

However, when new elections were held in July, the Liberal Democratic Party again came out on top, and the former bureaucrat Ikeda Hayato became prime minister. Ikeda turned away from the politically confrontational attitude of the Kishi cabinet toward a single-minded focus on economic growth and prosperity. He placed politically divisive issues like remilitarization and constitutional revision on the back burner. He also adopted the National Income Doubling Plan, which became state policy in December 1960. The plan's goal was to double national income within ten years, and to achieve this goal, the government committed itself to reforming the industrial structure and reinforcing Japan's competitiveness. Programs were launched to reorganize industries to meet the challenges of liberalization, to expand public spending on infrastructure, social security, and the development of human resources, and to reduce wage and other disparities between large and small enterprises. In the process, according to the sociologist Bai Gao, "the strategic attitude toward the economy in Japanese industrial policy developed to a new level."[5] Ikeda's new policy of focusing attention on productivity and prosperity was quite effective in sapping the strength from opposition parties and movements, which could offer no policy alternative of comparable popularity. In sum, the conference on the modernization of Japan came just as the new Japanese government was attempting to divert attention from struggles over democracy toward efforts to raise productivity and promote prosperity, so it is significant that "democracy" became the most controversial issue at Hakone.

## "SCIENCE" VERSUS "DEMOCRATIC VALUES"

Participants in the conference were invited to submit preliminary written statements, but the first day's discussion, which focused on definitions and conceptualizations of modernization, took as its starting point the position paper "Japan within the Concept of Modernization" by John Hall. Hall was a historian primarily of premodern Japan who had produced a pioneering study of the early modern statesman Tanuma Okitsugu and other works. In 1961 he was to become the A. Whitney Griswold Professor of History at Yale University and in addition to publishing prolifically on early Japanese institutional history would train virtually the entire next generation of historians of premodern Japan. In the position paper he attempts to define modernization by listing nine essential characteristics of a modern society, the first seven of which he borrowed from *The Politics of Developing Areas* (1960) by Gabriel Almond and James Coleman. They were as follows:

1. A comparatively high degree of urbanization;
2. Widespread literacy;
3. Comparatively high per capita income;
4. Extensive geographical and social mobility;
5. Relatively high degree of commercialization and industrialization within the economy;
6. An extensive and penetrative network of mass communication media;
7. Widespread participation and involvement by members of the society in modern social and economic processes;
8. A relatively highly organized bureaucratic form of government with widespread involvement by members of the society;
9. An increasingly rational and secular orientation of the individual to his environment based on the growth of scientific knowledge.[6]

The list was revised in the course of discussion, in part so as to make it less biased toward Western capitalist systems. An ancillary effect of further revision was to produce increasingly generic, objectivist characterizations like, "A relatively high degree of use of inanimate energy, the widespread circulation of commodities, and the growth of service facilities."[7] Nevertheless, Hall's nominalist and empiricist approach to definition, as well as the specific contents of his list, was subjected to criticism. Japanese intellectuals tended to comment favorably on the relative sophistication of the foreign Japan scholars' stated desire to avoid conceiving of modernization as a unilinear process equivalent to Westernization—that is, their seeming willingness to see the Western European and American experiences as only some of the various possible roads to modernity.[8] At the same time, Japanese critics were quick to point out that when defining features of modernity such as those produced by Hall were turned into criteria, or yardsticks, by which to measure a country's level of modernity, this very methodology subverted the theorists' best intentions and caused them, in Matsumoto Sannosuke's words, to "slip back into the old structure in which Western scholars 'scientifically' investigate non-Western societies from the outside." Despite the Americans' best intentions, their modernization theory failed to escape the Western perspective and problem consciousness.[9]

The political scientist and intellectual historian Maruyama Masao was apparently most prominent among those who objected from a different angle. According to Hall's later account of the conference, Maruyama "from the first considered our revised set of criteria too heavily weighted against the world of ideas and asked that the value system of the individual be given more consideration." Maruyama was joined by others, including Sakata and Toyama—and even Kosaka, who pronounced: "It is *modern man* who is of interest to us." Hall's irritation at this apparent skepticism toward "value-free" science is suggested in his recollection that "no sooner had we begun to consider the objective and quantifiable measures of rationalization in the material life of modern society than our discussion was drawn off in the direction of less tangible subjects." He admits that "unquestionably Mr. Maruyama and the others were right in insisting that greater recognition be given to the value changes affecting the individual in modern society." Nonetheless, he complains, "Unfortunately the problem of ethos and value as it was discussed at Hakone took a different and more political turn, becoming associated with the question of whether or not democracy was an essential element of modernization."[10]

In further elaborating what he took to be the Japanese side of the controversy, Hall quotes Kawashima's 1961 reflection: "Granted that 'political discussion' for purposes of achieving 'democracy' is not science . . . I believe that in the modernization of Japan such values as 'democracy' and 'human rights' have played an 'important role' in providing the motive force in social and political development, and that these have provided important 'issues' for the various ideological camps. These are matters of *historical fact,* and they should not be overlooked by empirical science."[11] Kawashima explained that Japanese social scientists like himself tended to respond to the question of modernization in a practical, subjective mode that reflected the political tensions latent in their efforts "to free ourselves from an autocratic political system and to actualize 'democratic' principles under circumstances in which, since the Meiji period, the state had more or less successfully mobilized scholarship and education for nationalist purposes."[12] Their sense of personal engagement with modernization and democracy caused them to view these as unfinished projects rather than just scholarly categories.

A number of the foreign participants apparently disagreed. Like their colleagues in the United States, who were similarly caught up in the ideology of modernization in their study of other parts of the world, the American Japan specialists who organized the Hakone Conference liked to think that "politics" had no place in science. In the words of Michael Latham, "Modernity and modernization, they argued before both foreign and domestic audiences, were not political constructions. They were objective phenomena revealed by social scientific inquiry. They were facts."[13]

Some Japanese participants criticized not only the content of the modernization theory that was sponsored by Hall and his American and European colleagues, but what they felt to be the high-handed manner in which the foreigners pressed it upon the Japanese. Indeed, it appears that the mood during some of the conference was darkened considerably by an undercurrent of Japanese dismay at the American and European participants' insistence on their own point of view and unwillingness to address topics that the Japanese believed to be vital, especially those related to democracy.

Kawashima's 1961 account focuses initially on the language problem, pointing out that the Japanese scholars found this meeting markedly different from most international forums in that, because Japanese was the primary medium of discussion, they "experienced no psychological tension and entered into debate quite freely." On the other hand, he reports that "the foreign scholars were relatively silent, and only two or three participated actively." This was because of the language policy; that is, it seemed clear to Kawashima that "even those scholars who spoke Japanese well sought opportunities to speak in English," and he felt that such scholars "had not fully anticipated" the seriousness of the language barrier.[14]

Of course, language dominance is intrinsically political in the sense that being prevented from using one's first language weakens one's ability to put across arguments, resulting in anxiety and frustration. Anxiety and frustration, in turn, are often expressed in irritation, which leads to conflict, and to some extent that seems to have been the case at Hakone, with important repercussions. Kawashima reports that "a kind of psychological pressure did become tangible and a certain barrier to communication did arise," with the result that really consequential discussion became impossible. According to Kawashima, the hiatus in communication was provoked by foreign scholars' misunderstandings of Japanese proposals that some attention be paid to the issue of democracy in the conference's definition of modernization. He writes: "The Japanese scholars [including himself] were understood by some of the foreign scholars to be mixing political argumentation (talking politics) with social scientific analysis, leading to a scene in which, in an accusatory manner, at one point it was sharply demanded of the Japanese scholars that they, 'First, reply to us regarding whether or not you are going to make an issue of democracy!' I had the impression that from that point forward the issues that most urgently needed to be discussed could no longer be taken up."[15] Kawashima's account is abbreviated, but suggestive of what he apparently felt to be a breach of etiquette as well as a certain obtuseness on the part of some of the foreign scholars.

There were other "gaps" in understanding. He goes on:

When a certain Japanese economist expressed some doubts as to whether it was appropriate to use the term "per capita income" (included by Hall as one of the "conceptual criteria" of modernization) in regard to both "capitalist" and "communist" societies, he was challenged by a certain foreign scholar who said, "What is capitalism? Are you saying that the contemporary U.S. is capitalist? I think you should begin by defining capitalism." The Japanese scholar had no response. I assume that this Japanese scholar—feeling that in Japan the term "capitalism" would never elicit *quite such a strong* reaction (among social scientists), and believing that a rather clear conceptual definition already existed—was now confronted with an American who displayed an unexpectedly extreme emotional reaction; he also discovered that perhaps the definition of capitalism was not necessarily so clear after all, and suspected that the American conception might be quite different from that employed in Japan (where the U.S.A. is considered an advanced capitalist nation and, indeed, the champion of capitalism); as a result, he abandoned any thought of explaining himself. . . .

Moreover, two or three American scholars reacted very negatively when Japanese scholars employed "feudalism" as a scientific term. . . . The Americans' point was that there is no clear definition of "feudalism," and it is an emotional word that evokes "dislike" or "evil." However, in Japan we went through an extended debate on feudalism [in the 1920s], and more recently the concept has again become an issue in relation to how to define Chinese feudalism, so I suspect that Japanese scholars—at least those who attended this conference—are unwilling to be admonished for using the term vaguely or amateurishly.[16]

In sum, one does not have to "read" very much "into" Kawashima's admittedly circumspect account to find there an indictment of the intellectual arrogance and sense of political mission that, at least in retrospect, seem clearly to have pervaded the American modernizationist discourse in that era. This was so in spite of the fundamental ambivalence surrounding Japan's modernization. From the American perspective, Japan was both a non-Western country that was politically at risk of falling eventually into Communist hands *and* a model of successful modernization worthy of emulation in the underdeveloped areas of the non-West. It seemed to Americans that even though the Japanese—at least some of them—were imbued with recognizably modern values and had achieved a markedly capitalist form of modernization, many Japanese intellectuals still failed adequately to understand the full import of their own success. They needed to be convinced, first, that they had succeeded (since they persisted in viewing their own development in negative terms), and, second, that they should make their experience available to countries that could profit from it, especially elsewhere in Asia.

It seems quite evident in retrospect that the Americans were in Hakone on a political mission fueled by values and ideology even as they seemed eager to promote a "value-free" definition of modernization. Although the Japanese were evidently quite frank about their own engaged, practical-political stance, the Americans were silent about theirs. As a result, the Hakone Conference has almost invariably been remembered in Japan as the occasion for disagreement between Japanese and non-Japanese participants regarding how and to what extent value-laden questions such as democracy should be included in the definition of modernization. Japanese intellectuals have repeatedly commented critically on the overly objectivist, descriptive nature of Hall's definition of modernization, confessing, along with Matsumoto Sannosuke (who did not attend the conference), that:

> When told that this [list] is what is meant by modernization, honestly speaking, we Japanese cannot help but feel dissatisfied, as if something is missing. . . . It is almost inevitable that in Japan the concept of modernization will be considered in conjunction with the *values* and *motivations* of realizing democratic principles and enhancing the rights of the individual in social life and relationships. . . . [T]he really important question is the degree to which [the various factors involved in modernization] are directed toward human liberation, and the extent to which the various systems and organizations of modern society advance the ideals of the modern human beings who built them. This is the kind of issue Japanese are especially concerned about.

According to Matsumoto and others, Japanese scholars were likely to believe that genuine modernization is based upon certain ideals or essences whose teleology could not be captured in the nominalistic inventories put forward by the Americans. Modernization was a value-driven practice that demanded commitment, including political commitment, rather than mere scientific observation.[17] By arguing in this manner, Matsumoto and the others were, in a manner of speaking, adhering to a certain mode of thought that had been evident in progressive discourse since the Meiji period, and that in the post–World War II period more or less dominated conceptions of modernity and modernization: a conviction that far more than in any institutions, patterns, or other objective manifestations, the crucial elements of modernity subsisted in qualities of human agency, or subjectivity, that were less epistemological than practical.[18]

At the same time, although here we are concerned primarily with the Japanese response to American initiatives, it might seem that in some ways the American participants' perspective needs more explanation than the Japanese one. Sociological approaches to modernization in the United States had always emphasized values and value change, and thus one wonders why Hall so thoroughly neglected the area of values in his list of the features of modernity. One of the major theoretical progenitors of modernization theory, Talcott Parsons, had confirmed the importance of values and voluntary action through a reading of the early twentieth-century German social theorist Max Weber, and assigned to shared values the role of integrating the social system. He also reached "optimistic conclusions about the potential for liberal values to ensure cohesive, healthy democracy," and recognized that "a society's values would have a profound impact on the direction that change would take."[19] Had Hall given full credence to the question of values in his definition of modernity, perhaps less conflict would have emerged.

## THE "REISCHAUER OFFENSIVE"

In January 1961, not long after the conference, President John F. Kennedy selected one of the leading American conference participants, Edwin Oldfather Reischauer, to be his ambassador to Japan. Around the time of the Hakone conference, Reischauer had written an article about the security treaty issue and the Japanese protests, and in October 1960 it was published in *Foreign Affairs* as "The Broken Dialogue with Japan." There he summed up the contrasting views of Japan-U.S. relations embraced by Japanese intellectuals and the American public, and contended, "After 15 years of massive contact, Americans and

Japanese seem to have less real communication than ever." The misunderstanding was especially serious between the American government and the "Japanese opposition," he argued. Opposition leaders were "right in their charge that the close contacts they once had with Americans during the Occupation no longer exist." This was, in part, the fault of the American diplomatic corps, which maintained contact primarily with "English-speaking businessmen and with conservative political leaders, who not only stand in the positions of responsibility but also share more of our point of view on world problems."[20]

Reischauer believed the *Foreign Affairs* piece to have been responsible in part for his selection as ambassador,[21] and he went to Tokyo determined to engage Japanese intellectuals and the general public in a new "dialogue" regarding not only bilateral relations but Japanese democracy and modernization. As he wrote in his article, even members of Japan's "moderate opposition" believed that "Japan . . . is far from being a true democracy. [They think that] however perfect the external forms may be, the inner realities are not there. The Japanese people, accustomed to centuries of authoritarian rule, do not have natural democratic reactions. Japanese society is still hopelessly 'feudalistic,' by which they mean that a high degree of social inequality and authoritarianism still remains in personal relations in the family, in education, business and government, and the individual still lacks the habit of depending on his own independent judgment."[22]

Reischauer began immediately to give speeches that often closely resembled university lectures, publish articles, and participate in roundtable discussions in Japanese journals.[23] Among his major objectives were to convince the Japanese that their modernization was a success and their government as democratic as could be expected. They should therefore more self-confidently present their historical experience to struggling new nations in Asia and Africa as a model of successful modernization of a liberal sort. Reischauer made these arguments straightforwardly in a published conversation with the prominent government adviser Nakayama Ichiro. Nakayama was an extremely influential economist who as chairman of the planning committee of the Economic Deliberation Council was the major figure behind the income-doubling plan and also a leader of the American-sponsored Japan Productivity Center.[24]

Although hardly a typical "opposition intellectual," Nakayama gave voice to several of the perceptions that Reischauer had set out to contest. Nakayama raised questions about the depth of Japan's historical and contemporary commitment to democracy, especially in the realm of labor relations; pointed to the legacy of familism and "paternal community" in Japanese social relations; and politely challenged the view of "some American economists" that peculiarly Japanese patterns like the seniority wage system and enterprise unions were creative adaptations of Japanese tradition that had supported modernization and therefore should be left alone.

Reischauer responded with a frank outline of his own approach to Japanese democracy and modernization. He insisted on the contemporary relevance of Japan's experience with democracy between the world wars, including the emergence of the labor union movement in the period 1918–21, and argued that without this prewar, indigenous foundation the institutional reforms carried out in the Occupation period would never have succeeded to the extent they had. He admitted, of course, that the relative rapidity of Japan's development had meant that its "premodern and predemocratic legacy" was strong, especially in comparison to North America. But didn't some European countries have to deal with even stronger premodern legacies in the midst of their modern societies? Not only was Japan relatively unencumbered by premodern residues; any sudden attempt to apply remedies might be more damaging than the residues themselves. Reischauer went so far as to caution that Japanese democracy might suffer more from too much change all at once than from too little: "Japan has changed more rapidly than any other country in the world, and if it now changes even faster there are sure to be more internal collisions and difficulties. . . . Japan has now reached the speed limit in growth."[25]

The aspect of Reischauer's comments that generated the most controversy, however, was his explicit recommendation that Japan's approach to modernization should be offered confidently as a model underdeveloped countries in Southeast Asia and elsewhere. Because Western Europe and the United States had modernized over too long a period of time, they were less relevant as object lessons than Japan, which had developed more rapidly with only selective reference to the experience of Europe. The only other possible model was the Communist one, exemplified primarily by China. Nevertheless, in

Reischauer's view, China's method of "forcing down the living standard in order to generate the capital for investment" showed that the Chinese "had decided to make progress in industrialization even at the expense of democracy"; as a result, it had made little progress and was much less attractive. Japan, by contrast, had allowed for the gradual development of democracy by "maintaining a very appropriate balance between government leadership and private initiative." The Japanese government had taken the lead, "but left enough social freedom for individual initiative to participate." In sum, Reischauer contended, Japan had "experienced a number of difficult problems like militarism, but overall [its modernization] was a great success."[26]

It was Reischauer's blithe willingness to downplay the historical importance of Japan's "fifteen-year war," from 1931 to 1945, that persuaded many to take his views as outright Cold War propaganda rather than reasoned historical analysis. Indeed, many progressive Japanese feared that his unqualified endorsement of Japan's modern history would fuel the nationalism that was rising precipitately in the early 1960s in conjunction with mounting economic growth figures and the Ikeda government's income-doubling plan. To some extent, their fears were undoubtedly justified. The new nationalism was able effectively to broaden its appeal by celebrating the goal of becoming an "economic great power."[27] The conservative literary critic Fukuda Tsuneari, for example, answered what he facetiously called the "Reischauer offensive" in a six-part series of articles, where he expressed fundamental approval of Reischauer's arguments while registering certain objections from the right. Most important, he took issue with Reischauer's view that the Japanese democratic movement had been relatively strong from Meiji onward but had been limited in its growth by the military, which was granted a special position under the Meiji constitution. Fukuda argued that, to the contrary, rather than being an impediment to modernization and democracy, the military had fostered modernization and gradual liberalization by acting as a "sea wall" protecting Japanese development. According to Fukuda, it was precisely by granting the military a "status largely independent of civilian government" that the Meiji government made modernization and democracy possible.[28] Furthermore, the army had been "the supreme actor in Japan's modernization, as well as its most noteworthy product." He argued that this was because the military thrived on mechanistic materialism, so that "in no other occupation could one feel and calculate so directly the level of modernization [of society]." Even in the "human realm," the military had "inculcated the kind of personality suitable to a member of a modern nation-state."[29] By pretending to take up Reischauer's brand of "value-free" analysis and extending it in order to demonstrate the importance of the military's role in modernization, Fukuda was contributing indirectly to the postwar movement for rearmament that was expanding under the cover of economic growth and prosperity.

What came to be called Reischauer's "new view of history" generated interest and controversy in other ways. In contrast, it seems, to some other Americans, he was convinced of the central role of values and ethics in Japan's modernization. For example, when he sought in 1963 to explain why Japan had succeeded in modernizing more rapidly than China, he turned immediately to a discussion of "value systems and guiding ideals."[30] Factors such as "goal orientation" and an "entrepreneurial spirit," which in his view were present in Japan but not in China, played a central role. He concluded, "No one can look at the history of China and Japan in the second half of the nineteenth century without coming to the conclusion that such factors as . . . value systems, and guiding ideals have an important bearing on modernization and economic growth—indeed, more bearing than physical factors such as natural resources or even the factor of outside stimulus."[31]

Moreover, given the importance of a negative conception of "feudalism" in both pre- and postwar Japanese analyses of Japan's modern development, about which more below, it is noteworthy that in Reischauer's view feudalism played a positive role in generating not only values but a social structure conducive to modernization. In contrast to the centralized, bureaucratic Chinese empire, whose "very solidity and strength . . . slowed up the process of modernization," Japan's "feudal divisions permitted a more varied and richer reaction to Western learning and power." Reischauer added that, by restricting social mobility and preventing non-samurai from aspiring to political power, feudal classes in Japan had actually contributed to early modern private economic initiative and achievement, while the samurai distain for commerce had prevented them from oppressively taxing economic activity. In Chinese history, on the other hand, one found repeated cases of "the powerful, centralized government crushing through taxation, or taking over through monopoly, any new economic development that proved profitable."[32] In Reischauer's view, therefore, feudalism had been a factor in Japan's favor, not something to be regretted.

## THE JAPANESE PARADIGM

Perhaps the differences between the American and Japanese sides that apparently occurred at the Hakone meeting were partly a function of circumstantial factors, such as fresh memories on the Japanese side of the security treaty struggle over precisely the question of democracy, and John Hall's unaccountably objectivist list of criteria. Nevertheless, that the Hakone conference has been remembered in Japan ever since as the occasion for disagreement between Japanese and Americans regarding the role of democratic values in modernization suggests that the Japanese response had deeper, more profound origins. Indeed, upon reflection, it appears that the Japanese reaction can be said to have emerged precisely from the major blind spot in Reischauer's conception of modern Japanese history: the "fifteen-year war." Reischauer treats the years of mobilization and war as an exceptional period of "hyper-nationalistic mysticism"[33] during which Japanese society experienced scarcely any lasting change. Once it was over, whatever little historical impact it might have had was effectively nullified, as the Japanese reconnected with the nascent legacy of democracy and free enterprise that had reached its apex in the mid-1920s. In other words, in Reischauer's scheme, Japan's highly successful postwar modernization owed virtually nothing to wartime development. Yet, clearly, the opposite was the case. To an extent far beyond what Reischauer was willing to recognize, not only important aspects of postwar Japanese society and economy but also the world view of major postwar intellectuals emerged directly or indirectly from the experience of total war.[34]

The generation of Japanese intellectuals that attended the Hakone conference and led the Japanese intellectual world of the 1950s and 1960s were those whose young adulthood had been dominated by right-wing resurgence, suppression of left-wing movements, regimentation, and war. Born between 1905 and 1915, most were in their thirties at the end of the war when, as the literary critic Ara Masato put it, they experienced a "second youth" of expressive freedom and optimism.[35] Moreover, they had not only weathered mobilization and deprivation, but had been imprinted with certain forms of thought, views of history, and what Tsurumi Kazuko has called an "ideo-affective posture" that were all grounded in wartime exigencies.[36] The following thumbnail sketch of their orientation is provided by one of the leading members of the same generation, the economist Uchida Yoshihiko: "Overwhelmingly influenced by Koza-ha ["Lectures School" Marxist] theory, they began their intellectual activities, each in a specific realm of expertise, in the era of political suffocation."[37] Uchida went on to label this generation, which led the postwar intellectual world and included most of the influential social scientists and historians, the "civil society youths," and more recently they have been called the "civil society" school.

What did Uchida mean by "Koza-ha theory"? The prewar influence of Marxism in Japanese thought may be said to have culminated in the early 1930s, just as the Japanese army was beginning its full-scale aggression on the Asian continent. In 1932 members of the dominant faction of Marxists published a seven-volume series of collected "lectures" that provided a definitive analysis of the historical development of capitalism in Japan. As a result, they came to be called the Lectures School (Koza-ha). The authors and editors of this series mostly belonged to the generation just before the "civil society" theorists, and their influence on the latter was formative. Their basic conclusions regarding Japanese development provided support for the program of the Japan Communist Party, which emphasized a two-stage approach to revolution in Japan: before attempting to bring about a socialist revolution it was necessary to complete the bourgeois-democratic revolution.

Because the first, bourgeois-democratic, stage of revolution depended, in part, on advanced capitalism, the Lectures School focused attention on the development of capitalism and was known for its emphasis on the pathological peculiarities of existing forms of Japanese capitalism. For example, in 1931 the famous Lectures School economist Yamada Moritaro set forth an abstract, normative model of capitalism and then used that model as the basis for a comparative diagnosis of the Japanese case. When measured against the normative model, Japanese capitalism emerged as pathological in at least three interrelated ways: First, the low agricultural wages prevalent in semifeudal agriculture had impeded the development of universal standards of value and perpetuated unequal exchange in the form of excessively low wages in other sectors of the economy. Second, profit in Japanese capitalism was generated not primarily from technological advances but from excessive exploitation of low-wage labor. Third, the economy was dominated not by the most technologically advanced sectors but by textiles and other light industries that were relatively labor-intensive. This backwardness in Japanese capitalist enterprise was compensated for in part by the role of the state in fostering high-technology defense industries, but again, the result was pathological, leading to the bifurcation of the economy into a dual structure in which small-scale manufacturers and enterprises coexisted with huge, capital-intensive industries. Overall, this amounted to "semifeudal capitalism"—capitalism in form but not in content.[38]

Major figures in the Lectures School were arrested in 1936, and accelerated mobilization for total war created an atmosphere in which revolutionary discourse—that is, discourse focused on strategies for directly transforming the relations of production—became strictly taboo. Under such circumstances, some of them searched for a way to respond to mobilization so as to maximize the benefits that might accrue to the working class. The eventual result of their effort came to be called "productive forces theory." This theory was based on the premise that the wartime turn to central planning and expansion of production would help rectify the excessive exploitation of labor that Yamada and others had identified in Japanese capitalism. That is, intentional expansion of the productive forces through government-led technological development and rationalization would expand the impact of technology in the economy as a whole and push high-tech industry decisively into a leading economic role, thereby gradually rendering the relatively labor-intensive, hyper-exploitative industries uncompetitive. It would at the same time accelerate demand for more highly skilled workers and expand the proportion of such workers in the labor force. The long-term result would be more equal, less exploitative industrial relations—that is, the development in the labor market of fair, equitable exchange of the sort called for by Yamada's normative model of pure capitalism. The result would also be new scope for initiative on the part of highly skilled, technologically competent workers who would increasingly develop as free, imaginative subjects.

Lectures School Marxists or former Marxists also responded to the extreme repression that accompanied all-out mobilization by devoting intensive study to the works of non-Marxists such as Max Weber and the eighteenth-century British political economist Adam Smith. Indeed, according to a recent account, the formative and most productive period of Weberian studies in Japan occurred between 1926 and 1945.[39] Such "civil society" school theorists as Okochi Kazuo, Otsuka Hisao, and Takashima Zenya devoted themselves to studying and translating Weber's sociology of religion, including *The Protestant Ethic and the Spirit of Capitalism.* They further explored the role of economic ethics by delving into Adam Smith's *Theory of Moral Sentiments* as well as his *Wealth of Nations.*[40]

Japanese scholars during and after the war were influenced by Max Weber's work in a number of ways: First, it had an impact in the realm of social scientific methodology and stimulated debates on the role of value judgments in social science. As this clearly suggests, the "civil society" school scholars who participated in the Hakone conference were every bit as familiar with the norms of "objective" social science as the Americans. Second, Weber's corpus had an impact in the realm of social policy, especially in regard to class conflict and the role of state intervention in addressing it. Third, it influenced Japanese views of Asia in the context of Japanese expansion in that area. Fourth, it affected analyses of the development of capitalism in Japan and the nature and role of economic values in that development.[41]

The last of these modes of influence is perhaps the most relevant to an attempt to explain the way leading Japanese intellectuals responded to the modernization theory of John Hall and his colleagues. That is, the dual impact of Marx and Weber (along with Smith and others) on members of the "civil society" school generation during the war caused them to pay close attention to the role of subjective values and ethics as components of otherwise objective processes of social change. Tsuzuki observes: "What the 'civil society' school got from the Lectures School of Marxism was a sense not just that the historical development of modern Japan was peculiar, but also that along with the material factors that drove the various processes of world history there were also human, spiritual factors involved. It happened that this notion was proposed to them by the work of Max Weber, and this led to a unique perspective on social science which combined Marx and Weber. In other words, the Lectures School provided the soil in which the Weberian approach could grow."[42] Of course, the legacy of Marx and Weber, and various theories of value and social change based on it, lasted well into the postwar period and may have contributed to the tendency of major Japanese participants to bridle at the American side's apparent neglect of values and ideals in their understanding of modernization. Moreover, some of the common themes of that legacy—including concern about what seemed to be "feudal" values as well as institutions and the fundamentally distorted ("semifeudal") nature of Japanese capitalism, an overriding concern about the working class and the importance of raising wages, and the key role granted to rural society in determining the form and limits of development—were latent in the conceptual orientation not only of many of the Japanese conference participants but of major thinkers and planners, some of whose ideas underlay government programs such as income-doubling.

As noted above, Maruyama Masao and Kawashima Takeyoshi were the conference participants most closely identified with the "civil society" school, but others such as Okita Saburo, whose career was spent largely in government economic ministries, went through a comparable trajectory and received some of the same influences. Nakayama Ichiro and other major government economic advisers such as Arisawa Hiromi and Tsuru Shigeto were influenced by Lectures School Marxism as well as classical and neoclassical economics, and the wartime strategies of planned economy and emphasis on productivity had a lasting impact on their thinking. They were concerned about democracy as well as productivity and growth. Their focus on the problem of "dual structure" in the economy—the bifurcation between a modern, highly capitalized sector and a less modern sector consisting of small firms—and their belief in a "high-wage, high-productivity" approach had roots in the Lectures School of Yamada Moritaro and others, and resonated with the productive forces theory of wartime. Moreover, these men were in a position to translate their ideas into action. As Laura Hein has pointed out, Nakayama and Arisawa joined with the civil society school economist Okochi Kazuo to focus the policy of the Japan Productivity Center on higher wages through increased productivity, and Nakayama's income-doubling plan was intended not primarily to accelerate growth but "to eliminate *low-wage* jobs by shrinking the bottom half of the dual structure."[43]

In sum, influential people throughout Japanese academia, government, and even private industry adhered to an approach to modernization that was forged in the crucible of total-war mobilization as well as strongly conditioned by postwar democratization. Their approach was influenced in varying degrees by Marxist analysis as well as broadly consistent with modern social science. They acknowledged the necessity of scientific objectivity but persisted in conceiving of modernization as not just an ongoing, objective process but an intentional, human project, aimed at realizing certain values such as peace and democracy and driven by ethics as well as profit. They disagreed sharply among themselves on many issues, but their overall approach did not divide them in any fundamental way from the Americans.

## NOTES

1. Quoted in John W. Dower, *Embracing Defeat: Japan in the Wake of World War II* (New York: W. W. Norton, 1999), 550.

2. On the accommodation implicitly reached between the United States and Japan after World War II in regard to racial hierarchy, see Yukiko Koshiro, *Trans-Pacific Racisms and the U.S. Occupation of Japan* (New York: Columbia University Press, 1999), chap. 1.

3. Bruce Cumings, "Boundary Displacement: Area Studies and International Studies during and after the Cold War," *Bulletin of Concerned Asian Scholars* 29, no. 1 (1997): 12–15.

4. Patricia Steinhoff, "Japanese Studies in the United States: The Loss of Irrelevance," *IHJ Bulletin* 13, no. 1 (winter 1993): 3.

5. Bai Gao, *Economic Ideology and Japanese Industrial Policy* (London: Cambridge University Press, 1997), 227.

6. John Whitney Hall, "Changing Conceptions of Modernization in Japan," in Marius B. Jansen, ed., *Changing Japanese Attitudes toward Modernization* (Princeton: Princeton University Press, 1965), 18.

7. Ibid., 19.

8. Kawashima Takeyoshi, " 'Kindaika' no imi," *Shiso* (November 1963): 3–4.

9. Matsumoto Sannosuke, *Kindai Nihon no chiteki jokyo* (Tokyo: Chuko Sosho, 1975), 193.

10. Hall, "Changing Conceptions of Modernization," 26–27.

11. Ibid., 28.

12. Kawashima Takeyoshi, "Kindai Nihonshi no shakai kagakuteki kenkyu," *Shiso* (April 1961): 108.

13. Michael E. Latham, *Modernization as Ideology: American Social Science and "Nation Building" in the Kennedy Era* (Chapel Hill: University of North Carolina Press, 2000), 50.

14. Kawashima, "Kindai Nihonshi no shakai kagakuteki kenkyu," 107.

15. Ibid., 108.

16. Ibid., 109.

17. Matsumoto, *Kindai Nihon no chiteki jokyo*, 194.

18. J. Victor Koschmann, *Revolution and Subjectivity in Postwar Japan* (Chicago: University of Chicago Press, 1996).

19. Latham, *Modernization as Ideology*, 32–33.

20. Edwin O. Reischauer, "The Broken Dialogue with Japan," *Foreign Affairs* (October 1960): 26.

21. Edwin O. Reischauer, *My Life between Japan and America* (New York: Harper & Row, 1986), 163.

22. Reischauer, "The Broken Dialogue with Japan," 18–19.

23. One of Reischauer's most university lecture-like articles was "Kindaishi o mitsumeru: futatsu no jigen ni yori hatten katei no bunseki," *Asahi janaru* 4, no. 23 (10 June 1962): 39–44.

24. Gao, *Economic Ideology and Japanese Industrial Policy*, 38–40.

25. E. O. Reischauer and Nakayama Ichiro, "Nihon kindaika no rekishiteki hyoka," *Chuo koron* (September 1961): 90.

26. Ibid., 97.

27. Furuta Hikaru, Sakuta Keiichi and Ikimatsu Keizo, eds., *Kindai Nihon shakai shisoshi* II [Kindai Nihon shisoshi taikei dainikan] (Tokyo: Yuhikaku, 1971), 320–22.

28. Fukuda Tsuneari, "Gunto no dokuso ni tsuite: Nihon kindaika shiron, sono go," *Bungei shunju* (April 1964): 84.

29. Fukuda Tsuneari, "Kindaika o habamu mono: Nihon kindaika shiron, sono roku," *Bungei shunju* (June 1964): 78.

30. Edwin O. Reischauer, "Modernization in Nineteenth-Century China and Japan," *Japan Quarterly* 10, no. 3 (July-September 1963): 302.

31. Ibid., 307.

32. Ibid., 300–305.

33. Reischauer, "The Broken Dialogue with Japan," 20.

34. Yamanouchi Yasushi, J. Victor Koschmann, and Narita Ryuichi, eds., *Total War and "Modernization,"* Cornell East Asia Series 100 (Ithaca: Cornell East Asia Program, 1998).

35. Ara Masato, "Daini no seishun," *Kindai bungaku* 2 (March 1946): 1, quoted in Tsuzuki Tsutomu, *Sengo Nihon no chishikijin: Maruyama Masao to sono jidai* (Tokyo: Seori Shobo, 1995), 13.

36. Kazuko Tsurumi, *Social Change and the Individual: Japan before and after Defeat in World War II* (Princeton: Princeton University Press, 1970), 30.

37. Uchida Yoshihiko, *Nihon shihonshugi no shisozo* (Tokyo: Iwanami Shoten, 1967), 39–40, quoted in Tsuzuki, *Sengo Nihon no chishikijin,* 16.

38. Yamada Moritaro, *Saiseisan hyoshiki bunseki joron* [*Keizaigaku zenshu*, vol. 11] (Tokyo, 1931). For a synopsis and discussion, see Asada Mitsuteru, "Taichoki shakai kagaku no shiso," in Sumiya Etsuji et al., eds., *Koza: Nihon shakaishisoshi* [Handoki no shakai shiso] (Tokyo: Haga Shobo, 1967), 273–300.

39. Wolfgang Schwentker, *Max Weber in Japan: Eine Untersuchung zur Wirkingsgeschichte 1905–1995* (Tübingen: Mohr Siebeck, 1998), quoted in Yamanouchi Yasushi, *Nihon no shakai kagaku to ueba taiken* (Tokyo: Chikuma Shobo, 1999), 46.

40. Okochi Kazuo, *Sumisu to Risuto* (Tokyo: Nihon hyoronsha, 1943); Otsuka Hisao, "Makkusu Ueba ni okeru shihonshugi no 'seishin': kindai shakai ni okeru keizai rinri to seisanryoku josetsu," *Keizaigaku ronshu* 13, no. 12; 14, no. 4; 15, no. 1 (1943–46).

41. Yamanouchi, *Nihon no shakai kagaku to ueba taiken,* 47. Schwentker takes the four types of influence from Maruyama Masao, "Senzen ni okeru Nihon no ueba kenkyu," in Otsuka Hisao, ed., *Makkusu ueba kenkyu* (Tokyo: Tokyo Daigaku Shuppankai, 1965).

42. Tsuzuki, *Sengo Nihon no chishikijin,* 18–19.

43. Laura Hein, "In Search of Peace and Democracy: Japanese Economic Debate in Political Context," *Journal of Asian Studies* 53, no. 3 (August 1994): 771.

## FURTHER READING

Dower, John W. "E. H. Norman, Japan, and the Uses of History." In Dower, ed., *Origins of the Modern Japanese State: Selected Writings of E. H. Norman.* New York: Pantheon, 1975.

Hein, Laura, "In Search of Peace and Democracy: Japanese Economic Debate in Political Context." *Journal of Asian Studies* 53, no. 3 (August 1994): 752–78.

Jansen, Marius B., ed. *Changing Japanese Attitudes toward Modernization.* Princeton: Princeton University Press, 1965.

Koschmann, J. Victor, *Revolution and Subjectivity in Postwar Japan.* Chicago: University of Chicago Press, 1996.

Yamanouchi, Yasushi, J. Victor Koschmann, and Ryuichi Narita, eds. *Total War and "Modernization."* Cornell East Asia Series 100. Ithaca: Cornell East Asia Program, 1998.

# KOREANIZING MODERNIZATION: MODERNIZATION THEORY AND SOUTH KOREAN INTELLECTUALS

GREGG ANDREW BRAZINSKY

The Republic of Korea occupies a somewhat paradoxical position in the mind-sets of many Americans. In the American media the country appears alternatively either as a successful example of capitalist industrialization or as a bastion of traditional, corrupt "Asian values." Americans contrast South Korea's "economic miracle" with the poverty and famine that exists in North Korea as evidence that American or Western models of modernization were superior to Communist ones. But as soon as South Korea's miracle economy stumbles, as it did in the Asian financial crisis of 1997, Americans are quick to blame the durability of the country's "traditional values" such as Asian cronyism or immoral familism for its failures. For Americans, South Korea has come to serve at once as an example of the promise of modernity and the danger of tradition.

For South Koreans, however, being modern and being traditional have not necessarily represented mutually exclusive possibilities. Nor have South Koreans always represented "tradition" as something that is intrinsically antithetical to modernity. Modernization discourse in

South Korea has often emphasized the ways that traditions can buttress or inform modernity rather than hinder it. At no time was this more apparent than during the fifties and sixties when Americans began an ambitious effort to disseminate concepts of modernization, especially modernization theory, among South Korean intellectuals. The first encounter of many South Korean intellectuals with concepts such as "traditional" and "modern" was marked by neither the acceptance nor the rejection of these concepts but instead by their adaptation.

## THE ROK DURING THE FIFTIES AND SIXTIES AND AMERICAN COLD WAR POLICY

The arrival of modernization theory in South Korean academic circles did not occur entirely as a consequence of the globalization of ideas and culture. It was also a by-product of a calculated American effort to spread these theories in South Korean academic circles in order to address very specific fears that Americans harbored about the destiny of their Asian ally. Americans understood modernization as a concept that could control dissent, maintain order, and ensure stability in a country that was vital to the United States' international reputation and strategic interests.

The United States had played a determining role in the liberation of Korea from Japanese colonial rule in 1945, the establishment of a separate South Korean government in 1948, and the physical preservation of the new South Korean state in the face of both internal dissent and armed conflict with the North Korean Communist regime.[1] During the years after the Korean War, South Korea became a keystone in American efforts to bolster the security of Japan and its other Pacific allies. The continuing presence of thousands of U.S. troops on the Korean peninsula combined with large infusions of American military and economic assistance to the Republic of Korea served to link the United States' legitimacy as a world leader to the preservation of a pro-American government in South Korea. Americans, especially American policymakers, were well aware of the association between the ROK and U.S. credibility in the world arena. One strategy paper on South Korea produced by the United States Agency for International Development (USAID) in the early sixties noted that the ROK "had become a symbol of the determination of the United States to assist the nations of free Asia to defend themselves against Communist aggression" and that the loss of South Korea could jeopardize "the entire strategic and psychological position of the U.S. in the Pacific area."[2]

During the late fifties and sixties, however, events and circumstances in South Korea heightened American anxieties about the country's capacity to remain a dependable ally. By the late fifties South Korean students and intellectuals were increasingly voicing their discontent with both the corruption and the authoritarianism of the Syngman Rhee government, which the United States had helped to install in 1948. Growing popular dissent and criticism from the media only seemed to exacerbate the Rhee government's proclivity for dictatorial tactics, and by 1960 confrontation between the ROK government and the growing ranks of its detractors had become inevitable. A blatantly fraudulent presidential election in March 1960 set off massive student demonstrations that the Rhee regime—with American permission—used the ROK military to put down. But a month later, when the body of a middle school student who had been shot dead by South Korean police was found in Masan harbor, demonstrations erupted again. On 19 April 1960 a crowd of more than 100,000 students converged on the presidential palace and demanded Rhee's resignation, and once again Rhee's government resorted to the use of the military to end the demonstration. But when demonstrations persisted even the United States began pressuring Rhee to resign, and he finally fled to Hawaii on 29 April 1960.[3]

Yet the government that succeeded Rhee's, although popularly elected, did little to placate American fears about the country being swept by chaos. The new government was comprised chiefly of members of the ROK's Democratic Party, which had served as the opposition party during the forties and fifties. The leadership in the Democratic Party was generally committed to the principles of democracy, but it also favored a political system with a weak central government. Street demonstrations, many in favor of a new approach toward reunification with North Korea, persisted, and both conservatives and military leaders in the country became increasingly alarmed.[4] Moreover, the new government did little to redress South Korea's severe economic problems. In 1960 South Korea was one of the poorest countries in the world. Its per capita GNP stood at only $78, significantly below that of North Korea, whose economy had taken off during the years after the Korean War. A report prepared by an American official in February 1961 that was widely circulated among officials in the incoming John F. Kennedy administration noted that Koreans had lost confidence in their "institutions, in themselves, and . . . in the U.S." The report warned that the "receptivity of a people in such a frame of mind to Communist and other extremist influence, after fifteen years of American presence is natural."[5]

In the end, South Korea's first experiment in democracy proved to be a very brief one. On 16 May 1961 a military junta led by Park Chung-Hee engineered a coup that replaced South Korea's existing government with a military dictatorship. Park dominated South Korean politics for nineteen years, switching to a quasi-democratic polity of which he was elected president in 1963 and 1967, but reverting to a harsh neo-authoritarian system called "yusin" in 1972. Although Park had temporarily subverted American control over the ROK military by using Korean troops with American permission, the U.S. government respected Park's desire to restore order and his zeal for stimulating economic growth. After temporary concerns that Park himself was a Communist were alleviated, the United States became increasingly supportive of Park's government although American policymakers pressured Park on issues such as human rights and free elections.[6] While somewhat greater stability ensued during the years after the military takeover, protests by both students and intellectuals against the government and sometimes against the United States never entirely ceased. Moreover, the military had traditionally not been accorded a great deal of prestige in Korean society, and many South Korean elites resented the new government even though they sometimes feared resisting it.

Throughout the late fifties and sixties American policy texts expressed a particularly strong concern about the dissident tendencies of South Korean intellectuals and college students and argued that the United States needed to engage these groups to assure that their intellectual orientation remained conducive to national development. One report circulated shortly after the April 19 Revolution said that "of the key power groups in Korea today the two key ones are the students and intellectuals and the U.S." and spoke of the need for the United States to make a "pitch to win the confidence of students."[7]

Although the military coup's leadership restricted the rights of students and intellectuals to meet and hold demonstrations, American policymakers remained extremely attentive to the atmosphere at Korean universities and continued to make gaining the confidence and trust of Korean intellectuals one of their top priorities. A task force report on Korea prepared just after the military coup had occurred contended that the United States should "encourage the evolutionary process of social change" and that "in its encouragement special attention needs to be paid to the intellectuals."[8]

The U.S. government continued to monitor and keep in contact with leading students and intellectuals during times of relative tranquility as well as during more turbulent periods. Bernard Lavin, a U.S. Foreign Service officer who worked with the United States Information Service between 1959 and 1967, became particularly well acquainted with groups of student activists and frequently invited members of activist student organizations to the embassy or to his home to discuss significant issues.[9] Lavin's efforts, however, were apparently only part of a much broader effort to monitor the activities of Korean intellectuals and students. Ten days after the military coup had occurred one embassy official assured the State Department that during the period after the coup the "embassy-USIS" had "kept in close contact with student communities in order to ascertain as much as possible their reactions to military takeover." The cable claimed that any assessment of the student mood could "at best be tentative" but pointed to a general ambivalence among Korean university students toward the coup. It also pointed to the possibility of future protests, claiming that the students saw themselves as the "principal segment of Korean society in which moral responsibility for [the] defense of freedom rests" and were likely to "make bolder statements and take actions calling for the return of political freedoms."[10] During the early sixties American officials tended to be sympathetic toward the democratic aspirations of such students but also were troubled by their potential to undermine political stability in the ROK.

Concerns about demonstrations by students and intellectuals remained constant during subsequent years and intensified when the demonstrations touched on issues involving the U.S. role in the ROK. After American soldiers committed an unwarranted assault on Korean civilians in Paju in 1962, for instance, demonstrations demanding the conclusion of a Status of Forces Agreement (SOFA) that would establish stricter standards of behavior and discipline for U.S. armed forces in the ROK arose at many South Korean universities. Samuel Berger, the American ambassador to the ROK, wrote that the demonstrators probably included those who had "malicious or subversive motives" and that such demonstrations "cannot repeat cannot be tolerated." Berger also warned that the demonstration could not be "brushed aside as of minor or temporary significance."[11]

Both American and ROK government officials were acutely aware that the restlessness of students and intellectuals was not simply the result of individual political issues, however, but a by-product of deeper grievances against the failures of both the United States and the South Korean government to improve socio-economic conditions in their country. One American official wrote, "The average student is still avowedly anti-communist in outlook but, perhaps, emotionally, more attracted to the left for possible solutions to his own and the nation's problems since, apparently, little if any progress has been achieved by the present system."[12] Similarly, in discussing the problem of student demonstrations with U.S. officials one Korean minister explained while Korean university students "aspired to positions with status and income appropriate to their higher education," they often ended up "living a meager hand to mouth existence looking for jobs and spending much of their time in tea rooms discussing politics."[13] Constantly dogged by such concerns about the capacity of the country's students and intellectuals to wreak political havoc, the United States became increasingly interested in finding ways to influence the content of what these groups taught, wrote, studied, and learned.

## INTRODUCING MODERNIZATION THEORY TO KOREAN INTELLECTUALS

Worried about the implications that student and intellectual dissent could have for the country's stability and security, Americans came to perceive the introduction of modernization theory to South Korean universities as an ideal tool for bringing about the intellectual reorientation of groups that seemed disillusioned with both the United States and their own government. Modernization theory's emphasis on the inevitability of social and economic progress, its critique of communism, and its inherent faith in the capacity of the "advanced" countries of "the West" to stimulate the development of the poorer regions of the world seemed like the perfect ideological counter to the growing tendency among South Korean intellectuals to look for radical solutions to their country's problems. As the U.S. government began to make increasing efforts to design intellectual and cultural exchange programs geared to groups such as youth, labor, and intellectuals, the promotion of modernization theory among academics and students in South Korea and other Asian countries became an important component of its cultural policy.[14] Encouraged by Washington, private American foundations and universities soon began making their own efforts to acquaint South Korean elites with modernization theory.

Among U.S. government agencies the United States Information Service (later United States Information Agency or USIA) played by far the most significant promotional role. In 1967 the USIS country plan for the ROK listed contributing to the "modernization of the ROK by promoting awareness and understanding of the requirements for economic growth, democratic social development and political stability" among its major objectives. One of the target audiences for such efforts was "university faculty," among whom the USIS determined to spread the idea that "the academic community has a responsibility to study, articulate and disseminate practical ideas on the modernization process."[15] Throughout the late fifties and sixties the USIS published magazines targeted specifically at Korean intellectuals, paid for the translation of books, and arranged for personal exchanges of both students and scholars between the United States and the ROK. Such initiatives were greeted with varying degrees of ambivalence and enthusiasm by their Korean targets.

Print media served as one of the USIS's most significant vehicles for introducing and promoting modernization theory at South Korean universities. The USIS's translation program made the works of several modernization theorists, especially economists, available to Korean students and intellectuals. By 1964 Rostow's *The Stages of Economic Growth* had already been through two printings and was credited by visiting American economists with widely influencing South Korean economists. The USIS also printed a low-cost series of book translations for students that included titles such as Max Millikan's *The Emerging Nations,* Edward S. Mason's *Economic Planning in Under-*

*developed Areas,* and Robert J. Alexander's *A Primer for Economic Development.* In the first printing, the USIS produced 2,000 copies of each of these titles, and all of them sold out within six months of publication. A USIS translation of J. K. Galbraith's *Economic Development in Perspective* proved particularly popular and went through several printings.[16] In addition to translating books into Korean, the USIS also published a quarterly magazine, *Nondan* (meaning forum), which contained translations of the most recent American scholarship in fields such as economics, history, and sociology. Unlike numerous other USIA publications targeting a broad range of South Korean elites, *Nondan* specifically targeted students and intellectuals. Articles in *Nondan* canvassed a wide range of subjects and sometimes included writings by well-known Korean as well as American scholars. Nevertheless, articles on modernization theory appeared with marked regularity in the journal. Some of these included: Lester M. Salamon's "Comparative History and the Theory of Modernization," David E. Powell's "Social Costs of Modernization," S. N. Eisenstadt's "Intellectuals and Tradition," and Robert Fluker's "Regional Cooperation and the Modernization of Southeast Asia."[17]

The USIS also teamed up with the staff of Joong-ang, a South Korean television network, to create a weekly news program with the theme "Modernization in Korea." The program, which began airing in December 1965, attempted to convey to its audiences "all aspects of the modernization process that is taking place with accelerated speed in Korea." Initial programs consisted of 25-minute roundtable discussions by prominent South Korean professors in the field of economics. Subsequent programs in the series focused on a broad array of different issues including: national planning, educational development, sociological changes, and rural development. American experts in different fields were also frequently featured on the program. For instance, Oswald Nagler, an Asia Foundation–sponsored adviser to the ROK government, hosted a series of programs on national physical planning that included subjects such as comprehensive planning and community development. Although only a fraction of the South Korean population owned televisions at the time the series first appeared, the programs were probably viewed by 70,000 to 100,000 people. Moreover, Joong-ang television edited the series for reproduction in pamphlet form for use in university and other discussion groups.[18]

Personal exchange programs managed by the USIS served both to bring prominent American modernization theorists to teach or lecture at South Korean universities and to send Korean scholars to the United States to study. Academic exchanges occurred, of course, in a wide variety of disciplines, but the United States Educational Commission (USEC) often brought lecturers in fields such as political science and economic development where modernization theory was in vogue, and many such lecturers spoke on the topic of modernization during their tenures in the ROK. For instance, William Douglas, a political scientist who was brought to South Korea as Fulbright lecturer in 1963, delivered an address titled "The Role of Political Parties in the Modernization Process" at a conference held in Seoul on the "Modernization Process in Korea." Although most of the professors going to South Korea to spend full years or semesters at various universities tended not to be very well known, the USIS also ran an "American Participant" program that brought some of the best-known modernization theorists to the country for short periods. In 1964, for instance, the USIS brought Walt Rostow to speak at Seoul National University and asked him specifically to comment on where the ROK stood in terms of his "stages of economic growth." Rostow told his South Korean audience that their country was in the "take-off" stage but his speech was attacked by the country's media. The press did not criticize modernization theory itself, however; rather, it complained that the United States had brought a "foreign expert" for the purpose of making Koreans "feel good" at a time when their country's economic poverty was readily apparent.[19]

The USIS also played a very active role in encouraging American philanthropic organizations such as the Asia Foundation, the Ford Foundation, and the American Korea Foundation to develop cultural exchange programs with the ROK. The Asia and Ford Foundations took a particularly active interest in promoting social science research, including studies that deployed modernization theory, among South Korean scholars. Because South Koreans did not necessarily associate the activities of these organizations directly with U.S. government policies they were often more capable of promoting particular ideas or types of research than the USIS itself was.

The Asia Foundation was instrumental in both establishing and providing continuing financial support for the Korean Research Center.

Founded in 1955, the center was designed to facilitate social science research in the ROK and sought particularly to support research on Korean society, culture, and history. The Asia Foundation donated money to support the center's library, which contained a large number of English-language volumes and provided annual research fellowships to leading Korean scholars. Among the goals of these fellowships were: "providing materials, foreign experience and services to enable Korean scholars to understand modern social science methodology" and "developing studies of modernization especially as they relate to the Korean experience." Studies done under the auspices of the center were later published in book form.[20]

The impact of Ford Foundation funding on academic research in South Korea was even more widespread and enduring. The Ford Foundation established a particularly close relationship with Korea University, one of the top three universities in South Korea, where it was instrumental in helping to strengthen the Asiatic Research Center (Asea Munje Yŏnguso). The Asiatic Research Center had been formed as an adjunct research institution at Korea University in 1957 with the purpose of promoting research on both Korea and East Asia. The Ford Foundation furnished the center with nearly $700,000 between 1962 and 1967.[21] The funding was put to a large variety of different uses including financing advisory visits by American scholars, holding national and international conferences, and publishing research journals. Nearly all these activities accelerated both the transmission of modernization theory from the United States to the ROK and its dissemination in South Korea. Scholars brought to the Asiatic Research Center through Ford Foundation funding included the renowned expert on modern Chinese history John Fairbank, and George M. Beckmann, who had written on the modernization of Japan and China. These scholars both helped the ARC's leadership to formulate a research agenda and delivered lectures in their areas of specialization to students and faculty. During 1960, for instance, Fairbank delivered a lecture titled "Problems of Modern China" in July and Edwin Reischauer spoke on "Korea and Modernization" in October.[22] The center also utilized external sources of funding to publish its biannual scholarly journal, the *Journal of Asiatic Research* (Asea Yŏn'gu), which it also attempted to distribute abroad. Conferences supported by the Ford Foundation included an international conference, "Problems of Modernization in Asia," held in 1965 and another, "Problems of Communism in Asia," held in 1966. The conference on modernization was a particularly impressive week-long event that gathered not only the foremost South Korean scholars but also top-notch American scholars such as Lucian Pye, Marion Levy, and Robert Scalpino.[23] Such activities enabled the Asiatic Research Center to become perhaps the most significant indigenous institutional vehicle for the dissemination of modernization theory in South Korea. Many of the best-known South Korean historians, economists, and sociologists who deployed modernization theory in one way or another either studied or taught at Korea University during the fifties and sixties.

Individual American universities also sometimes played significant roles in introducing modernization theory and some of its applications to South Korean scholars. Harvard University's Yenching Institute was particularly significant in this regard. The Yenching Institute both offered funding directly to research institutions in the ROK and, more significant, managed an exchange program that enabled South Korean scholars in different fields of the humanities and social sciences to study or do research at Harvard for one-year periods. While the number of scholars the institute could invite was limited, many of those it supported became important figures in their individual fields. Some scholars who attended the institute studied in disciplines where modernization theory had relatively little impact such as literature and linguistics. But a significant proportion of South Korean scholars attending the Yenching Institute focused on either history or the social sciences. Some of those whose work later deployed modernization theory in one form or another included: Yi Kwang-Rin (1957–58) who became a pioneer in the field of modern Korean history, Kim Jun-Yŏp (1958–59), a specialist on Chinese politics who later became director of the Asiatic Research Center at Korea University, and Choi Jae-Sŏk (1966–67), a sociologist whose research focused on Korean family institutions.[24] Kim Jun-Yŏp's position in the Asiatic Research Center enabled him to play a particularly significant role in promoting research on modernization in Korea through both channeling funding to appropriate scholars and using the center to launch publications and organize conferences.

Scholars from Korea, Japan, and Taiwan who attended the Yenching Institute later formed the Visiting Scholars Association (VSA) with branches in each of the individual countries. The Korea Branch began holding academic conferences in the mid-sixties, some of which were attended by scholars from Taiwan and Japan as well. A conference held in Seoul in December 1966 focused on the "Modern History of the Far East" and included presentations titled "Modernization in the Far East" and "Historical Studies of Modern East Asia in Korea." A similar conference held five years later focused on "Tradition and Change in East Asia" and featured a paper by the Korean historian Chun Hae-Jung titled "Tradition and Change in China and Korea." In his remarks at the session Kim Jun-Yŏp claimed that "modernization" was a "time consuming task" that needed to be studied for a "considerable period of time."[25]

Other South Koreans specializing in the social sciences were able to attend American universities either through lesser-known scholarship programs or occasionally through their own resources. Nearly 7,000 South Korean exchange students studied in the United States between 1953 and 1967, and approximately 25 percent of these majored in the social sciences.[26] Many studied economics and came into contact with American scholars whose work focused on economic development and tended to contain assumptions similar to those of modernization theorists when it did not deploy modernization theory itself. One South Korean who studied at the University of Minnesota recalled meeting Walter Heller, who later became an economic adviser to the Kennedy administration. Kim Wan-Sun earned a Ph.D. in economics at Harvard and took courses with economists such as Simon Kuznets and John Kenneth Galbraith. Similarly, Kim Ch'ae Pang studied monetary policy at the University of Southern California, where he took a course on comparative economic history taught by Spencer D. Pollard. Pollard taught that economic and cultural development did not occur spontaneously but was a result of humanity's endless creative activity and that if man lost his will to develop, civilization would become stagnant or fall into ruin.[27] Although many of the South Koreans who studied independently in the United States did not became academics when they returned home, a high proportion of them remained guided by the assumptions of modernization theory.

American modernization theories reached South Korean students and intellectuals with diverse backgrounds through a wide array of different mechanisms. By the early sixties the problems and possibilities of modernization in South Korea had become one of the most talked-about and written-about subjects among the country's elite. In 1966 the Korean historian Han Woo-Keun noted that "the problem of the 'modernization' of Korea" had been "much discussed in recent years both in individual articles and in various conferences and symposiums" and that such topics were not "limited to the academic research of historians, but discussed by scholars both at home and abroad as an urgent practical problem of Korean society."[28] The Korean word for modernization, "kŭndaehwa," had been used in some instances before 1950, but it began to take on a meaning more similar to the American concept of modernization from the late fifties onward. By the early sixties the term had become nearly ubiquitous in South Korean academic and popular journals. Articles appeared on different facets of modernization in a wide array of magazines, journals, and newspapers, and South Korean scholars from a variety of academic disciplines took part in conferences on the subject. A relatively select group of academics played the most significant role in adapting and disseminating modernization theories, and this group will be given the most detailed attention in the discussion that follows. It is also clear, however, that the views of these scholars had a significant influence on both university students and the media.

## MODERNIZATION, KOREAN STYLE

Long before the United States became an inevitable part of Korea's destiny in 1945, Koreans had acquired hundreds if not—as many Koreans would claim—thousands of years of experience at adapting different foreign philosophies to their own needs and values. Smaller and militarily weaker than most of its neighbors, Korea had little choice but to enter into hegemonic systems that were not of its own making. Until the late nineteenth century, Korea had been part of the Chinese tributary system and its intellectual and cultural life frequently came under the influence of its "middle kingdom" neighbor. The entry of religions and philosophies such as Buddhism and Confucianism was not entirely a product of Koreans' own choosing, but Koreans nevertheless chose the ways that they made some of these belief systems their own. An old proverb "when the whales fight the shrimp gets crushed" has long been used as an expression of Korea's precarious geographic position in between great power rivals. But when it came to negotiating the different social and cultural orders that stronger powers sought to impose on it, Korea just as often proved to be the dolphin that outsmarted the whales. Or, to borrow Michel de Certeau's phrase, Koreans' "use of the dominant social order deflected its power, which they lacked the means to challenge; they escaped it without leaving it."[29]

It should not come as a surprise then that during the fifties and sixties, when South Koreans confronted a new hegemonic power which sought to impose a new intellectual order upon the country, they could marshal a considerable array of tactics to reconcile this new order with their own goals and desires. American modernization theories contained an inherent set of rules and assumptions that established intellectual parameters for what South Koreans who became engaged in these discussions of modernization could say or write. Even when working within the rules of recognition prescribed by modernization theory, however, Korean intellectuals found ways to articulate cultural difference and to remain critical of both the ROK government and the United States. While some South Korean scholars conceptualized and applied "modernization" in terms that were almost entirely consistent with those laid out by American scholars, more often than not these intellectuals articulated hybrid conceptions that were responsive to their own fears and desires. The hybrid nature of South Korean understandings of modernization was particularly apparent in the ways that they came to conceptualize their country's modernization process.

Many South Korean scholars were genuinely inspired by the sense of possibility that modernization seemed to offer and consequently sought both to delineate the ways that Korea's modernization might occur and even to act to propel their nation along a path toward modernity. It was in their efforts to delineate Korea's modernization process, however, that South Korean scholars began to generate conceptions of modernization itself that most stridently asserted cultural difference. Such cultural difference found its most certain expression in debates that occurred both among South Korean scholars and between South Korean and foreign scholars on two interrelated issues. The first was the question whether "modernization" was conceptually the same as "Westernization." The second was the question whether

Korean "traditions" could or should inform the country's modernization process.

Neither Americans nor Koreans answered the first question in a uniform manner. Moreover, definitions of both terms varied from scholar to scholar. Nevertheless, the tone and content of South Korean writing on this subject differed from those found in American scholarship. Moreover, for South Korean scholars, explicating the relationship between modernization and Westernization often served as a means of evading implications of modernization theory that elevated the United States and the West over Korea and the East.

American scholars did not always contend that modernization and Westernization were one and the same. But many did argue that modernization entailed Westernization, especially in the context of discussions about Korea. When Edward Wagner, a professor of Korean history at Harvard, spoke in South Korea on the subject of "Korean Modernization" in 1963, for instance, he announced that "Modernization" was a concept "essentially identical in nuance with 'Westernization' " and that when applied to "a cultural entity that may be termed backward or underdeveloped, modernization signifies the process through which such an entity strives to Westernize itself."[30] To be fair, the vast majority of Wagner's scholarship did not focus on the issue of modernization, but his conflation of modernization and Westernization reflected both a broader trend in American thinking and some of the specific ideas that leading American scholars presented to South Koreans.

While American scholars tended to argue either that modernization was Westernization or, at best, that modernization *need not* be the same as Westernization, South Korean scholars tended to write articles contending that in Korea's case, modernization *must not* be the same as Westernization. They pointed to a range of historical and sociological reasons why the modernization process in Korea should or could not duplicate the process that had occurred in Europe and the United States. In elaborating the distinction between the two concepts that American scholars had partially defined, South Korean intellectuals also disclosed an anxiety about the effects that change was having and could have on their society. Drawing an analytical distinction between Westernization and modernization enabled South Korean scholars to accept the American proposition that modernization was desirable while simultaneously remaining guarded against the possibility of future economic or cultural subordination.

Many South Korean intellectuals acknowledged that "the West" had achieved modernization first or that the modernization of Asia had been stimulated by the West, but nevertheless contended that "modernity" or "modern values" were inherently just as much a part of Korean or Asian culture as they were of Western culture. Thus, they believed finding a way for Korea to become modernized but not Westernized was a realizable objective. In an article titled "Will Korea's Modernization Be Westernization?" one South Korean scholar wrote that "modern values were discovered and converted into ideology in the West" and that the success of the West in "effecting historical changes, reorganizing society and achieving a dazzling culture" had "stimulated the late awakening countries of Asia and Africa and hastened the process of modernization" in those societies. At the same time, however, the author contended that modern values were by no means the exclusive province of the West. He argued instead that "the most purely modern value was human liberation" and that the "values of human liberation had by no means been absent from either the East or Korea." The values of human liberation, according to the author, had even been manifest in past events in Korean history such as the farmers' protest movement that occurred during the Three Kingdoms period and the slave uprisings during the Koryo dynasty.[31] Thus, rather than following the pattern in the West, Korea's "modern values" needed to be "searched for in the 'peoples' spirit' which ran through the everyday life of the common people."[32] Along similar lines, Cho Ki-Jun, one of South Korea's leading economic historians, argued in a brief article that he wrote for a popular women's magazine that modernization did not mean "simply imitating the West without criticism." Cho noted that while some equated modernization with Westernization "the seeds of modern society had been planted not only in the West but also in Eastern societies during the Middle Ages" and that "Western culture did not contain only modern elements" but had its share of "pre-modern elements" as well.[33]

Intellectuals in South Korea not only tried to explain how and why Korea's modernization could be different from Westernization but also frequently became engaged in criticizing the process and outcome of modernization in the West. A four-day conference titled "Modernization of Korea, the Ideas and the Orientation" held at Dongguk University in 1966 to commemorate the university's sixtieth anniversary even had a one-day session devoted to a "Critique on Western Ideas for Modernization." In the opening address Joh Myung-Gee, the president of the university, sought to delineate a concept of modernization that would get around the problems of the modern ego and its emphasis on material interests that for Joh were a part of Westernization. Joh expressed hope that modernization would be viewed "as the creation of a welfare society on so vast a scale that it involves the entire world and mankind rather than assimilation into the self-centered realities of life." He warned that such assimilation "may bring [a] near sighted, make shift effect; but such an effect is doomed to destruction." This tendency, he claimed, "was more or less connected with the western ideas for modernization." Joh criticized the penchant that had existed in Korea's past for the "blind worship of Western ideas" and urged the panel that was scheduled to discuss Western ideas for modernization to "draw a useful conclusion through their discussion[,] useful to 'our' modernization" through focusing "not only on the advantages and disadvantages of the western ideas but also on the way they are to be and how they are to affect our tradition."[34]

As South Korean scholars began to conceptualize their country's modernization, they increasingly rejected the possibility that it could be guided by the same principles that had guided the modernization process in Europe and the United States. The question remained, however, of how exactly Korea's process would be differentiated from those of Western countries and whether it could or should be informed by Korean "traditions." Intellectuals in South Korea sought to answer this question by breaking down some of the conceptual barriers between tradition and modernity erected by American scholars, arguing that the presence of one did not necessarily mean the absence of the other. American East Asia specialists, especially experts on Japanese history and society, had, in some instances, pointed to the ways that traditions had contributed or could contribute to the modernization process, but South Korean scholars strove for an even more thorough rebuttal of the notion that traditions were dysfuntional in modernization by actively seeking principles that could guide Korea's modernization in its traditional religions and philosophies. This meant that these scholars implicitly accepted both the basic binary between modernity and tradition and the characterizations of particular aspects of Korean culture as traditional that were created by American scholars. Even in the process of mimicking these constructions, however, South Korean scholars managed to implicate cultural difference through infusing their conceptions of modernization with what they considered the philosophical and spiritual essence of Korean traditions. Through doing so, they sought to create a conceptual basis for Korea's modernization that assured that the process would not result in the same emphasis on materialism that they perceived in Western modernity.

Among Korean "traditions," Confucianism was most frequently discussed in terms of its relevance to the modernization process. Confucianism itself had changed significantly in the course of its long history in Asia, a fact which makes it difficult to say what exactly Confucianism was. Nevertheless, American experts on East Asian history and society almost always viewed Confucianism as an obstacle to modernization, and South Korean scholars sometimes agreed with this assertion. American scholars tended to argue that through failing to distinguish between state and society, emphasizing the rule of man rather than the rule of law, and refusing to recognize the dignity of the individual, Confucianism had obstructed modernization.[35] Yet other South Korean scholars argued that Confucianism possessed certain inherent features that would enable it to inform their country's drive toward modernity. They asserted that Confucianism's emphasis on fostering virtuous public servants and encouragement of political activities that benefited the people gave it the capacity to serve as a moral compass for Korea's modernization efforts.[36]

The conflicting sentiments over Confucianism's potential role were exemplified in a dialogue that took place at the International Conference on the Problems of Modernization in Asia held at Korea University in 1965. Western scholars and some of the South Korean scholars attending argued that Confucianism could not possibly inform Korea's modernization. Cho Kah-Kyung, a professor of philosophy at Seoul National University, argued that Confucianism "could never be made into a spiritual backbone of modernization." In a later discussion, Robert Scalpino, a political science professor at the University of California at Berkeley, elaborated this point, arguing that "Confucianism inclines away from modernity" and that it had "something in common with Marxism-Leninism—that both of these systems appeal essentially to authority." But such negative characterizations were disputed by both Chinese scholars from Hong Kong and Taiwan and by some of the other South Koreans. Tang Chun-I, a professor from the New Asia College in Hong Kong, for instance, argued that "we may find in Confucianism something universal and permanent and yet having a certain connection with modern problems." Along similar lines, one South Korean scholar contended that "there are fundamental values to be preserved and promoted in Confucianism" and that such values "have a religious force that may function as a rallying point for modernization."[37]

Buddhism's potential as a guiding ideology for Korea's modernization also drew significant attention. Several South Korean scholars spoke of the ability of Buddhism to contribute to their country's modernization process, disputing the claims made by Western scholars that Buddhism's stress on determinism, glorification of poverty, and emphasis on the spiritual rather than the material precluded political and economic development. They contended instead that Buddhism's view of man as a being capable of both degeneration and improvement and its emphasis on the cultivation of goodness sanctioned the exertion of distinctive human reasoning for the improvement of everyday life.[38] Rhi Ki-Yong, for instance, authored and edited several books in both English and Korean on Buddhism's place in history and in the modern world. During the sixties he argued on a variety of occasions that Buddhism could play an important role in Korea's modernization process. Rhi maintained that conceptions of modernization itself needed to be broadened beyond their typical emphasis on rationalism and efficiency. "Modernization in this country," he contended during one conference, "should not be a selfish movement." He listed the aims of modernization as the security of "peace, safety and [the] welfare of human life," respect for "human reason," and the enactment of laws for "harmony and [the] development of human society." Such an idea of modernization, he argued, could "be found in the basic thought of Buddhism." According to Rhi, Buddhist theory on human reason had listed the "virtues and wisdom that human beings ought to acquire and argued that [the] acquirement of these virtues and wisdom would lead to happiness, prosperity and peace of human beings which are [the] ultimate aims of modernization."[39]

The use of discussions of modernization theory by South Korean scholars to reaffirm the value of Korean "traditions" and criticize the West underscores one of the central ironies of American efforts to influence South Korean thought and to blunt the rising tide of Korean nationalism. Americans hoped that modernization theory's tendency to elevate the West and its focus on the need for underdeveloped countries to imitate advanced ones would serve to legitimate their involvement in South Korean affairs. Discussions of modernization among South Korean scholars frequently ended up doing exactly the opposite. Scholars in South Korea utilized modernization theory as a means of criticizing the West and fueling the kind of antiforeign nationalism that Americans had come to dread.

The appropriation of modernization theory by intellectuals in the ROK speaks to the appeal that the theory sometimes carried for people in the developing world, but it also speaks to the ways that the concept of modernization has limited Americans' ability to understand change in other societies. For South Korean elites, frustrated with their nation's poverty, the concept offered a means of articulating the process of change that they hoped to stimulate in their country. Yet at the same time they also understood modernization as a process that they could shape through their own historical agency. For Americans, however, changes in Korea that have not conformed to preconceived notions of modernity have served as signs of Koreans' otherness. By failing to look at South Korean conceptions of modernization, they have been precluded from understanding the subjectivity of Koreans in forging their own history during the last fifty years.

## NOTES

The author thanks Tim Borstelmann, J. Victor Koschmann, Sherman Cochran, Michael Shin, Martina Deuchler, Barry Strauss, and the editors of this volume for their helpful comments and suggestions on drafts of this essay. All Korean names and words have been Romanized according to the McCune-Reischauer System except in the cases of Korean names that have been Romanized differently either by the individuals themselves or by popular media (such as Syngman Rhee).

1. The best source on America's involvement in the creation of the Republic of Korea and the Korean War is Bruce Cumings's two-volume work *The Origins of the Korean War:* vol. 1, *Liberation and the Emergence of Separate Regimes, 1945–*

*1947* (Princeton: Princeton University Press, 1981), and vol. 2, *The Roaring of the Cataract, 1947–1950* (Princeton: Princeton University Press, 1990).

2. "Field Proposed Program for 1963: Korea," USAID Library and Learning Resource Center, Washington (hereafter USAIDL).

3. Bruce Cumings, *Korea's Place in the Sun: A Modern History* (New York: Norton, 1997), 339–47.

4. Ibid., 346–47.

5. "The Situation in Korea, February, 1961," National Security Files, box 127, John F. Kennedy Library, Boston (hereafter JFKL).

6. Cumings, *Korea's Place in the Sun*, 346–54.

7. "The Situation in Korea, February, 1961," NSF box 127, JFKL.

8. "Report of the Korea Task Force, June 5, 1961," NSF box 127, JFKL.

9. Bernard J. Lavin, "Witness to Korean History"; the author retains a copy of the paper in English which was translated into Korean and published in installments by the *Korea Times* in Hawaii in 1999.

10. Marshall Green to Secretary of State, 27 May 1961, NSF box 128, JFKL.

11. Berger to Secretary of State, 6 June 1962, NSF box 128, JFKL.

12. Ibid.

13. "Underlying Causes of South Korean Student Discontent," 8 June 1964, NA/RG 59 Records of the Department of State, General Foreign Policy Files, 1964–66, Political and Defense, box 2401.

14. L. D. Battle's "Report to the President on International Cultural Presentations Programs," 30 November 31961, NSF box 296, JFKL, called for an increase in spending on cultural exchange programs and recommended specifically that these programs target youth, labor, and intellectuals.

15. "USIA Country Plan for Korea, 1967," USIA Declassified Materials Collection, Washington (hereafter USIAL). The author retains copies of all documents from this collection. The U.S. government's recent decision to merge the USIA with the State Department has made the future location of these materials uncertain.

16. USIS Seoul, "Assessment Report—Korea, 1964," Educational and Cultural Exchange, USIAL.

17. Although *Nondan* is mentioned in USIS documents, there are not many surviving issues of the magazine. The articles mentioned above were taken from issues published in the late sixties and early seventies and scattered throughout the "Records of the USIA," in the Lyndon Baines Johnson Library, Austin, Tex. (hereafter LBJL).

18. "Inauguration of New USIS-supported TV series on Modernization in Korea," 29 December 1965, Korea—Incoming, USIAL.

19. Lavin, "Witness to Korean History." William A. Douglas's lecture "The Role of Political Parties in the Modernization Process" is included in a book containing

all of the lectures from the conference titled *The Modernization Process in Korea,* which is available in the Harvard Yenching Library.

20. Asia Foundation, "The Asia Foundation in Korea 1964," brochure published by the Asia Foundation. A list of some of the grants awarded by the Asia Foundation in South Korea was also supplied to the author by the local offices of the Asia Foundation in Seoul.

21. This information was supplied to the author by the Ford Foundation Archives.

22. Koryŏ taehakkyo asea munje yŏn'guso, *Koryŏ taehakkyo asea munje yŏn'guso isimnyŏnji* [A Twenty-Year History of the Asiatic Research Center], (Seoul: Asea munje yŏn'guso, 1977), 1–22, 146–47.

23. The Asiatic Research Center eventually published the entire proceedings of this conference. See Asiatic Research Center, ed., *International Conference on the Problems of Modernization in Asia* (Seoul: Asiatic Research Center, 1966).

24. *Bulletin of the Korea Branch of the Visiting Scholars Association, 1972,* Harvard University Archives, Cambridge, Mass.

25. Ibid., 1967 and 1972 issues.

26. Im Taesik, 1950 nyŏndae Miguk ŭi kyoyuk wŏnjo wa ch'inmi ellit'ŭi hyŏngsŏng [American Educational Assistance in the 1950s and the Formation of a Pro-American Elite], in Yŏksa munje yŏnguso, ed., *1950 nyŏndae Nambukhan ŭi sŏntaek kwa kulchŏl* [1950 North and South Korea's Choices and Reflections], (Seoul: Yŏksa pip'yŏngsa, 1998), 164.

27. Maeil kyŏngje sinmun, ed., *Na ŭi yuhak sijŏl: myŏngsadŭl ŭi p'yŏlch'inŭn chŭlmŭnnal ŭi kkum kwa yamang* [My Years as an Exchange Student: Well-Known Individuals Youthful Dreams and Desires] (Seoul: Maeil kyŏngje sinmunsa, 1986), 3:107–36, 183–214, and 1:130–45.

28. *Bulletin of the Korea Branch of the Visiting Scholars Association, 1967.*

29. Michel de Certeau, *The Practice of Everyday Life* (Berkeley: University of California Press, 1984), xiii.

30. Edward Wagner, "Korean Modernization: Some Historical Considerations," *Korea Journal* 3, no. 8 (August 1963): 27–30.

31. During the "Three Kingdoms Period" what is now known as Korea was divided into three competing states—Silla, Paekche, and Koguryŏ. This period lasted between roughly 300 and 676, when Silla assumed control of the entire Korean peninsula. The Koryo dynasty was formed in 918, unified the Korean peninsula in 935, and remained in power until 1392. Peasant and slave uprisings in the twelfth century demanded changes in the hereditary status system.

32. Im Hŭ isŏp, "Han'guk ŭi kŭndaehwanŭn sŏguhwa in'ga [Will Korea's Modernization Be Westernization?]," *Ch'ŏngmaek* 1, no. 4 (December, 1964): 146–51.

33. Cho Kijun, "Muŏsi kŭndaehwa in'ga [What Is Modernization?]," *Yŏwŏn* [Women's Garden], March 1964: 62–65.

34. Myung-Gee Joh, "The Ideas for Modernization of Korea: Opening Address," in Tongguk taehakkyo, *Han'guk kŭndaehwa ŭi inyŏmkwa panghyang: Tongguk taehakkyo kaegyo yuksip chunnyŏn kinyŏm haksul simp'ojiŭm nonmunjip* [Modernization of Korea, the Ideas and the Orientation: Symposium in Commemoration of the 60th Anniversary of the Founding of Dongguk University], (Seoul: Tongguk taehakkyo, 1967) (hereafter Tongguk).

35. Several American scholars expressed these views at, among other places, the International Conference on the Problems of Modernization in Asia. See Asiatic Research Center, *International Conference on the Problems of Modernization in Asia,* 111–13.

36. On these points see Sang-Eun Lee, "Confucian Thought from the Viewpoint of Humanism," *Asea yŏn'gu* [Journal of Asiatic Studies] 4, no. 2 (December 1961): 189–99.

37. Asiatic Research Center, *International Conference on the Problems of Modernization in Asia,* 111, 113, 125.

38. See for instance, Rhi Ki Yŏng's paper in ibid., 71–74.

39. Ki-Yŏng Rhi, "Buddhism and Modern Man," in Tongguk, 576–77.

## FURTHER READING

Cumings, Bruce. *Korea's Place in the Sun: A Modern History.* New York: Norton, 1997.

Eckert, Carter, et al. *Korea Old and New: A History.* Cambridge: Harvard University Press, 1990.

Henderson, Gregory. *Korea: The Politics of the Vortex.* Cambridge: Harvard University Press, 1968.

Lee, Yur-Bok, and Wayne Patterson, eds. *Korean-American Relations, 1866–1997.* Albany: SUNY Press, 1997.

Macdonald, Donald Stone. *U.S.-Korean Relations from Liberation to Self-Reliance: The Twenty Year Record: An Interpretive History of the Archives for the U.S. Department of State for the Period 1945 to 1965.* Boulder, Colo.: Westview, 1992.

# CONTRIBUTORS

MICHAEL ADAS is the Abraham Voorhees Professor of History at Rutgers University. He has written extensively on European colonialism, peasant protest, and more recently technology and Western global dominance. His *Machines as the Measure of Men* (1989) focused on British and French variations on the last of these themes, and he is completing a new book titled *Dominance by Design: Technological Imperatives and America's Civilizing Mission.*

LAURA BELMONTE is an associate professor of history at Oklahoma State University. Her research focuses on social and cultural factors in modern U.S. foreign relations. She is currently completing *Defending the American Way: National Identity, Propaganda, and the Cold War, 1945–1959*. Her *Speaking of America: Readings in U.S. History* will appear in 2003.

GREGG ANDREW BRAZINSKY is an assistant professor in the history department and the Elliot School of International Affairs at The George Washington University. He is writing a book on American nation building in South Korea during the 1950s and 1960s.

DAVID C. ENGERMAN is in the history department at Brandeis University, where he teaches courses on American intellectual history, foreign relations, and radicalism. His first book, currently titled *Modernization from the Other Shore: American Intellectuals and Russian Development*, is forthcoming.

NILS GILMAN holds a doctorate from the University of California, Berkeley, and is the author of *Mandarins of the Future: Modernization Theory in Cold War America*, forthcoming in 2003.

MARK H. HAEFELE received his Ph.D. in history from Harvard University. His recent publications include "John F. Kennedy, USIA, and World Public Opinion," *Diplomatic History* 25 (winter 2001). He divides his time between teaching at Harvard and managing a hedge fund.

CHRISTINA KLEIN is an associate professor of literature at MIT. She has published articles on American representations of Asia in *Minnesota Review* and in Christian Appy, ed., *Cold War Constructions: The Political Culture of United States Imperialism, 1945–1966* (2000). Her first book, *Cold War Orientalism: Asia in the Middlebrow Imagination, 1945–1961*, is to be published in 2003.

J. VICTOR KOSCHMANN is professor of history at Cornell University. He has written *The Mito Ideology: Discourse, Reform, and Insurrection in Late Tokugawa Japan, 1790–1864* (1987) and *Revolution and Subjectivity in Postwar Japan* (1996), in addition to editing several volumes including *Total War and "Modernization"* (1998).

MICHAEL E. LATHAM is an associate professor of history at Fordham University. He is the author of *Modernization as Ideology: American Social Science and "Nation Building" in the Kennedy Era* (2000) and has published articles on American Cold War culture, social analysis, and the legacies of imperialism.

MICHAEL MAHONEY is assistant professor of modern African history at Yale University. He specializes in the colonial and postcolonial state in southern Africa, and the state's interactions with the governed. His publications include "The Millennium Comes to Mapumulo: Popular Christianity in Rural Natal, 1866–1906," *Journal of Southern African Studies* 25, no. 3 (1999). He is working on a study of political culture in nineteenth- and early twentieth-century colonial South Africa.

# INDEX